ANCIENT POTTERY, CUISINE, AND SOCIETY AT THE NORTHERN GREAT LAKES

MIDWEST ARCHAEOLOGICAL PERSPECTIVES
Donald Gaff, *series editor*

The American Midcontinent, stretching from the Appalachians to the Great Plains, and from the boreal forests of Canada to the Gulf of Mexico, is home to a rich and deep multiethnic past that even after 150 years of exploration continues to fascinate scholars and the public alike. Beginning with colonization by the first Native American big game hunters, through the origins of domestic food production and construction of the largest earthen monuments in North America, and ultimately the entry of multiple colonial empires and their varying interactions with native populations, the story of the region is an exciting one of changing cultural and environmental interactions and adaptive strategies. The diverse environments that characterize the region have fostered a multiplicity of solutions to the problem of survival, ranging from complex sedentary agriculturally intensive societies to those with highly refined seasonal resource strategies keyed to timed movement and social flexibility.

To explore this region from new and different vantage points the Midwest Archaeological Conference Inc. and the University of Notre Dame Press are pleased to launch the Midwest Archaeological Perspectives series, a unique collaborative book series intended for a broad range of professional and interested lay audiences. The books published in Midwest Archaeological Perspectives will be the most compelling and current works of archaeological narrative and insight for the region, with a temporal scope encompassing the span of human use of the region from the first colonizing Paleoindian cultures to the more recent historical past. The series will explore both old questions tackled from new perspectives, and new and interesting questions arising from the deployment of cutting-edge theory and method.

ANCIENT POTTERY, CUISINE, AND SOCIETY AT THE NORTHERN GREAT LAKES

SUSAN M. KOOIMAN

University of Notre Dame Press
Notre Dame, Indiana

Midwest Archaeological Conference, Inc.

University of Notre Dame Press
Notre Dame, Indiana 46556
undpress.nd.edu

Copyright © 2021 by Susan M. Kooiman

All Rights Reserved

Published in the United States of America

Library of Congress Control Number: 2021943170

ISBN: 978-0-268-20145-6 (Hardback)
ISBN: 978-0-268-20146-3 (Paperback)
ISBN: 978-0-268-20144-9 (WebPDF)
ISBN: 978-0-268-20147-0 (Epub)

CONTENTS

List of Figures		vii
List of Tables		xi
Acknowledgments		xiii
ONE	Introduction	1
TWO	Environmental and Cultural History of the Northern Great Lakes	9
THREE	Cuisine and Pottery Technology in the Northern Great Lakes	27
FOUR	Pottery and Cuisine: Theoretical and Methodological Perspectives	43
FIVE	Pottery Taxonomy, Chronology, and Occupational History of the Cloudman Site	59
SIX	Pottery Function	83
SEVEN	Diet and Cuisine at the Cloudman Site	109
EIGHT	Ethnographic and Ethnohistorical Accounts of Diet and Cooking	129

| NINE | Culinary and Technological Tradition and Change at the Cloudman Site | 143 |

	Appendix A. Cloudman Pottery Data	159
	Appendix B. Cloudman Pottery Vessels Sampled for Microbotanical, Stable Isotope, and Lipid Residue Analyses	177
	Appendix C. Selected Vessels from the Cloudman Pottery Assemblage	183
	References	189
	Index	213

FIGURES

Figure 1.1. Location of the Cloudman site (20CH6) and select Woodland sites in the Great Lakes. Courtesy of Adriana Martinez. 3

Figure 2.1. Map of the Great Lakes with the Northern Great Lakes region indicated. Courtesy of Adriana Martinez. 10

Figure 2.2. Distribution of cultural groups ca. 1630. Courtesy of Erin Beachey. 24

Figure 3.1. Drummond Island and the Cloudman site (20CH6). Courtesy of Adriana Martinez. 34

Figure 6.1. Rim diameter frequencies of the Cloudman pottery assemblage. 86

Figure 6.2. Interior carbonization patterns for the Cloudman site (20CH6) pottery assemblage. Courtesy of Erin Beachey. 99

Figure 6.3. Interior carbonization Pattern 1 (boiling). 99

Figure 6.4. Interior carbonization Pattern 2 (stewing). 100

Figure 6.5. Interior carbonization Pattern 3 (boiling + stewing). 100

Figure 6.6. Proportions of interior carbonization patterns by component (percentages of total analyzed vessels displayed). 102

Figure 7.1. Plot of δ15N/δ13C values of Cloudman pottery residues. 111

Figure 7.2. Frequencies of lipid residue food categories by component (percentages of total sampled vessels displayed). 112

Figure 7.3. Microbotanical frequencies of maize, wild rice, and squash by component (percentages of total sampled vessels displayed). 114

Figure C1. Vessel 5, Laurel Pseudo-scallop Shell. 184
Figure C2. Vessel 20, Laurel Dentate Stamped (oblique). 184
Figure C3. Vessel 109, Laurel Banked Linear Stamped. 184
Figure C4. Vessel 6, Laurel Dentate Rocker Stamped. 184
Figure C5. Vessel 131, North Bay Linear Stamped. 184
Figure C6. Vessel 35, Late Laurel (cf. Laurel Incised or Mackinac Banded). 184
Figure C7. Vessel 33, untyped (incipient Blackduck?). 184
Figure C8. Vessel 80, Mackinac Punctate. 185
Figure C9. Vessel 191, Mackinac Punctate. 185
Figure C10. Vessel 50, Mackinac Banded. 185
Figure C11. Vessel 120, Mackinac Banded. 185
Figure C12. Vessel 76, Mackinac Undecorated. 185
Figure C13. Vessel 55, Mackinac ware. 185
Figure C14. Vessel 81, Blackduck Banded. 185
Figure C15. Vessel 88, Blackduck Banded. 185
Figure C16. Vessel 199, cf. Bowerman Plain v. Cordmarked. 185
Figure C17. Vessel 200, untyped (ELW/MLW Transition). 186
Figure C18. Vessel 42, Bois Blanc ware. 186
Figure C19. Vessel 24, "Proto-Juntunen" ware (plain). 186
Figure C20. Vessel 102, Juntunen Drag-and-Jab. 186
Figure C21. Vessel 204, Juntunen Linear Punctate. 186
Figure C22. Vessel 25, Juntunen ware. 186
Figure C23. Vessel 43, Traverse Decorated v. Punctate. 187
Figure C24. Vessel 150, Traverse Plain v. Scalloped. 187
Figure C25. Vessel 162, Iroquoian-style (cf. Lawson Incised). 187
Figure C26. Vessel 64, Iroquoian-style (cf. Ripley Plain). 187
Figure C27. Vessel 74, Iroquoian-style (cf. Huron Incised). 187
Figure C28. Vessel 156, Iroquoian-style (cf. Huron Incised). 187
Figure C29. Vessel 166, Iroquoian-style (cf. Huron Incised). 187
Figure C30. Vessel 39, Laurel ware (Middle Woodland). 188
Figure C31. Vessel 201, untyped (Middle Woodland). 188
Figure C32. Vessel 52, Mackinac Undecorated (Early Late Woodland). 188

Figure C33. Vessel 53, Mackinac Punctate (Early Late Woodland).   188
Figure C34. Vessel 83, Mackinac ware (Early Late Woodland).   188
Figure C35. Vessel 202, Mackinac ware (Early Late Woodland).   188
Figure C36. Vessel 63, untyped (Early Late Woodland).   188
Figure C37. Vessel 75, Traverse Plain v. Scalloped (Late Late Woodland).   188
Figure C38. Vessel 54, untyped (cf. O'Neil site cup; Late Woodland).   188
Figure C39. Vessel 167, Iroquoian-style (Late Precontact).   188
Figure C40. Vessel 182, Iroquoian-style, cf. Huron Incised (Late Precontact).   188

TABLES

Table 5.1.	Cloudman Pottery Vessels by Site Component	61
Table 5.2.	Middle Woodland Vessels by Type	62
Table 5.3.	Miscellaneous Woodland and Unknown Vessels	64
Table 5.4.	Early Late Woodland Vessels by Type	65
Table 5.5.	Late Late Woodland Vessels by Type	69
Table 5.6.	Late Precontact Vessels	70
Table 5.7.	Miniature Vessels by Type	74
Table 5.8.	AMS Dates from Carbonized Pottery Residue Samples	77
Table 6.1.	Mean Temper Size of Pottery Vessels by Component	85
Table 6.2.	Temper Size Relationships, Welch's Unpaired T-Test (significant outcomes boldfaced)	85
Table 6.3.	Mean Rim Diameter of Pottery Vessels by Component	87
Table 6.4.	Rim Diameter Relationships, Welch's Unpaired T-Test (significant outcomes boldfaced)	87
Table 6.5.	Vessel Wall Thickness by Component	89
Table 6.6.	Body Thickness Relationships, Welch's Unpaired T-Test	90
Table 6.7.	Technical Properties of Pottery Vessels by Type/Ware	91

Table 6.8.	Comparison of Mean Temper Size and Mean Body Thickness of Pottery Vessels by Component	94
Table 6.9.	Frequency of Use-Alteration Traces by Component	95
Table 6.10.	Interior Carbonization Pattern Frequency by Component	101
Table 6.11.	Primary Interior Carbonization Pattern Frequency by Component	102
Table 6.12.	Interior Carbonization Pattern Relationships, Kruskal-Wallis	103
Table 6.13.	Interior Carbonization Pattern Frequency by Type/Ware	104
Table 7.1.	Vessel Clusters by Microbotanical Species Content (Jaccard's Coefficient)	116

ACKNOWLEDGMENTS

Although this book bears only my name, it is the result of the effort and support of many others without whom this body of work would not have been possible. First and foremost, I would like to thank my doctoral adviser, William Lovis, for his support, wisdom, patience, and guidance throughout the process of writing my dissertation and for his continued mentorship as I turned that research into this book and other articles. I am also grateful for the constant flow of support, encouragement, and good advice I received from my doctoral committee members, Jodie O'Gorman, Mindy Morgan, and Ryan Tubbs, as well as from Lynne Goldstein, a valued mentor. Jim Skibo has continued to be an inspiring mentor and collaborator, and I am indebted to him for his excellent advice on writing and publishing.

I must acknowledge Rebecca Albert for her excellent and hard work in contributing to this project, and I am thankful for her friendship. The works of Sean Dunham and Chris Stephenson were essential building blocks for my research, and I am extremely grateful for these intelligent and gracious colleagues and friends. I owe deep gratitude to Eric Drake and Mary Malainey for their invaluable contributions, and I must also thank Timothy Figol of the Residue Analysis Laboratory at Brandon University and Shari Effert-Fanta of the Illinois State Geological Survey for their vital roles in this research. I am grateful to the Michigan State University (MSU) Department of Anthropology for laboratory space for my analysis and to the MSU Museum for access to the Cloudman pottery assemblage. This research would not have been possible without funding and support from the National Science Foundation, the MSU Graduate School, the MSU College of Social Science, and the MSU Alumni and Friends of Archaeology Fund. Thank you to Southern

Illinois University, Edwardsville, Department of Anthropology, and Julie Zimmermann for their support while reframing and editing the manuscript. I am forever indebted to the Midwest Archaeological Conference and the University of Notre Dame Press for their sponsorship of this publication. Thanks to Eli Bortz and Matthew Dowd for their editorial advice and expertise, to Sheila Berg for copyediting, and to the reviewers whose comments made this a stronger work.

I would be nothing without the constant love and support of my family and friends. To my siblings—Scott, Keith, Julie, Dan, and Joe—I am ever grateful for your presence in my life, along with Monica, Holly, Jake, Abby, Emma, and many other loving family members who are too numerous to name here. I am grateful to Erin Beachey for a lifetime of friendship and for her graphic design skills that created some of the figures in this work. Thanks to Didi Martinez for drafting all the maps and for her emotional support during this process. Amy Michael, Mari Isa, Jack Biggs, Nicole Geske, Caitlin Vogelsberg, Kate Frederick, Micca Metz, Emma Meyer, Lisa Bright, Josh Burbank, and Jeff and Autumn Painter also warrant special thanks and gratitude.

I would like to thank my parents, Calvin and Elaine, who instilled in me the strength, determination, and work ethic required to achieve my goals and who always supported my dreams. This book is dedicated to their memory.

Finally, I would like to acknowledge the ancient Indigenous people of the Great Lakes, who occupied the region for millennia. Their true stories live on in their descendants, and this work represents an outsider's interpretation. I hope I have respectfully portrayed aspects of their complex and dynamic lifeways and cultures across time.

Introduction

Food and cooking are vital components of human culture and survival. Understanding subsistence-related behaviors and technologies used for cooking and food preparation is important for unveiling the lifeways of past societies because of their close association with identity, social and political relationships, and ideologies, as well as adaptive decisions rooted in environment and environmental change. Food remains and pottery are among the most widely studied artifacts in archaeology because of the depth of information they can provide about those who lived before us, allowing us to see ourselves reflected in commonalities and to marvel at the ingenuity of people living in often-challenging environments without our modern amenities.

The Northern Great Lakes region of North America was occupied by Indigenous groups for thousands of years before the arrival of Europeans. Despite this rich history of occupation, these inhabitants were largely mobile and left behind limited archaeological remains that were further impacted by the generally poor preservation of organic materials common across the region. In areas such as the Northern Great Lakes, multidimensional analysis is necessary to tease more information out of minimal archaeological remains. Fortunately, new analytic techniques for extracting increasing amounts of information from these artifacts are constantly being developed and refined. Expansion of routine archaeological pottery and dietary analyses to include a variety of analytic methods, old and new, holds the potential to improve interpretations of ancient lifeways and amplify evidence for adaptive and social behaviors at archaeological sites across the globe. The intersection of foodways and pottery is a promising arena for multidimensional research yielding robust interpretations of the past.

This book examines changing settlement, subsistence, and social patterns from the perspective of food processing technology, food and resource selection, and cooking methods based on a pottery assemblage from a pre-European-contact Indigenous occupation site on the shores of Lake Huron in the Upper Peninsula of Michigan. The results contribute to the growing body of data about precontact Northern Great Lakes dietary behaviors and provide clarification about diachronic behavioral change in the context of social and environmental factors. They also demonstrate the effectiveness of using multiple diverse yet complementary methods for examining ancient cuisine and culinary technology.

CERAMICS, COOKING, AND CUISINE AT THE CLOUDMAN SITE

A combination of ceramic and dietary analytic methods was used to examine the ceramic assemblage from the multicomponent Cloudman site (20CH6), located on Drummond Island in northern Lake Huron (figure 1.1). Over the past several decades a debate has arisen about regional subsistence and settlement patterns in the Northern Great Lakes. While some scholars have argued for a distinct transition from broad spectrum hunting-gathering to an intensified focus on specific, productive wild or cultivated foods during the Woodland period (200 BC–AD 1600) (Cleland 1982, 1989; O'Shea 2003), there is another argument for greater or complete continuity in settlement and subsistence patterns throughout the period (Martin 1989); yet others have observed a more gradual and nuanced transition in these patterns over time (Drake and Dunham 2004; Dunham 2014; Smith 2004).

Most scholars would now agree that both social and adaptive changes occurred in the Northern Great Lakes over the course of the Woodland period, although the exact nature of these changes is still in dispute. Most evidence shows that Late Woodland groups in the region were focusing

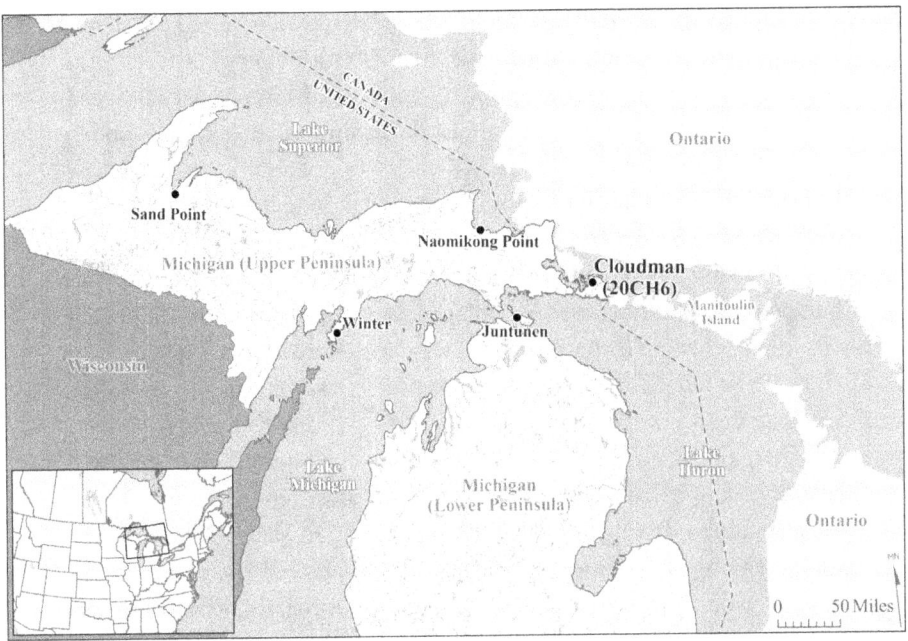

Figure 1.1. Location of the Cloudman site (20CH6) and select Woodland sites in the Great Lakes. Courtesy of Adriana Martinez.

on specific seasonally abundant foods, but it is not known whether they were turning primarily to fall-spawning fish (Cleland 1982), fish and wild starchy resources such as wild rice and acorns (Dunham 2014), or, like many other Late Woodland peoples of the Midwest, domesticated foods like maize (O'Shea 2003).

It has been observed that alongside these possible dietary alterations, cooking methods and cooking technology may also have changed to accommodate new food processing demands. Regional trends in cooking techniques, as observed through changing patterns of interior carbonized food residues, show a transition from stewing to boiling foods during the Late Woodland period (Albert et al. 2018; Kooiman 2016). Starchy resources such as acorns, wild rice, and maize all require prolonged boiling to become edible or optimally nutritious, so this pattern may be related to the changing subsistence regimes noted by other scholars. If more intensive cooking practices were employed to properly process new foods, then alterations to pottery technology may have been required to accommodate them. Seemingly small adjustments to a pottery vessel, such as thinning the vessel walls or reducing the size of temper particles, can improve its performance and durability during intensive cooking episodes.

The Cloudman site was periodically occupied by pottery-making Indigenous groups between approximately AD 50 and AD 1500, making it an ideal site for observing a range of variables in one place over a long period of time, thereby minimizing the effects of distance or social and microenvironmental variation on the observed changes and allowing diachronic changes in pottery function to be related to broader adaptive and social change. The Cloudman site pottery assemblage is used to investigate the overarching question of whether pottery technology, pottery use, diet, and cooking habits changed over time and, if so, how these changes relate to hypothesized transitions in subsistence, settlement, and social patterns among pottery-making groups in the Northern Great Lakes region. The themes of site context and chronology, pottery technology, cooking styles, diet and environment, cuisine, and identity are explored here using a combination of methods centered on ancient pottery vessels and their associated absorbed and adhered food residues.

LEGACY, TRADITION, AND INNOVATION

Examining the ceramic assemblage from the Cloudman site from the perspectives of foodways and technology demonstrates the effectiveness of multidimensionally constructed research for providing clarification to long-standing questions using existing archaeological collections. The Cloudman site was excavated and its artifact assemblage initially analyzed between 1990 and 1995; its ceramic assemblage has remained on storage shelves, untouched, since that time. Artifact assemblages from sites excavated long ago and left on museum shelves long after their initial analysis are affectionately referred to as "legacy collections" by archaeologists. These collections provide ample potential for testing new and innovative collections-based research without the expense of and disturbance caused by excavating new sites and material culture (Bawaya 2007; Lovis 1990).

Traditional pottery or ceramic analysis conducted by archaeologists focuses on placing vessels into typological (taxonomic) categories based on style and decoration. Typologies based on style are extremely useful to archaeologists since they connect a site to a specific time, place, and society (Sackett 1977). Functional pottery analysis, however, views "pots as tools" (Braun 1983) and endeavors to discover how people in the past made and used ceramic vessels (Skibo 1992, 2013). Technical properties and use alterations (evidence of past use) provide insight into the role of pottery in both the daily and ceremonial lives of past groups. Since basic pottery analysis has traditionally included only typological categorization, this means there is a plentitude of legacy collections ripe with potential for reanalysis through a functional lens.

Likewise, interpretations of past diet have historically been based on plant seeds and animal bones found in archaeological contexts. While providing a great deal of information, these bones and seeds do not always preserve well. Recent scientific innovations have allowed archaeologists to examine past diet using a suite of microscopic and chemical food remains associated with pottery and other food processing tools. These remains are often better preserved and can be directly associated with food processing tools, allowing for more precise analysis of cooking traditions.

Application of a combination of both traditional and innovative analytic methods can extract a broader range of information that serves to enrich our interpretations of the past. This research exemplifies the importance of analyzing old data from different perspectives to bring to light new information.

GOALS OF THIS BOOK

This book explores how diet, cooking, and ceramic cooking technologies changed throughout the course of the Woodland and Late Precontact periods in the Northern Great Lakes and their associated environmental and social implications. The 1,500-year history of the occupation of the Cloudman site by Indigenous pottery-making groups played out against the backdrop of broader sociocultural trends occurring both locally and regionally. To understand cuisine and cooking technology at the site level, it must be situated in the context of these broader regional and historical trends. Chapter 2 discusses the cultural history of the Northern Great Lakes region, while chapter 3 provides a more detailed context for the problem of local Woodland period subsistence, settlement, and social interactions.

Chapter 4 discusses the theoretical underpinnings of this research, as well as the methods employed to explore the research questions according to those theoretical perspectives. Pottery style, pottery function, and foodways studies reveal that a wide and complex variety of social and cultural factors are tied to cooking technology and cuisine. These perspectives guided the methods employed here to extract maximum data from the broken remains of humble ancient cooking pots.

To properly investigate diachronic change, the occupational history of the Cloudman site must first be established, a process that is outlined in chapter 5. Pottery, the material culture that serves as the focus of this book, provides two methods for dating archaeological sites. Pottery typologies based on style have long been used by archaeologists as an indicator of the time period in which sites were occupied. The Cloudman site pottery assemblage includes types associated with the Middle Woodland, early, and Late Late Woodland periods, as well as vessels stylistically similar to those produced by Iroquoian groups (Huron/Wendat-Petun) from southern Ontario. Accelerator mass spectrometry (AMS) radiocarbon dating of carbonized food residues adhered to the interior of ceramic cooking vessels allows further refinement of the occupational chronology of the Cloudman site.

Understanding pottery function is useful for interpreting the behaviors and motivations of past peoples. Functional pottery analysis of the Cloudman assemblage, detailed in chapter 6, reveals a variety of changes in cooking and vessel manufacture at the site over time. Chapter 7 focuses on analysis of food residues associated with pottery, which provides important information about ancient diet that supplements and enhances more traditional methods used to define past foodways. Three different types of food residue analysis (microbotanical, lipid residue, and stable isotope) are used together to create a more comprehensive picture of past diet than is possible by application of each technique alone.

Finally, chapter 8 documents ethnographic and ethnohistoric accounts of local Indigenous culinary habits and traditions. These provide rich insights into how people interacted with their social and natural environments to create a stable and sustainable cuisine that enabled them not only to cope with the harsh northern climate but also to establish unique identities through food and cooking. Comparison of the research results against recorded observations of cooking and dietary behaviors among Indigenous peoples occupying the Northern Great Lakes during the past two centuries offers clues about ancient cuisine that cannot be found in archaeological data alone.

Over the course of 1,500 years, there were notable changes in Indigenous cooking methods, food resource selection, pottery technology, and pottery style at the Cloudman site. These changes may be connected to a complex series of dynamic environmental, social, and even ideological factors that altered the way Northern Great Lakes peoples interacted with their environment and with each other. Typological and functional pottery analyses highlighted these changes from a technological perspective, while the combination of proxies for ancient cuisine—food residues, use-alteration or cooking pattern analysis, and ethnographic analogy—revealed how ancient peoples may have adapted to new social and environmental conditions through flexible foodways and evolving identities and social relationships.

Ultimately, the data obtained from the application of a series of diverse yet complementary pottery and dietary analysis methods contribute valuable new insights into the ongoing discussion of resource intensification, technological adaptation, and social transformation in the precontact Northern Great Lakes. The combined results demonstrate the efficacy of a multidimensional approach to studying subsistence and technology that can be applied to archaeological assemblages from a wide variety of contexts while also resulting in a fuller yet more nuanced picture of the dynamism of Northern Great Lakes Woodland foodways and technology.

CHAPTER 2

Environmental and Cultural History of the Northern Great Lakes

The Northern Great Lakes region, although often overlooked in the archaeological literature, has a rich, millennia-long cultural history characterized by complex and dynamic human interactions with both the social and natural environments. The archaeological history of the Northern Great Lakes, situated on the perimeter of the midwestern United States, is integrated into the overall cultural trajectory of the region. However, a number of phenomena distinguish the Northern Great Lakes from the rest of the Midwest, from environment to sociocultural trends. It is within this unique microcosm that questions concerning foodways and technological change are considered. This chapter details the broader ecological and social contexts of the research problem.

Clarification of geographic terms used in this book is required to properly convey the scope of the trends discussed below. The Great Lakes region constitutes land surrounding Lakes Superior, Michigan, Huron, Erie, and Ontario in northeastern North America, including portions of modern-day United States and Canada. "Upper Great Lakes" refers to the subset of this region lying north and west of Detroit, encompassing lands surrounding Lakes Huron and Superior and much of Lake Michigan. The focus of this study, the Northern Great Lakes, encompasses Lake Superior and the northern portions of Lake Huron and Lake

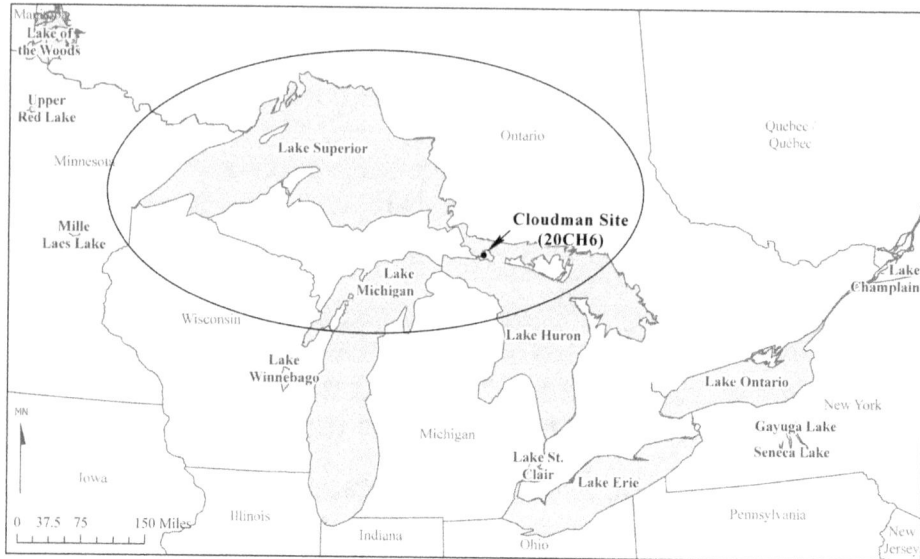

Figure 2.1. Map of the Great Lakes with the Northern Great Lakes region indicated. Courtesy of Adriana Martinez.

Michigan and includes the Upper Peninsula of Michigan, northern Lower Michigan, parts of northern Wisconsin and Minnesota, and parts of southern coastal Ontario (figure 2.1).

Consistent communication of dates is also required for clarity given the diachronic nature of the study. Henceforth, dates related to paleoclimatic trends are reported as "BP" (before present, i.e., 1950). Sociocultural dates and time periods are reported as calendrical years "BC" and "AD," and direct radiocarbon dates are reported in calibrated form ("cal BC" or "cal AD"), correlating with calendrical years, rather than in radiocarbon years.

PALEOCLIMATE AND ENVIRONMENTAL BACKGROUND

The onset of human occupation in northern Lower Michigan and the Upper Peninsula of Michigan occurred later than in other parts of the

Midwest because of glacial ice coverage during the retreat of the Wisconsin ice sheet (Cleland, Holman, and Holman 1988; Larson and Schaetzl 2001). Michigan was deglaciated between approximately 20,000 and 9000 BP. This deglacial phase was time transgressive, with the southern parts of Lower Michigan uncovered initially and northern Upper Michigan the last area to become ice-free (Blewett, Lusch, and Schaetzl 2009).

The first evidence of human occupation in southern Lower Michigan appears between 12,000 and 10,000 BP, after the forest cover became more extensive, thus creating an environment more amenable to human habitation (Kapp 1999; Lovis 2009; Shott and Wright 1999, 61). During this time, known as the Paleoindian period, the northern Michigan environment was composed of tundra and boreal forest (Hupy and Yansa 2009) and was occupied by large herbivores such as caribou and the last of the megafauna (Holman and Brandt 2009).

Although glacial retreat from the Upper Peninsula had occurred by the beginning of the Younger Dryas, the Marquette Re-advance again covered the area with ice around 11,500 BP and retreated, for the final time, around 9900 BP (Larson and Kincare 2009; Pregitzer et al. 2000). By this time, all of Michigan except the south shore of Lake Superior in the Upper Peninsula was ice-free (Kapp 1999). However, a long period of sparse vegetation development in northern Lower Michigan and Upper Michigan following deglaciation precluded occupation of these areas prior to 10,500 BP (Cleland, Holman, and Holman 1988).

What followed was a period of overall warming but frequent fluctuations in rainfall and lake levels (Kapp 1999; Larsen 1999), affecting vegetational and faunal composition (e.g., extinction of megafauna) as well as human habitation patterns (see, e.g., Lovis, Donahue, and Holman 2005). At this time, the eastern Upper Peninsula was covered by pine-dominated forests (Hupy and Yansa 2009). By 8000 BP, forest zones across the Eastern Woodlands were relatively similar to their modern composition, with hemlock and birch trees major components (Crawford 2011; Hupy and Yansa 2009).

For a time, the climate shifted to cooler and moister conditions, causing a decrease in pine and an increase in hemlock around 6800 BP (Hupy and Yansa 2009) and the rise in lake levels, resulting in the Nipissing maximum phase of Great Lakes level by around 5000 BP (Kincare and Larson 2009; Robertson et al. 1999). However, between about 4000 and 3000 BP, lake levels dropped to levels known as the Algoma Stage. This was due to a very warm, dry period known as the Mid-Holocene Climatic Optimum, which again altered the vegetation composition across the landscape (Hupy and Yansa 2009; Kapp 1999; Robertson, Lovis, and Halsey 1999).

Major ecological and biotic changes took place across the state beginning around 3000 BP, when the climate become moister and cooler, resulting in widespread marsh formation in the Upper Peninsula of Michigan (Kapp 1999, 57). Between 3000 and 2000 BP, the forest in the eastern half of the peninsula stabilized to the hemlock-dominated forest (composed of birch, cedar, beech, and maple) that covers the region today (Hupy and Yansa 2009). Terrestrial and aquatic faunal species in the Midwest likewise became more similar to those present in the region under modern conditions around this time (Shott 1999, 72). However, fluctuations in lake levels and forest compositions influenced the abundance of and accessibility to certain species throughout time, and the human advent of new technologies, such as the bow and arrow and fishing nets, also affected the species that were exploited (Styles 2011). The Medieval Climatic Optimum (ca. AD 900–1100), also referred to as the Medieval Warm Period, has been connected to widespread demographic and cultural change across North America (Foster 2012; Lovis, Arbogast, and Monaghan 2012) and corresponds to technological and social shifts seen across Michigan (Brashler et al. 2000).

Changes in climate and environment over such deep time segments are important for understanding past behavior, as many of the major and minor ecological changes mentioned above can be correlated to settlement-subsistence patterns evident in the archaeological record. However, environment and climate are not determinate factors of sociocultural change or decision making but rather provide parameters that constrain variation. Although groups living in the Northern Great Lakes were most certainly reactive to their environment, interactions with other groups and the development of new ideas and technologies played a part in the overall trajectory of Northern Great Lakes history.

CULTURAL BACKGROUND: OVERVIEW OF UPPER AND NORTHERN GREAT LAKES ARCHAEOLOGY

Pre-Woodland Periods

The first humans moved into modern-day Michigan between 10,000 and 8000 BC (Shott and Wright 1999), commencing the Paleoindian period. Sites dating to this period are sparse throughout Michigan. Paleoindians were highly mobile hunter-gatherers reliant on megafauna, fish, plants, and large herbivores such as caribou (Holman and Brandt 2009; Lovis 2009).

The subsequent Archaic period (8000–1000 BC)—typically divided into Early, Middle, and Late subperiods (McElrath, Fortier, and Emerson 2009)—is an important time interval in the trajectory of foodways in Eastern North America. Four indigenous seed-bearing plants (squash, sunflower, marshelder, and chenopod), known as the Eastern Agricultural Complex (EAC), were brought under domestication in the mid-south region of Eastern North America during the Archaic period, between 3000 BC and 1800 BC (Smith and Yarnell 2009). Evidence for the contemporaneous cultivation of several cultigens and cultivars were found at the Riverton Site (1800 cal BC) in southern Illinois, which was occupied by a partially mobile, small-scale society (Smith and Yarnell 2009). Thus, the development of the earliest crop complex in the Eastern Woodlands was likely not the result of population pressure but instead a long-term response to a resource-rich environment (Smith and Yarnell 2009). However, there is little, if any, evidence of the EAC or any other domesticates in the Northern Great Lakes region during the Archaic period, despite their presence as far north as the Saginaw drainage basin.

There is little known about Early and Middle Archaic (8000–3000 BC) Northern Great Lakes lifeways, a result of few identified and intact sites dating to these periods (Lovis 1999; Lovis, Donahue, and Holman 2005; Shott 1999). The Late Archaic period (3000–200 BC) may represent a period during which certain subsistence and mobility practices emerged that would characterize regional group behaviors in subsequent periods. Evidence of food remains and food processing tools suggests intensive, repeated fall occupations of various sites on Grand Island, Michigan, located in Lake Superior (Neubauer 2016, 2018). Local Indigenous bands came together to gather and process seasonally abundant foods such as whitefish and acorns (Neubauer 2016, 2018). This pattern of seasonal aggregation of groups at important fishing and gathering locales, particularly in the autumn, set a precedent for similar scheduling and returns to "persistent places" observed in much of the Northern Great Lakes during the following Woodland period (Dunham 2014).

Woodland Period

The Woodland period is generally recognized as a "stage marker" representing a suite of cultural developments between about 1000 BC and AD 1000/1600 in the Eastern Woodlands of North America (Anderson and Mainfort 2002). The Woodland period is usually associated with the advent of ceramic technology and is typically divided into three subperiods: Early, Middle, and Late. The beginning of the Early Woodland period is generally signaled by the appearance of pottery; by about 500 BC, sites containing technologically rudimentary and thick-walled "Marion" or "Schultz Thick" vessels appear in parts of the Midwest (Garland and Beld 1999). The subsequent Middle Woodland (200 BC–AD 500/600) period is dominated in much of the Midwest by the appearance of Hopewell, "diverse sets of specific Middle Woodland societies, each internally bound through several diverse spheres of alliance" (Abrams 2009, 172).

The Northern Great Lakes constitute a unique region within the Eastern Woodlands of North America relative to Woodland societies living farther to the south. Some groups occupying this northern area adopted pottery nearly a thousand years after other midwestern societies, and therefore in the absence of an "Early Woodland" (Mason 1970), the Middle Woodland (200 BC–AD 500/600) and Late Woodland (AD 500/600–1600) remain the primary temporal divisions for this area (Brose and Hambacher 1999). While groups to the south were transitioning to characteristic Woodland lifeways, such as the manufacture and use of pottery and the construction of burial mounds, those in the north persisted in Archaic lifeways until the Middle Woodland period despite undoubted centuries of contact with pottery-making neighbors to the south. The Hopewell phenomenon that prevailed over much of the Midwest during the Middle Woodland had little effect on the groups living in the Northern Great Lakes besides their participation in long-distance trade or down-the-line exchange of goods (Brose and Hambacher 1999; Martin 1999b). Southern Middle Woodland ceramics have been found as far north in Michigan as the northwestern lower peninsula (Holman 1978; Lovis 1971; Lovis, Rajnovich, and Bartley 1998).

The Middle Woodland period in the Northern Great Lakes (which is sometimes referred to as the Initial Woodland, particularly among Canadian researchers) witnessed the first adoption of pottery in the region. Previous assessments dated the outset of the Middle Woodland at about AD 1, but recent dates of early pottery in the Northern Great Lakes suggest the adoption of pottery as early as 200 BC (Albert et al. 2018). There is a lack of clear geographic attribute clustering of pottery types throughout the Middle Woodland period, which reflects fluidity of regional populations rather than stable and formally geographically bounded social relationships (Brose and Hambacher 1999). This fluidity was necessitated by the mobility of the populations, who still relied on a broad spectrum of resources spread over large geographic ranges. Middle Woodland groups seem to have increased aggregation at coastal villages for procurement of spring-spawning fish species; they also continued to come together along lakeshores for limited fall fishing or along inland streams and lakes for wild rice gathering (Brose and Hambacher 1999; Cleland 1982; Smith 2004).

Middle Woodland social fluidity is demonstrated by the large geographic distribution of Laurel ware, which is found in southern Manitoba, northern Minnesota and Wisconsin, the Upper Peninsula of Michigan, and Ontario (Janzen 1968; Stoltman 1973; Wright 1967). The finely made and highly decorated pottery vessels characteristic of Laurel do not seem to be stylistically derived from any other established regional ceramic tradition, although exchange of certain stylistic elements occurred with neighboring, contemporary traditions (Rajnovich 2003). Ceramic types found in adjacent regions include North Bay pottery, found in the Door Peninsula of Wisconsin and the western Upper Peninsula of Michigan (Mason 1966, 1967); Goodwinian Middle Woodland wares, local to the northeastern lower peninsula of Michigan (Fitting et al. 1969); and Point Peninsula wares of southeastern Ontario (Mason 1981; Ritchie 1969). All traditions utilized coil-constructed pottery with subconoidal bases, and stylistic variation occurs in a continuum across the region with little regional restriction, suggesting high levels of group movement and interaction (Brose and Hambacher 1999).

The Laurel culture is typically defined by a mobile hunting-gathering-fishing lifeway, a lithic industry dominated by end scrapers and stemmed or notched projectile points, bone-antler tools, and harpoons (Stoltman 1973). Laurel pottery is grit tempered with smoothed, rarely cordmarked exterior surfaces, and upper rim surfaces are often decorated, sometimes ornately, with a variety of dentate stamps (Janzen 1968; Stoltman 1973). Most sites are located on islands or sandy beaches along lakeshores or river mouths, places accessible by canoes or dugouts, and most residential sites suggest occupancy by a single family or small groups of relatives (Brose and Hambacher 1999, 191).

Major Middle Woodland sites in the Northern Great Lakes include Naomikong Point (Janzen 1968), Winter (Bianchi 1974; Richner 1973), Gyftakis (Fournier 2007), Summer Island (Brose 1970), Cloudman (Branstner 1995), Portage (Lovis, Rajnovich, and Bartley 1998), Arrowhead Drive (McPherron 1967), Nina (Dunham and Hambacher 2002), and Bark Dock (Dunham and Hambacher 2007), as well as Pic River (Wright 1966), Heron Bay, Michipicoten Harbor, and Sand River (Wright 1967) in Ontario. These sites are or were once located along the shoreline, and several are the earliest components of multicomponent sites, speaking to the increased interest in occupying prime fishing locales in the Woodland period.

The adoption of pottery at the outset of the Middle Woodland in the Northern Great Lakes is likely indicative of some social or economic change, the nature of which is still under debate. Skibo, Malainey, and Drake (2009) posited that the adoption of pottery was prompted by the need for improved efficiency of acorn processing, as demonstrated by lipid residue analysis of both fire-cracked rock and early pottery on Grand Island. However, lipid residue analysis of Middle Woodland pottery from the nearby Naomikong Point site did not contain nut lipids (Kooiman 2012, 2016; Malainey and Figol 2015). Interior carbonization patterns found in pottery across the Upper Peninsula suggest that vessels were routinely filled to the top during cooking (Kooiman 2012, 2016), a habit possibly carried over from a long tradition of cooking in organic vessels, which can be placed over fire without burning if filled with liquid (Speth

2015). The use of organic vessels fulfilled the needs of upper Great Lakes cooks for thousands of years, and the reasons for transitioning to clay cooking pots may have varied across the region (Skibo, Malainey, and Kooiman 2016).

The Late Woodland period (AD 500/600–900/1600), which is also referred to as the Terminal Woodland in the Northern Great Lakes, may be described as a time of significant economic and cultural change that varied considerably across Eastern North America, change possibly spurred by increased populations from the Middle Woodland to the Late Woodland (Anderson and Mainfort 2002; Holman and Brashler 1999). The shared artifact styles seen among many areas during the Middle Woodland gave way to increasing heterogeneity of ceramic styles throughout the period, suggesting greater social distinction and territoriality as resources were in more demand (Braun and Plog 1982; Holman and Brashler 1999; McElrath, Emerson, and Fortier 2000).

The Late Woodland was a time of technological and subsistence change in the Eastern Woodlands of North America. The bow and arrow made its first appearance during this time, and cultivated crops became increasingly important in many regions (McElrath, Emerson, and Fortier 2000). The adoption and dietary incorporation of domesticated plant species was gradual across the Woodland period, and most groups remained semimobile until the intensification of maize cultivation after AD 800/900. Throughout much of the Eastern Woodlands, Late Woodland period traditions were followed by a variety of new cultural manifestations marked by maize agriculture and increased sedentism (Schroeder 2004). In contrast, Late Woodland period sociocultural practices and lifeways generally persisted until European contact in much of the upper and Northern Great Lakes, although they did not remain static (Schroeder 2004).

Major Late Woodland sites in the Northern Great Lakes include Sand Point (Dorothy 1978, 1980), Scott Point, Juntunen (McPherron 1967), Wycamp Creek (Lovis, Arbogast, and Monaghan 2012), O'Neil (Lovis 1973), Bark Dock (Dunham and Hambacher 2007), and Cloudman (Branstner 1992, 1995), mostly large coastal sites interpreted as seasonal aggregation fishing sites. However, according to Dunham (2014), smaller interior sites were just as important for the seasonal subsistence rounds but are less visible due to their size and location in less developed areas (e.g., the Inland Waterway sites [Lovis 1978]). While some argue that populations grew over the course of the Late Woodland period and required new food procurement and mobility strategies (Cleland 1982), others believe populations and settlement/subsistence strategies remained steady throughout (Martin 1989, 1999a).

Unlike the preceding Laurel Middle Woodland, Late Woodland pottery was formed by slab construction instead of coiling and was frequently cordmarked. Ceramic wares from across the Northern Great Lakes continued to share many stylistic attributes in the Early Late Woodland period (AD 600–1000) (Holman and Brashler 1999). Bowerman and Skegemog wares common to the Traverse corridor in the northeastern lower peninsula of Michigan bear resemblance to wares farther to the south (Hambacher 1992; Holman and Brashler 1999). Juntunen sequence vessels, most closely associated with the Straits of Mackinac, predominate in the eastern Upper Peninsula throughout the Late Woodland period (Martin 1999a). The sequence includes Mackinac, Bois Blanc, and Juntunen wares (McPherron 1967). The earliest, Mackinac ware, is common between AD 750 and AD 1000 (Lovis 2014; McPherron 1967), and while distinct from most lower Michigan wares, it bears some resemblance to Skegemog pottery (Holman and Brashler 1999). Blackduck ware, a possible stylistic descendant of Laurel ware, is found across and beyond the Northern Great Lakes, from Saskatchewan to Quebec, and from northern Minnesota to the Upper Peninsula of Michigan across variable durations of time (Hamilton, Graham, and Nicholson 2007; Lugenbeal 1978; McHale Milner 1998; McPherron 1967; Reid and Rajnovich 1991). Blackduck closely resembles Bois Blanc ware, the second of the Juntunen sequence wares, which was manufactured in the Straits region between AD 1000 and AD 1200 (Lovis 2014; McPherron 1967).

Pottery style generally became more heterogeneous during and after the Late Late Woodland (Holman and Brashler 1999), reflecting greater social localization and reduced mobility and territories (McHale Milner 1991, 1998). Traverse ware replaces Bowerman and Skegemog pottery in the Traverse corridor (Hambacher 1992), while Juntunen ware, the last of the Juntunen sequence, predominates in the Straits and eastern Upper Peninsula after AD 1200 (McHale Milner 1998; McPherron 1967). Juntunen wares display stylistic attributes that suggest interactions with Iroquoian groups of Ontario (Brashler et al. 2000; Holman and Brashler

1999; McHale Milner 1998), using similar decorative motifs but employing drag-and-jab decoration techniques rather than incising, which is the characteristic decorative technique employed by Iroquoian potters. Upper Mississippian (Oneota) wares associated with southern Wisconsin and northern Illinois also make an appearance at certain sites across the Upper Peninsula (Dorothy 1978, 1980; Dunham and Hambacher 2002, 2007; Holman and Brashler 1999; McPherron 1967). Distinct local pottery wares also more frequently co-occur at Late Woodland coastal aggregation sites, suggesting both an increased sense of group identity and the importance of extralocal relationships during this time (Holman and Brashler 1999; McHale Milner 1991, 1998; O'Shea and McHale Milner 2002).

Whereas people producing Mackinac pottery in the Early Late Woodland period maintained a more mobile lifestyle similar to that of their Laurel Middle Woodland predecessors, a greater number of distinct pottery styles with more limited geographic distributions during the Late Late Woodland suggest a time of greater group identity formation, smaller territories, and decreased residential mobility (Holman and Lovis 2008). Some have argued that population increases in the Late Late Woodland period resulted in new cultural adaptations to these pressures. Social localization demonstrated by pottery style has been interpreted as the result of the development of a tribal-level societal structure (O'Shea and McHale Milner 2002).

A tradition of earthwork construction in parts of the Northern Great Lakes emerged after AD 1000, a change that has been associated with the development of regional ritual tradition that facilitated and maintained social and trade networks between dispersed tribes or groups (Howey 2007; Howey and O'Shea 2006). Earthwork enclosures and burial mounds may have served as locales for seasonal group aggregation and/or as demarcations of resources and territories on the landscape (Howey 2007; Howey and O'Shea 2006). To deal with decreased territories and increasing population, Late Late Woodland/Late Precontact groups also began intensified efforts to store food, represented by the appearance of cache pit sites, which have been identified at various inland locales in northern Lower Michigan (Hambacher and Holman 1995; Howey 2015; Howey and Frederick 2016; Howey and Parker 2008). Cache pits would have served as redundant storage to mitigate risk of cold-season food shortages (Frederick 2019).

These phenomena, however, appear isolated primarily south of the Straits of Mackinac. There are no reported earthen enclosures or cache pit clusters in the eastern Upper Peninsula of Michigan (Howey, Palace, and McMichael 2016; Frederick 2019). There are, however, mounds located at several island locations in the eastern Upper Peninsula, including the Juntunen site on Bois Blanc Island in the Straits of Mackinac (McPherron 1967), and on Drummond Island, at the Potagannissing Bay Mounds site (20CH245) and the Cloudman site (20CH6) (Branstner 1995; Demers 1991; Hinsdale 1931). The mounds on Drummond Island, however, have been associated with the Middle Woodland period, although this has not been confirmed (Branstner 1995; Demers 1991). A large Late Woodland mound group, the Sand Point site, is located in the western Upper Peninsula and may be more closely associated with mound-building traditions in Wisconsin (Dorothy 1978). Ultimately, the archaeological record suggests significant social, settlement, subsistence, and possibly even ideological changes taking place in the Northern Great Lakes during the Late Woodland/Late Precontact period.

Iroquoian Period

Iroquoian-speaking people occupied portions of modern-day New York and southeastern Ontario. Iroquoian groups that settled in modern-day Ontario during the Late Precontact and early Contact periods include the Wendat (Huron), Tionnontati (Petun), Neutral, and St. Lawrence Iroquoians (Warrick 2000). Although the emergence of sedentary agriculturalists with pottery and a language system quite distinct from surrounding Algonquian groups caused many to believe that the Iroquoians migrated into the region, most archaeologists now believe that these groups developed in situ from Woodland populations (Smith 1990; Warrick 2000).

Late Woodland Princess Point groups in southern Ontario (AD 600–1000) have been interpreted as being the direct ancestors of later Iroquoian groups based on the continuity of material culture and settlement-subsistence patterns. They were among the first to experiment with maize agriculture in northeastern North America (Fox 1990a). Princess Point people lived in small year-round villages with warm-season camps for hunting and gathering, since wild resources still made up most of their diet (Snow 1980; Warrick 2000).

Immediate descendants of Princess Point are referred to as "Early Iroquois" (AD 1000–1300) (Warrick 2000; Williamson 1990). Wright (1973) divided the early Iroquoian stage of Ontario into two distinct regional variants: the Glen Meyer branch in southwestern Ontario and the Pickering Branch of southeastern Ontario. While the two branches are no longer considered discrete sociocultural entities, they are still recognized as distinct regional populations (Williamson 1990). Glen Meyer and Pickering peoples lived in unstable, semisedentary villages composed of small longhouses and began to rely more heavily on maize (Bamann et al. 1992; Kuhn and Funk 2000). The subsequent Middle Ontario Iroquoian stage (AD 1300–1400) is marked by the growing intensification of horticulture subsistence (particularly maize cultivation). This was accompanied by the establishment of stable, year-round residences, which gradually became populated with longhouses of increasing size (Bamann et al. 1992; Kuhn and Funk 2000). Households were located in small to medium-sized villages that were widely dispersed across the landscape and were not yet incorporated into regionwide identities, as signaled by ceramic motifs (Hart et al. 2017).

The emergence of Wendat-Petun (Huron) populations (distinct from other Ontario Iroquoian groups, such as the Neutral and St. Lawrence Iroquois) arose around AD 1400, in south-central Ontario, between the Trent River, the Niagara Escarpment, and Lake Ontario, an area historically known as "Huronia" (Ramsden 1990). The Wendat-Petun developed as population increases solidified regional identities. Villages were autonomous and highly organized, with each matrilineage contained within a longhouse; both village and house sizes were larger than in the Middle Iroquoian period (Warrick 2000). Along with villages, farming hamlets and logistical resource extraction camps associated with the Wendat-Petun have also been found (Ramsden 1990). The population migrations, social restructuring, and coalescence of smaller villages into larger ones that occurred after AD 1500 have been attributed to the indirect effects of European contact, although this has been disputed in recent years (Ramsden 1990). While there is some stylistic overlap between "Huron/Wendat-Petun" and "Neutral" pottery, these groups are also associated with specific ceramic typologies emblematic of distinct social identities (Wright 1973).

Proto-Iroquoian and Iroquoian populations witnessed the gradual intensification of cultivated foods. Although maize first appeared in southern Quebec by 391 to 209 cal BC (St-Pierre and Thompson 2015), northern New York by cal AD 1 (Hart, Brumbach, and Lusteck 2007), and southern Ontario between cal AD 260 and 660, these early groups only began to experiment with maize cultivation and consumption (Fox 1990a). Maize was not a significant part of the diet until the Early Iroquoian period (AD 1000–1300), when it still only constituted between 20% and 30% of the diet among Ontario groups, who continued with predominantly hunter-gatherer subsistence strategies (Warrick 2000). Evidence for beans, squash, and sunflower does not surface until the middle of the eleventh century; the "Three Sisters" subsistence regime (maize, beans, and squash) became dominant between AD 1300 and AD 1525, and sunflower and tobacco were also grown (Bamann et al. 1992; Kuhn and Funk 2000). Although the Huron were sedentary agriculturalists by this time, their diets were supplemented by wild game, fishing, and some wild plant resources (Williamson 1990). They may have also traded maize in exchange for fish and wild game, often via the Odawa, with northern hunting-gathering Algonquian groups as a form of risk buffering against periodic crop failure (O'Shea 1989; Smith 1996).

Late Precontact/Early Contact Period

Despite the persistence of Late Woodland traditions in the Northern Great Lakes until the time of contact with Europeans, a series of new cultural manifestations—such as the Mississippian, Upper Mississippian/Oneota, Fort Ancient, and Iroquoian societies—that were focused on maize agriculture and increasingly sedentary lifestyles were forming in other parts of the Eastern Woodlands and had an impact on local groups (Schroeder 2004). Copper from the western Upper Peninsula of Michigan was shaped into ornaments or implements and incorporated into the vast Mississippian trade network (Ehrhardt 2009), while Ramey Incised-style vessels similar to Ramey Incised ones (believed to be emulations of special-purpose vessels manufactured at the site of Cahokia in southern Illinois) have been found at the Juntunen site in the Straits of Mackinac (McPherron 1967) and the Sand Point site, which is located at the base of the Keweenaw Peninsula on Lake Superior (Dorothy 1980). A number of sites with pottery assemblages containing shell-tempered Oneota wares have been found across the Upper Peninsula as well, which in some cases appear to represent movement of Oneota groups into the area rather than the result of trade (Brose 1970; Dunham and Hambacher 2002, 2007; Halsey 1999; McPherron 1967). Although sites associated with Oneota groups appear in Wisconsin, Iowa, and northern Illinois around AD 1000 (Henning 1998), components associated with Oneota occupations at sites in the Upper Peninsula generally date to about AD 1300 or later (Brose 1970; Halsey 1999; McPherron 1967). Iroquoian and Iroquoian-style vessels appear in very limited quantities west of southeastern Ontario during the period from AD 900 to AD 1300, while their appearances become much more frequent across the Northern Great Lakes after AD 1300 (McHale Milner 1998, 212–13).

The Anishinaabeg people, which includes the Ojibwe, Potawatomi, and Odawa, are believed by scholars to have originated from east of the Great Lakes, migrating west in the late sixteenth or early seventeenth century (Danziger 1978, 7). This is corroborated by Anishinaabe oral tradition, which recounts their origins on the North Atlantic coast and subsequent 500-year westward migration along the St. Lawrence River, culminating in their arrival at the western end of Lake Superior by the seventeenth century, settling among resident Algonquian groups (Benz and Williamson 2005). Therefore, the resident Woodland groups in the Northern Great Lakes appear to have experienced increased social interactions and population movements between AD 1300 and AD 1600, a period hereafter referred to as the Late Precontact period.

The arrival of Europeans in North America further complicated the social landscape of the Northern Great Lakes (figure 2.2). When the French arrived in Ontario in 1615, they encountered Algonquian-speaking bands of mobile hunter-gatherers living adjacent to Huron territory (Fox 1990b). These people were identified as the Odawa. At the time, these groups occupied the Bruce Peninsula, Manitoulin Island, and other parts of the coast of Georgian Bay (Fox 1990b). Early historical accounts and archaeological excavation of Contact period Odawa sites indicate that they were mobile hunter-gatherers who heavily fished and practiced marginal horticulture (Fox 1990b).

Fox and Garrad (2004) argue that substantial exchange between precontact Huron-Petun groups in southern Ontario and Algonquian groups occupying the south shore of Georgian Bay (assumed to be the Odawa) commenced in the fourteenth century and that Iroquoian-manufactured and imitation Iroquoian pottery located along the Georgian Bay region is evidence of this exchange. Archaeological sites from

Figure 2.2. Distribution of cultural groups ca. 1630. Courtesy of Erin Beachey.

this time have been identified as Odawa based on Algonquian lithics and ritual signatures (e.g., dog burials), despite the Huron/Wendat pottery and pipes (or locally produced copies), which are argued to be the result of trade with the Wendat (Fox 1990b; Ross 1975). Proponents of this model claim hunter-gatherer Odawa groups exchanged fish for maize with the Wendat (Fox 1990b; Fox and Garrad 2004). Alternatively, Warrick (2000, 442) interprets these findings as evidence of early Iroquoian occupation of south Georgian Bay, mapping Middleport (AD 1330–1420) Iroquoian sites in the area.

B. A. Smith (1996) found evidence of an exchange network centered on the exchange of food items, where northern Algonquian groups, primarily the Ojibwe, traded meat to middlemen Odawa for their own consumption and for trade with Huron/Wendat and Petun groups in southern Ontario, who in turn provided maize for distribution to the north. The Odawa themselves provided fish, reed mats, and other products to the system but primarily served the role of transporters of food items (Smith 1996, 278).

Groups known historically as the Ojibwe (also known as Ojibay, Ojibwa, and Chippewa) settled in the Upper Great Lakes primarily around all shores of Lake Superior, although some migrated and settled as far as the western plains of Minnesota and the Dakotas (Danziger 1978, 8). Odawa is a dialect of the Ojibwe language, the mutual intelligibility of which would have facilitated trade among the different Anishinaabeg groups (Mithun 1999). Most Ojibwe lived a mobile, hunter-gatherer lifestyle, following seasonal economic cycles based around subsistence activities such as fishing, hunting, and gathering, much like resident Woodland populations (Danziger 1978, 9, 11–13). Anishinaabeg people in the Great Lakes retained a flexible social structure that frustrated the European traders who attempted to trade and make treaties with them (Witgen 2012). Although local Indigenous groups often held the upper hand in their early interactions with European traders, European diseases and intensified colonization efforts eventually depleted Indigenous populations and reversed the balance of power throughout the Great Lakes of North America (Milner, Anderson, and Smith 2001; White 1991; Witgen 2012).

CONCLUSION

The sociocultural history of the Northern Great Lakes is complex, despite the superficial appearance of simplicity when compared to the cultural histories of neighboring regions. Indigenous societies in this region had to contend with harsh climatic and environmental fluctuations and conditions. While these challenges sometimes delayed or precluded the types of cultural developments that occurred elsewhere in the southern Great Lakes, the riverine Midwest, and southeastern Canada, it also led to local and regionally successful adaptations and behaviors that resulted in the long-term endurance of groups occupying the region and a cultural dynamism reflected in the material culture.

The paucity of sites and artifacts resulting from low population densities and relatively poor preservation of archaeological materials contributes to the initial appearance of the Northern Great Lakes as a "less interesting" region of scholarly inquiry. It also makes interpretations of past behavior among these local groups difficult. However, the collective results of the many decades of research in this region, when examined closely, reveal the complex nature of Northern Great Lakes societies through time. The application of analytic techniques both old and new can provide new data and inform different or standing unanswered questions, highlighting both the intriguing history of the Northern Great Lakes and the scope of human flexibility and creativity in the face of social and environmental change.

CHAPTER 3

Cuisine and Pottery Technology in the Northern Great Lakes

In the broader cultural context of the Northern Great Lakes outlined in the previous chapter, changing subsistence traditions, social interactions, and settlement patterns during the Woodland period have become central issues for archaeologists studying the region. Pottery and food remains have provided useful information about these topics, yet many questions remain, and answering these lingering uncertainties is at the core of this study. The use of updated pottery and dietary analytic methods in the past decade has uncovered more pieces of this ongoing puzzle of the past, and their application to a substantial yet understudied site in the Northern Great Lakes holds the potential to offer more clues about ancient subsistence, society, and technology.

SUBSISTENCE AND SETTLEMENT IN THE NORTHERN GREAT LAKES

The subsistence and settlement patterns of the Woodland occupants of the Northern Great Lakes have long been topics of archaeological inquiry and therefore have been much debated. Various models for Upper Great

Lakes (including the Northern Great Lakes) Woodland settlement-subsistence patterns have been proposed. The most prominent model for Middle Woodland subsistence centers on seasonal aggregation at coastal sites, where groups took advantage of spring-spawning fish in shallow waters using, according to Cleland (1982), the seine net. Summer Island was interpreted by Brose (1970) as a spring coastal site, with evidence of a return to a generalized mixed economy following the spawning runs. These groups likely moved to different coastal sites, or to interior lakes or streams, during the remaining warm season to exploit various other seasonal resources before retreating to small interior hunting encampments for the summer (Brose 1970; Brose and Hambacher 1999).

Cleland (1982) proposed that the invention of the gill net in the Late Woodland period allowed inhabitants to exploit deep-water spawning fish, leading to a series of widespread changes marking the Middle Woodland–Late Woodland transition, including increased populations, larger and denser shoreline sites, and subsistence strategies that relied on exploitation of seasonally abundant fish and plant materials. Seasonal aggregation at coastal sites therefore also occurred in the fall, when deep-water spawning fish (such as whitefish and lake trout) could be harvested en masse.

Martin (1989) disputed Cleland's "inland shore fishery" model of change over time, citing a lack of evidence for increasing population size, instead attributing perceived site size increase to the palimpsest effect of repeated occupations. Questioning Cleland's evidence for the invention of the gill net at the outset of the Late Woodland period, Martin presents data suggesting that some deep-water fishing occurred during the Middle Woodland period. She also disputes alteration of settlement patterns resulting from new seasonal fishing habits in the Late Woodland, arguing instead for subsistence and residential continuity throughout the Woodland period. In rebuttal to Martin, Cleland (1989) reiterates evidence supporting the intensified exploitation of fall-spawning fish during the Late Woodland and claims Martin failed to demonstrate the use of gill nets, which are necessary for deep-water fishing, during the Middle Woodland period.

In a reexamination of this issue and debate, B. A. Smith (2004) uses multiple lines of evidence to demonstrate that fall-spawning fish were exploited during the Middle Woodland but that the intensive use of gill nets to procure them in large quantities did not become common until the Late Woodland period, particularly after AD 1100 in the Lake Michigan basin and after AD 1400 throughout the rest of the Upper Great Lakes. Drake and Dunham (2004) likewise advocate for greater continuity in the use of coastal sites between the Middle and Late Woodland periods than was suggested by Cleland but acknowledge broader shifts in social, subsistence, and settlement patterns moving forward into the Late Woodland period.

Most recently, Dunham (2014) highlighted alterations in settlement, subsistence, and social structures over the course of the Late Woodland period in the eastern Upper Peninsula of Michigan, the approximate center of the Northern Great Lakes region. People in the Early Late Woodland period (AD 700–1000) were more residentially mobile, meaning that they frequently moved their base camps across the landscape in pursuit of new patches of food resources, and they also produced more homogeneous ceramic styles (similar to the stylistic and social homogeneity observed during the Middle Woodland). Groups in the Late Late Woodland period (post–AD 1200) transitioned from residential mobility to logistic mobility, sending out logistical parties on long foraging or hunting forays to bring resources back to base camps occupied for longer periods of time. Late Late Woodland people also occupied sites with greater resource diversity, exploited greater amounts of starchy resources (such as wild rice and acorns), increased their use of storage, and displayed greater social heterogeneity.

Dunham (2014) hypothesizes these changes were in response to more dynamic lake levels resulting from the Medieval Climatic Optimum, which began after AD 900 (Lovis, Arbogast, and Monaghan 2012). This period caused environmental and resource instability, resulting in reactions from groups occupying the region as described above. These are all economic or social mechanisms for risk buffering, or protection against both short- and long-term food shortages. Reliance primarily on the exploitation of spring- and fall-spawning fish, as posited by Cleland, was too risky, and therefore both wild rice and acorns were exploited and stored as buffering resources against periodic fish shortages. Dunham (2014) did not find maize to have been included as a major component of even the Late Late Woodland buffering mechanisms in this portion of the Northern Great Lakes.

An alternative view of Late Woodland subsistence regimes states that the ceramic heterogeneity seen in the Late Late Woodland is indicative of the formation of horticulturalist coastal societies (such as groups using Juntunen wares) and inland groups, who remained foragers (O'Shea 2003). This model proposes that coastal societies who were maize agriculturalists occupied large aggregation sites used for rituals and exchange of maize and aquatic resources with inland foraging groups. Its interpretation is based on the finding that maize constituted 18% to 20% of the diet of individuals buried at the Juntunen site, located on Bois Blanc Island in the Straits of Mackinac (Brandt 1996), and the discovery of earthwork enclosures with associated storage pits in northern Lower Michigan (Howey 2007, 2015; Howey and Frederick 2016; Howey and O'Shea 2002, 2006; O'Shea and McHale Milner 1998).

WOODLAND POTTERY STYLE IN THE NORTHERN GREAT LAKES

As discussed in chapter 2, Middle Woodland period populations in the Northern Great Lakes were highly mobile and maintained fluid social relationships and group compositions, necessitated by their reliance on a broad spectrum of resources spread over large geographic ranges (Brose and Hambacher 1999). This is evidenced by broad stylistic similarities in pottery seen across much of the Upper Great Lakes (Brose and Hambacher 1999). Laurel ware is found broadly across the northern and southern shores of Lake Superior and parts of northern Lake Michigan, while North Bay wares predominate in the Door Peninsula of Wisconsin and the western Upper Peninsula of Michigan, although the two stylistic families have many similarities (Brose 1970; Brose and Hambacher 1999; Mason 1981).

The Late Woodland period, on the other hand, appears to have been a time of increasing localization in the Northern Great Lakes, during which subsistence efforts were concentrated within decreased geographic ranges on productive but localized resources (potentially including maize, fall-spawning fish, and certain wild resources) (Dunham 2014; McHale Milner 1991, 42–43). The Late Woodland pottery types local to the Straits of Mackinac and the eastern Upper Peninsula of Michigan are found in a more limited range than Middle Woodland Laurel ware and are more distinct from other regional pottery types, particularly those manufactured after AD 1200 (McHale Milner 1991, 1998; McPherron 1967). This trend continues throughout the Late Woodland, where differences observed between Mackinac (Early Late Woodland) and Juntunen (Late Late Woodland) pottery distributions and settlement patterns indicate a decrease in residential mobility over time (Holman and Lovis 2008).

Using ethnohistorical information and stylistic ceramic analysis of Juntunen phase (AD 1200–1450) sites in the Upper Peninsula of Michigan, McHale Milner (1991) argued that Late Woodland peoples developed increasingly bounded social groups at the local level while also maintaining long-distance social ties for risk-buffering purposes in times of local food shortages. Distinct pottery styles found within specific, limited geographic ranges provide evidence of bounded social groups, while extralocal (long-distance) relationships are indicated by the unexpected presence of "foreign" (nonlocal) stylistic elements on Juntunen pottery (McHale Milner 1998). According to McHale Milner (1991, 1998), these social relationships were formed, maintained, and solidified through integrative social events at seasonal aggregation sites. A number of such aggregational sites dating to the Late Woodland period have been identified along the coasts of the Northern Great Lakes, such as the Juntunen (20MK1), Cloudman (20CH6), and Sand Point (20BG14) sites. These served as locations where independent hunter-gatherer bands would come together to fish or gather other seasonally abundant resources such as acorns or wild rice and form and solidify social relationships that could facilitate trade and support. In certain parts of the Northern Great Lakes, sites where disparate groups came together for social and ceremonial purposes are marked on the landscape by mounds and earthen enclosures (Howey and O'Shea 2006; Howey 2007; Howey, Palace, and McMichael 2016; McHale Milner and O'Shea 1998). Dog burials have also been located at sites thought to be important locales of feasting and exchange between groups in the Northern Great Lakes during the Late Precontact and Historic periods (Smith 1996).

Ceramic evidence, alongside environmental and settlement data, suggests that Northern Great Lakes Woodland groups increasingly employed a series of risk-buffering techniques throughout the Late Woodland period to minimize potential food shortages in the face of restricting territories. These strategies include integrative social events and shifting intensification of targeted resources (fish and starchy foods) as responses to environmental instability. While the social aspects of this transition are well documented and studied, the change in resource selection and resource cooking and processing has yet to be critically analyzed through the lens of pottery. Technological pottery traits, or nonstylistic physical characteristics, can be subtle yet important indicators of broader adaptive and social change, since potters react to altering cooking and food processing needs by adjusting the physical characteristics of cooking vessels to perform optimally and fulfill new cooking requirements.

COOKING AND COOKING TECHNOLOGY IN THE NORTHERN GREAT LAKES

Ceramic cooking vessels and associated culinary evidence can reflect subsistence and settlement changes, which may in turn be rooted in alterations to social and natural environments. Seemingly simple changes in pottery technology—such as thickness, size, shape, and composition—and cooking habits may, therefore, provide evidence of broader changes in how past groups negotiated with each other and with the environment.

Previous analyses of pottery function among assemblages in the Northern Great Lakes revealed possible shifts in cooking techniques between the Middle Woodland and Late Woodland periods. Patterning of carbonization (i.e., burned food residue) on interior surfaces of Middle Woodland ceramic cooking vessels from the Naomikong Point (20CH2) and Winter (20DE17) sites indicated the prevalence of stewing, while Late Woodland vessels from the Sand Point site (20BG14) were more frequently marked with carbonization patterns indicative of boiling practices (Albert et al. 2018; Kooiman 2012, 2016). Stewing is a low-temperature, long-term cooking process that reduces liquid content; boiling requires higher temperatures and maintenance of a more aqueous mixture. The observed increase in boiling practices at these Northern Great Lakes sites prompted the hypothesis that the observed change in cooking habits signaled broader dietary shifts, possibly connected to the intensification of starchy foods in the Late Woodland, which require intensive boiling to be made digestible (Braun 1983; Wandsnider 1997).

These changing dietary trends and cooking styles over the course of the Woodland Period may have been necessitated by alterations in settlement and subsistence patterning as suggested by several regional scholars (Cleland 1982; Dunham 2014; Smith 2004).

To understand why cooking techniques and pottery technology may have been altered, it is important to first determine which foods were being processed in cooking pots. Microscopic and chemical food remains in adhered and absorbed residues associated with pottery vessels are the only direct evidence of which foods were being processed in cooking pots. Limited analysis of lipid residues extracted from cooking pots from the the Naomikong Point and Sand Point sites revealed only slight differences in vessel contents and therefore offered few answers about the differences in cooking styles at the two sites (Kooiman 2012, 2016; Malainey and Figol 2015). Analysis of microscopic plant remains found in food residues adhered to pottery vessels from the Winter site (20DE17) offered valuable insights into Middle Woodland period diet, but without a similar analysis of Late Woodland materials, change through time could not be assessed (Albert et al. 2018).

Ultimately, the ways in which technology, diet, cooking, and social relationships relate to one another and change from the Middle Woodland through the Late Woodland and Late Precontact periods are unclear. Pottery occupies a unique position at the crossroads of subsistence and society and offers the ideal pathway by which to explore these issues together. Examination of legacy collections, in this case, the Cloudman site pottery assemblage, can aid in the search for answers to decades-long archaeological debates, evidence that has been sitting on shelves for just as long, waiting to be mined for answers.

CASE STUDY: THE CLOUDMAN SITE (20CH6)

The Cloudman site is located on Drummond Island in the eastern Upper Peninsula of Michigan near the southern outlet of the St. Mary's River into Lake Huron (figure 3.1). It lies on the northern bank of the Potagannissing River, occupying a series of river terraces. The site covers approximately 30,000 square meters and contains four occupational components that are both vertically stratified and horizontally separated (Branstner

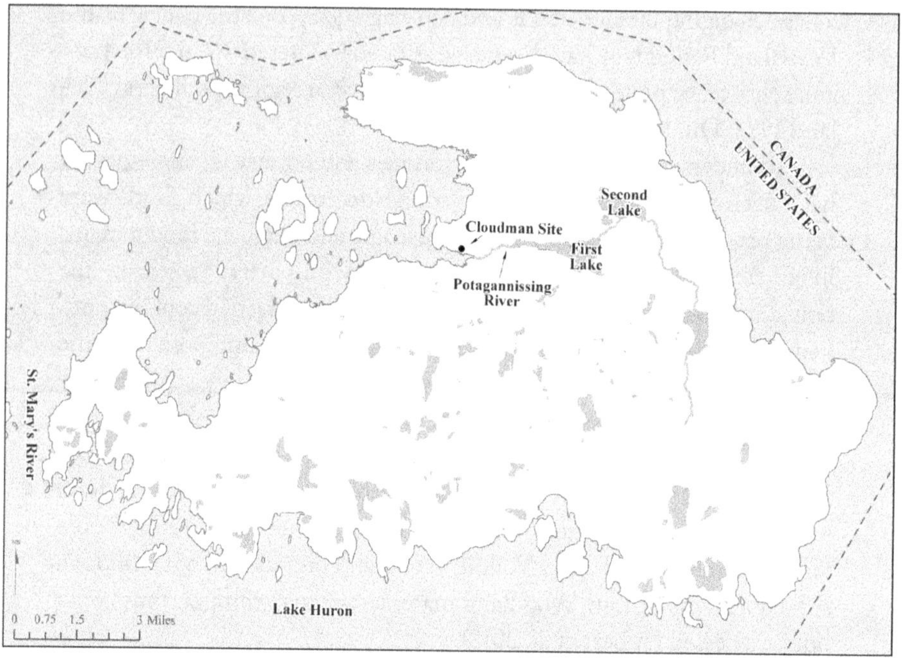

Figure 3.1. Drummond Island and the Cloudman site (20CH6). Courtesy of Adriana Martinez.

1995). Branstner (1995), using relative dating of artifact styles, interpreted the timing of occupation for each component of the site: Middle Woodland (AD 0–400); Late Woodland (AD 800–1500); "Protohistoric" (AD 1500–1650); and two Historic period homesteads (ca. AD 1880 and 1920).

History of Investigations

The Cloudman site consists of a habitation area and a large burial mound. The mound was the focus of amateur excavations in the 1920s, during which a couple of catlinite pipes, a copper hatchet, stone tools, and pottery sherds with "geometric designs" were recovered (Branstner 1995, 19). The whereabouts of these artifacts are currently unknown. The site (specifically, the mound) was first officially reported by Hinsdale (1931).

A thorough assessment of the Cloudman site was not conducted until 1974, when John Franzen assessed the locale as part of a survey of

Chippewa County. He initially reported Cloudman as containing Middle Woodland and Historic period occupational components (Franzen 1975). The St. Mary's River Archaeological Project, under the auspices of Michigan State University, visited the site in 1990 and 1991 to identify its components and spatial extent. The habitational zones were found located to the west of the mound, with the entirety of the site located within a 500-meter span along the shore of the Potagannissing River (Branster 1992; Demers 1991). The site was excavated under the supervision of Charles Cleland and Christine Branstner of Michigan State University in 1992 and 1994, during which 102 square meters of the habitational zone were excavated and thirty-three features uncovered (Branstner 1995). An additional unit was also excavated in 1995 by Cleland, although a report of the results from this work was not completed (Christine Stephenson pers. comm.).

Gradual lowering of lake levels over time led to the formation of three distinct river terraces at the site, which roughly correspond to each of the three primary occupations (Branstner 1995, 23). Middle Woodland materials are largely confined to the upper terrace (181 m and above); the middle (179–81 m) and lower (177–79 m) terraces contain mostly Late Woodland and Protohistoric materials, respectively (Branstner 1995, 23). There was only minimal spatial overlap between the different temporal occupations (Branstner 1995).

Branstner (1995) conducted preliminary analysis of the ceramic assemblage from all components of the Cloudman site, which included typological categorization of pottery vessels. Vessels from the Middle Woodland, Middle Woodland/Late Woodland transitional, Early Late Woodland, Late Late Woodland, and Contact/Protohistoric periods were sorted and identified. There were also several miniature vessels that were not described.

Identified Middle Woodland vessels at Cloudman are almost exclusively varieties of Laurel ware, while those vessels identified by Branstner (1995) as Early Late Woodland are primarily Mackinac ware varieties (see chapter 5 for typological descriptions). In accordance with McHale Milner (1991, 1998), Late Late Woodland vessels demonstrate great stylistic diversity. Branstner noted that thirty-one (72%) of the Late Late Woodland vessels represented hyper-localized styles not yet identified in the existing literature. Identifiable Late Late Woodland types primarily consisted of Juntunen ware.

Originally, one component of the site containing European-made trade goods and Iroquoian-style pottery types was interpreted as a "Protohistoric" Odawa occupation dating to approximately AD 1615–30 (Branstner 1995; Cleland 1999). This was based on apparent association of Iroquoian-style pottery and European-made trade goods, which were preliminarily dated to the early seventeenth century (Branstner 1995; Cleland 1999). According to Trigger (1976, 294), the Bruce Peninsula, Manitoulin Island, and Drummond Island were "Ottawa" territory around 1615, which also shows trade routes between the Odawa territory and the Huron (Wyandot) settled on the eastern shore of Lake Huron. A critical reassessment of both the Iroquoian-style pottery and the glass trade beads has since demonstrated that the pottery dates to between AD 1300 and 1500, while the beads most likely date to after AD 1670 (Kooiman and Walder 2019; Walder 2018). Soil compaction likely made these two occupations indistinguishable from each other in the site stratigraphy (see chapter 5 for an updated occupational history of the site).

Environmental Setting

Drummond Island lies within the eastern Upper Michigan regional landscape ecosystem, which is forested by northern conifers, northern hardwoods, and patches of oak (Albert, Denton, and Barnes 1986). This would have supported a variety of wild plants and animals that could be used for human exploitation. Although the region is cool and has rather sandy soil, it has a relatively long growing season due to climatological amelioration from Lakes Superior, Michigan, and Huron (Albert, Denton, and Barnes 1986). This means that the growing season would have been just long enough for maize to be successfully cultivated at the Cloudman site. In addition, the site is located close to modern wild rice stands, although it is difficult to determine their antiquity (Dunham 2008, 2014).

Some limited dietary and seasonality data are available for the Cloudman site based on floral and faunal remains. Flotation samples were taken from most features, and analysis of macrobotanical remains extracted from these samples revealed a great diversity of plant species (Egan-Bruhy 2007). Cloudman occupants ate a variety of fruits (including strawberry, raspberry, elderberry, and wild plum), nuts (such as hazelnut, walnut, and acorn), and seeds and cultigens such as chenopod, maize, and wild rice (Egan-Bruhy 2007). These resources would have been available during the summer and fall seasons.

Faunal remains from only two features were analyzed. Feature 26, attributed to the Late Woodland period, contained woodchuck and beaver, spring- and early summer-spawning fish (northern pike, sucker, catfish, bass, perch, walleye), and fall-spawning fish (whitefish and drum) (Cooper 1996). Feature 27, associated with the later occupations of the site, contained a dog burial and most of a snapping turtle but also contained portions of beaver, muskrat, black bear, caribou, common loon, spring- and summer-spawning fish (sturgeon, pike, sucker, catfish, perch, and walleye), and fall-spawning fish (whitefish and drum). Sample sizes of various species in both features were too small to assign strict occupational seasonality, although the large proportion of sucker (39% of fish elements) from Feature 27 suggests targeted spring-spawning species exploitation (Cooper 1996). The presence of the dog burial, alongside a wide variety of other species in the same feature, could represent ceremonial activities at the site (Smith 1996).

Large, multicomponent sites available for study in the Northern Great Lakes, and particularly in the Upper Peninsula, are rare. Arrowhead Drive/Juntunen, Summer Island, Scott Point, and Cloudman are the only sites with substantial ceramic assemblages attributed to Middle Woodland, Late Woodland, and/or Late Precontact periods; the Cloudman assemblage is the only assemblage with pottery from all three periods. This made Cloudman an excellent site for the investigation of the problem of changing subsistence strategies and cooking techniques throughout the Woodland and Late Precontact periods.

RESEARCH TOPICS AND EXPECTATIONS

In the context of what is known—and what is unknown—about cooking technologies and culinary habits in the Northern Great Lakes, this book investigates a series of topics using the Cloudman site pottery assemblage. The first topic of inquiry is whether there are *differences in technical properties* (specifically, thickness, temper size, and rim diameter) between Middle Woodland, Early Late Woodland, Late Late Woodland, and Late Precontact period pottery from the Cloudman site. Braun (1983) first proposed that the increased consumption of starchy seeds from the Middle Woodland to Late Woodland in the Midwest prompted technological alterations in cooking vessels. The palatability and digestibility of starchy seeds is improved by cooking them to the point of gelatinization in liquid broth, although this process requires both longer cooking times and higher temperatures (Braun 1983, 116). Late Woodland vessels from western Illinois and eastern Missouri have thinner walls and smaller temper particles, which improve thermal conductivity and thermal shock resistance, respectively. Braun (1983) concluded that technical alterations to Late Woodland vessels were directly related to the incorporation of more starchy foods in the diet. For example, dried maize requires long periods of boiling before it is edible and digestible. Using bulk $\delta^{13}C$ analysis, Hart (2012) also found a direct correlation between an increase in water-based maize cooking and wall thinning in Woodland vessels in central New York.

Given Dunham's hypothesized intensification of starchy food use in the Late Woodland of the eastern Upper Peninsula, it was expected that the trend of wall thinning and temper size reduction throughout the Woodland period would be reflected in the Cloudman assemblage. However, there was no significant statistical difference between vessel wall thickness and temper size of the Laurel Middle Woodland vessels from Naomikong Point and the Late Woodland vessels from Sand Point (Kooiman 2012, 2016), the possible result of the geographic difference between the sites. The Cloudman site assemblage allowed an investigation of vessel wall thickness and temper size through time at a single locale. Although diachronic trends in vessel wall thickness among the Cloudman pottery assemblage remain unclear, temper size was found to alter in significant ways through time, suggesting conscious decisions on the part of potters to alter technology to suit new cooking requirements.

Vessel size (or vessel volume) is a less understood aspect of formal variability. Size variation has been connected to utilitarian function (Rice 1987, 299), household size (Nelson 1981; Tani 1994; Turner and Lofgren 1966), and utilitarian versus ceremonial functions (Blitz 1993; Kooiman 2012, 2016; Potter 2000). Neither McHale Milner (1998) nor Kooiman (2012, 2016) found any correlation between vessel function and vessel size (inferred from rim diameter) among Late Woodland vessels in the Northern Great Lakes, although vessel size was possibly linked to the context of vessel use (ceremonial vs. utilitarian) at the Sand Point site (Kooiman 2016). The Cloudman site does include a mound, which is located away from the excavated habitation zones. The vessel assemblage analyzed here is unlikely to have derived from either the early twentieth-century excavations or any subsequent looting of the mounds since they originate from intact, subsurface contexts (Branstner 1995). Feature 27 contained a dog burial and might be associated with ritual or ceremonial activities, but none of the vessels used in this study were found in this feature (Branstner 1995; Cooper 1996). With no other clear demarcations of ceremonial space within the habitation zone, there is no basis for comparing contexts of use between the identified pottery vessels at the Cloudman site, although context of use may have still influenced vessel capacity. Although vessel size was not expected to change through time, the results proved otherwise. The nature of and possible reasons for this change are discussed in chapter 6.

Second, this book explores whether there were *changes in ceramic vessel use and cooking habits* evident through time. Large proportions of the Middle Woodland vessels from the Naomikong Point (20CH2) site and Late Woodland vessels from the Sand Point (20BG14) site were used for cooking (Kooiman 2012, 2016), based on high frequencies of use-alteration traces such as exterior sooting and interior carbonization, which demonstrate use of a vessel over fire (Skibo 1992, 2013). A change in cooking styles (from stewing to boiling), as discussed above, was also observed. Intensified exploitation of various starchy resources that require intensive boiling prior to consumption could result in these changing patterns. The Cloudman assemblage allowed comparison of use-alteration patterns through time in one location with a more refined time line. As anticipated, a change in cooking styles through time was also observed at the Cloudman site, reflecting observed regional trends.

Third, this study investigates whether *diachronic changes in subsistence strategies* (and possible attendant changes in cooking habits) are detectable through lipids, stable isotopes, and microbotanical remains extracted from pottery. Lipid residues, stable isotopes, and microbotanical remains present in absorbed and carbonized (burned) food residues provide direct evidence of foods cooked in ceramic vessels. While these food residues may not be representative of the diet as a whole, the evidence is optimal for exploring technical change in pottery because the vessels might be altered to suit the components of the diet processed in ceramic vessels. It was predicted that starchy foods (maize, wild rice, acorns) would become more common through time given the results of similar research in adjacent regions (Hart and Lovis 2013). However, the results presented a more complex series of events that demonstrate that subsistence change is not always simple or straightforward.

The fourth topic of inquiry is *synchronic variation* in ceramic vessel use, subsistence strategies, and cooking habits. If the nature of social relationships is reflected in ceramic style, then pottery vessels can also be used to examine the relationship between diet and cooking and identity. As discussed earlier, the similarity of pottery styles across the swath of the Northern Great Lakes and beyond during the Middle Woodland period is believed to reflect great social fluidity and the lack of distinction between social groups (Brose and Hambacher 1999). Late Woodland peoples, on the other hand, seemed to have become more localized, with restricted territories and identities, based on increased numbers of local, distinct pottery styles (McHale Milner 1991). Cuisine (which constitutes both food selection and cooking methods) can be a strong marker of identity (Montanari 2006; Smith 2006), and therefore, if distinct pottery types, representing distinct social groups, were occupying the Cloudman site during the same general period of time, then distinct culinary traditions might also be apparent.

Some increased degree of difference in vessel function, cooking styles, and food selection between vessels from distinctly different stylistic types in post–Middle Woodland occupations of the Cloudman site was anticipated. Even though distinct social groups may have been coming together at Cloudman for coordinated large-scale fish exploitation, they also may have maintained some of their unique food and cooking preferences while inhabiting the site. Alongside learning different stylistic traditions, Late Woodland potters may have learned to endow their vessels with unique technical properties suited to their specific culinary needs. However, the results of these comparisons of food residues, style, use, and technical properties among contemporaneous pottery vessels generally demonstrate that humans are not as predictable as archaeologists often believe them to be.

Fifth and finally, *ethnographic and ethnohistorical accounts* of Indigenous diet and cooking in the Great Lakes are explored to enhance interpretations of the archaeological data. Ethnographic and ethnohistorical accounts of foodways and cooking of societies that historically occupied regions geographically adjacent to the Cloudman site, including the Ojibwe to the west and Iroquoian groups to the east, provide context for the results of the archaeological analyses. Reference to observations to people with historical and cultural ties to the Great Lakes who also inhabit a similar environment and use similar resources served to greatly enrich and enhance archaeological interpretations. Methods of food preparation and food combinations practiced by Ojibwe and Iroquoian cooks strengthen interprtetations of the data derived from the use-alteration and dietary analyses applied to the Cloudman pottery assemblage. They also help delineate potential culinary differences between ethnic groups and enable recognition of identity through archaeological food remains.

CONCLUSION

This study follows a strong, decades-long tradition of research on subsistence and ceramics in the Upper and Northern Great Lakes. Although previous studies have created a substantial base of knowledge on these topics, questions about the nature of dietary, technological, and social change throughout the Woodland and Late Precontact periods remain. The use of new perspectives and techniques applied to a pottery assemblage from the multicomponent Cloudman site will enhance our understanding of how precontact Indigenous peoples negotiated changing natural and social environments.

CHAPTER 4

Pottery and Cuisine

Theoretical and Methodological Perspectives

This research employs multiple methods to answer a set of diverse yet related questions, thereby necessitating the integration of several theoretical perspectives. In this case, pottery function, foodways, and pottery style are the overarching theoretical frameworks on which the data are laid and the interpretations constructed. The theoretical framework, in turn, shapes the methods employed to investigate ancient technology and cuisine in the Northern Great Lakes. These include typological/taxonomic pottery analysis, functional pottery analysis, stable isotope analysis, microbotanical analysis, lipid residue analysis, and AMS radiocarbon dating. The combined use of both traditional and modern analytic techniques allows archaeologists to derive new information from old pottery assemblages.

AN INTEGRATED THEORETICAL FRAMEWORK

Pottery Style

Style has long been used to define what archaeologists call time-space systematics, in which style denotes both temporal affiliation and geographic spread (Sackett 1977). In other words, artifact style can signify a specific time and place, or spatiotemporal affiliation. Given this connection to the time and space within which human groups behave, it is often considered symbolic, whether actively or passively, of ethnicity or identity. Archaeological pottery in particular has been used to separate groups into "cultures" or "ethnicities" based on stylistic differences (Peelo 2011; Rice 1996a), largely because the plasticity of the ceramic medium provides endless possibilities in terms of form and decoration, making it a sensitive measure of learned behavior. After stone tools, which also possess stylistic elements but are not as plastic as clay, pottery is one of the most prevalent artifacts encountered at archaeological sites worldwide, making it a standard medium for assessing spatiotemporal affiliations (Skibo 2013). Style is used by archaeologists to create subjective typological categories that aid in the categorization of pottery styles and facilitate comparisons of pottery assemblages across sites. One danger of this practice is the conflation of archaeologically defined stylistic types (subjective categories created by archaeologists) and actual past identities or ethnicities (categories created and lived by people who made and used the pottery), which has been a topic of critique over the decades (Rice 1996b; Sackett 1977; Shepard 1968). However, geographic variation in ceramic vessel style does suggest that style is influenced by social interaction, even if types recognized today do not directly represent distinct social groups of the past (McHale Milner 1998; O'Shea and McHale Milner 2002).

Wobst (1977) states that style serves the function of symbolic communication and information exchange. Symboling, a learned behavior, allows individuals to interact with their social environment through the medium of artifacts, often in the expression of identity by means of style (Wobst 1977, 320). Items that are the most visible and used in arenas of interaction with other groups are the most likely to be used to communicate group affiliation, while less visible items, particularly those used within the home, are less likely to be used to carry such messages and will instead display clinal variation.

Weissner (1983) identifies two types of style: emblemic, which transmits a clear message about group affiliation or identity; and assertive, which is variation in form and style that carries information about personal identity, either consciously or unconsciously, but that does not directly symbolize identity. Within small-scale societies with somewhat fluid, cooperative risk-buffering relationships, the need to distinguish between groups symbolically (using emblemic style) is not as strong as in larger-scale societies with increased competition for resources. Instead, hunter-gatherer artifacts are more likely to transmit assertive style (Weissner 1983, 258). Weissner's (1983) study of San metal projectile points demonstrated stylistic differences only between noninteracting linguistic groups, which she attributes not to conscious distinction between groups but to nonoverlapping social spheres. Thus, with many utilitarian items, such as projectile points and domestic pottery, style is more useful for interpreting social interaction and relationships and less useful for defining social or cultural identities among cooperative small-scale societies.

McHale Milner (1998) and Carroll (2013) found that among pottery from the Straits of Mackinac and southwestern Michigan, respectively, the degree of visibility of stylistic elements transmits information in accordance with social distance. Low-visibility elements, such as lip shape, were shared among local groups, while high-visibility elements, such as rim shape and decoration, were shared among geographically broad but interacting groups. In both cases, stylistic similarities of high- versus low-visibility items correlated with multiple scales of group interaction based on geographic or social distance.

According to Wobst (1977) and Weissner (1983), utilitarian pottery, because of its use in the household and subsequent low public visibility, is a medium unlikely to carry strong, emblemic messages about identity. In small-scale societies, media displaying style, such as pottery and lithics, are more likely to carry information about breadth of social interaction. In regions and time periods with high social fluidity, pottery is even less likely to convey strong or distinct markers of identity, as demonstrated by Middle Woodland pottery in the Northern Great Lakes (see chapter 2). Within societies with more restricted social boundaries and/or increased resource competition (such as Late Woodland societies of the Northern Great Lakes), pottery styles might become more geographically restricted and more diverse within a given region (Carroll 2013; McHale Milner 1998; Wobst 1977). In these contexts, pottery style might not be a consciously created symbol of identity but rather an assertive representation of the interactive group, in which craft traditions are shared with little outside influence, such as within the matrilineal longhouses in late precontact Iroquoia (Hart and Brumbach 2009).

Pottery Function

Ceramic analysis has traditionally been focused on style because of its perceived social and temporal symbolism. Linton (1944) was among the earliest proponents of viewing pottery not for its symbolic, ideological, and social meanings but instead for its role as a utilitarian household item. He states that a cooking pot must have certain physical characteristics to effectively serve its functions, such as a mouth large enough to prevent sudden overboiling and to allow the cook access to the contents but small enough to prevent all liquid from evaporating during the boiling process. However, Linton's contemporaries largely carried on with traditional stylistic analyses, which served as frameworks for constructing chronologies and cultural spatiotemporal units in regions across the world.

Another mid-twentieth-century archaeologist, Anna O. Shepard (1968, 309–10), agreed that typological categories were the creation of archaeologists rather than of the culture being studied, and it was therefore "strange that pottery should be studied without considering its relations to the people who made it." She encouraged attention to the materials and construction techniques used to make pottery and championed the use of temper and clay paste properties for its classification, which she believed were better indicators of social relationships than were subjective categories. Shepard began a long tradition of compositional studies of ceramic assemblages worldwide. Her area of expertise, petrographic analysis, which examines the mineralogical and structural composition of ceramic material, was practiced more commonly in Europe than in North America but became more popular in the latter following Stoltman's (1989) revised methodology (Rice 1996b). Compositional studies have now expanded to include a variety of geochemical methods for identifying the composition of both clays and inorganic temper inclusions, such as X-ray fluorescence (e.g., Ligman 2013; Morgenstein and Redmount 2005; Tykot 2016), neutron activation (e.g., Falabella et al. 2013; Glascock and Neff 2003; Wallis, Pluckhahn, and Glascock 2016), and laser ablation–inductively coupled plasma–mass spectrometry (LA-ICP-MS) (e.g., Druc, Inokuchi, and Dussubieux 2017; Duwe and Neff 2007; Stoner 2016).

Braun (1983) helped introduce the most recent wave of interest in pottery function, calling for archaeologists to begin to view pots as *tools*, made by people to be used for a variety of functions beyond symbolizing social identity. Focused study of pottery can reveal manufacturing processes, and Braun urged the examination of mechanical performance characteristics to recognize why a vessel was constructed. He emphasized that the physical properties of a pot could have been controlled by potters in order to achieve certain desired performance characteristics; in other words, the technical characteristics of a pot have the potential to reveal what functions it was designed to fulfill.

Schiffer and Skibo (1987) adopted and expanded Braun's ideas under the "behavioral archaeology" theoretical framework. Decisions made by potters (technical choices) are aimed at imbuing a vessel with the most desirable performance characteristics, sometimes at the expense of other characteristics. Performance characteristics for ceramic vessels include ease of manufacture, cooling effectiveness, heating effectiveness, portability, impact resistance, thermal shock resistance, permeability, gripability, and abrasion resistance, which can be influenced by physical characteristics such as vessel size, wall thickness, vessel shape, paste composition, temper density, and temper type (Schiffer and Skibo 1987).

Analysis of pottery function is detailed by Skibo (1992, 2013). He divides function into two types: intended and actual. Intended function is rooted in the premise that "all pots are designed to be used" (Skibo 2013, 27; see also Schiffer and Skibo 1987, 1997). More specifically, potters are intentional in the decisions, or technical choices, they make about vessel form and composition. These choices determine the technical properties or physical characteristics of a ceramic vessel (i.e., shape, size, etc.), and each technical property affects one or more of a vessel's performance characteristics. The most important performance characteristics for cooking vessels are thermal shock resistance (the ability of a vessel to resist breakage when exposed to heat) and heating effectiveness (how quickly the contents of a vessel can be heated). Some technical properties enhance certain performance characteristics while detracting from others; for example, adding temper to a paste will increase a vessel's thermal shock resistance while simultaneously decreasing its impact resistance. Style, including form and decoration, is also a performance characteristic, because it can visually signal vessel function, group identity, or socioeconomic status (Schiffer and Skibo 1987, 1997).

A series of studies over the decades have tested the performance characteristics of other various physical properties. Rye's (1976) initial investigation into the effects of temper on various stages of manufacture set the stage for other temper studies. Bronitsky and Hamer (1986) tested the effects of tempering materials for impact and thermal shock resistance and found that all smaller-grained grit temper improved ceramic wall strength and that shell temper was better for shock resistance than grit temper. Feathers (2006) found that although shell temper increases workability and overall vessel strength, its adoption in Eastern North America was not widespread until widescale agriculture was practiced, limiting fuel for fire and requiring pottery that could be fired at lower temperature, which shell tempering allows. Surface treatments, such as slips and resins applied to the surfaces of vessels, increase heating effectiveness (Schiffer 1990) but have variable effects on abrasion resistance (Skibo, Butts, and Schiffer 1997). Organic temper, the earliest type used across the world, is thought to have been used for expedient pottery manufacture but was later replaced by inorganic tempers as a result of its poor performance characteristics (Skibo, Schiffer, and Reid 1989).

Intended function attributes can be used to distinguish between pottery manufacturing traditions among groups. Chilton (1998) found that vessels used by mobile Algonquian groups in the Northeast differed from those produced by neighboring Iroquoian groups, who were more sedentary. Iroquoian vessels were larger and thinner, possibly because they did not need to be transported, and they were more homogeneous in temper and form because they may have been produced in communal settings where manufacturing materials and habits were shared. Algonquian vessels, on the other hand, were thicker and smaller in order to facilate transportation, and the greater variety of temper materials and formal properties observed among them may reflect the more diverse geographic and social settings in which these vessels were produced.

Actual function entails the ways in which pottery was used, regardless of its technical properties (Skibo 1993, 2013). Actual function is assessed by looking at what Hally (1983) termed use-alteration traces. These traces include exterior sooting, exterior carbonization, interior carbonization, and attrition (Skibo 1992, 2013). *Exterior sooting* forms from contact of smoke with the pottery surface, indicating the use of a vessel over fire. *Exterior carbonization* and *interior carbonization* refer to burned food residues and provide direct evidence not only of cooking but also of cooking methods. Various cooking methods (e.g., roasting, stewing, boiling) result in different patterns of interior carbonization. *Attrition* refers to the removal of ceramic material by abrasive or nonabrasive processes and can occur through contact with other objects or surfaces, water vaporization, salt crystallization, and fermentation occurring within the vessel (Skibo 2013, 122). These traces provide a more refined perspective of pottery use, allowing inferences about use over fire, cooking practices, cuisine, and more.

Foodways and Cuisine

The study of foodways has its roots in folklore studies and is a growing topic of cross-disciplinary interest in anthropology. In archaeology, food-related research was traditionally concerned with "diet" and "subsistence," focusing on human acquisition of necessary nutrients to ensure survival. The terms "foodways" and "cuisine" place past food production, preparation, and consumption in the context of politics, ideologies, and economies (Twiss 2012, 357).

Examining food from an adaptive, environmental perspective has been the traditional avenue for dietary studies. Perhaps the most famous model for hunter-gatherer adaptive subsistence behavior is Binford's (1980) foraging-collecting spectrum. He identifies two major poles of subsistence-settlement strategies: foraging, which entails high residential mobility (frequent residential relocation based on resource abundance or availability) and daily procurement of food resources; and collecting, which employs logistical mobility (lower residential mobility, with base camps from which task groups disperse on logistical forays) and some form of food storage. Foraging and collecting represent two extreme ends of a continuum of strategies employed by hunter-gatherers, and where groups land on this spectrum is often dependent to a large degree on environment (particularly resource distribution across time and space) and competition for resources (Binford 1980).

In temperate zones, such as the Northern Great Lakes, seasonal fluctuations in resource availability require regular short-term predictive risk buffering to counteract potential caloric and nutritional shortfalls. Speth and Spielman (1983) found that diets consisting primarily of lean protein caused heightened metabolism, requiring increasing amounts of food to maintain proper energy intake. This is important in the lean time of late winter and early spring, when plant food sources are low and wild animals are at their leanest, the consumption of the latter leading to what some hunter-gatherer groups called "rabbit starvation" (Speth and Spielman 1983). Carbohydrates and fats both counteract this metabolic response, although carbohydrates provide a stronger counteractive effect.

The role of carbohydrates is, therefore, critical in predictable short-term food shortage risk buffering and explains the importance of selecting foods for storage. The Sami of subarctic Scandinavia use the inner bark of Scots pine to add carbohydrates and fiber to their diet throughout the year and to counteract the effects of protein starvation (Bergman, Ostlund, and Zackrisson 2004). Early use of seed crops in the Eastern Woodlands has also been linked to carbohydrate storage for consumption during lean periods (Gremillion 1996, 2004).

Not only does a balance of time, energy, and efficiency influence food choice, but so does nutritional balance. Maize and beans were grown and consumed together by many Late Prehistoric (post–AD 1300) North American Indigenous societies. The two crops grow well together, and beans provide protein otherwise lacking in maize-based diets (Hart 2008; Hart and Scarry 1999; Hart et al. 2002; Monaghan, Schilling, and Parker 2014). Maize is present rather early in portions of the Great Lakes (ca. cal 200 BC) (Albert et al. 2018) and may be related to the greater use of wild rice, which, like beans, is relatively rich in amino acids and would also have been a good complement to the nutritionally devoid maize (Hart and Lovis 2013). The selection of food for nutritional needs is clearly a complex process involving a mosaic of decisions, and it is further complicated by the addition of cultural factors.

The intersection of biological food requirements and cultural food preferences is best summarized by the "omnivore's paradox," which states that humans have incredible freedom and adaptability in food choices, but they also mistrust new foods. A social or cultural group's traditions of food choice and preparation (i.e., cuisine) work to resolve an omnivore's anxiety by limiting options and setting parameters for preparation (Fischler 1988, 277–79). The parameters are culturally defined and vary based on accessible resources, cultural traditions, and acceptable behaviors.

Food is a culturally defined term, and therefore what is conceptually accepted as food varies from group to group. Consequently, cuisine, or food culture, is used to differentiate between economic classes, ethnicity, gender, and religious beliefs, serving as a proxy representation of social diversity and identity (Twiss 2012). Food is also an integral part of everyday life. It is an avenue by which to socialize and unite families and communities, making food a physical need fulfilled in social contexts (Atalay and Hastorf 2006).

Food can serve "diametrically opposed semiotic functions" (Appadurai 1981, 496); it acts to both unify and divide. It can create a sense of belonging within and between groups or emphasize differences between groups, both of which solidify identity (Appadurai 1981; Smith 2006). In other words, food can serve as both a cultural mediator, setting a common ground between disparate groups, and as a device for "othering," or distinguishing groups or individuals from the self based on cultural behaviors (Montanari 2006). Othering is most common between groups defined by ethnicity (Jones 1997; Kalčik 1984; see also Barrett, Beukins, and Nicholson 2001; Egan-Bruhy 2014; Scott 1996). Even when common foods are shared, food preparation and cooking methods can be used to distinguish members of a community from those of other groups (Beoku-Betts 1995) or from others of differing ethnicities or classes within their own communities (Chase 2012) as an act of dietary identity formation.

Like food selection, cooking is "related in complex and varied ways to issues of gender, work, politics, economic life, and social differentiation" (Rodríguez-Alegría and Graff 2012, 5). Cooking techniques are often aimed at maximizing the digestibility and nutritional value of foodstuffs (Wandsnider 1997), but cultural traditions or taste preferences are not always geared to nutritional maximization (Rodríguez-Alegría and Graff 2012). Cooking is directly related to food production, food collection, and the manufacture of cooking tools, all factors critical to the overall economy (Rodríguez-Alegría and Graff 2012), and the tools involved in cooking can also be symbolic of identity (MacLean and Insoll 1999). This makes cooking a useful lens through which to view the intersection of resource selection and ceramic technology.

Changes in food selection and subsistence strategies are traditionally couched in terms of adaptation to new or changing environments, climatic changes, or increasing population pressure (Binford 1968; Childe 1936; Flannery 1973), but some archaeologists have begun to investigate dietary shifts from social, political, and ideological perspectives. Spielmann (2002) has argued that the mechanism driving the intensification of food production in small-scale societies is neither economic nor political but communal ritual activity, specifically, feasting and craft specialization. She claims that demand for items critical to communal ritual participation common among many small-scale societies was more important for the development of agricultural intensification than subsistence provisioning. Hastorf and Johannessen (1994) argue that the timing and patterning of the intensification of maize production and consumption in both North and South America was not advantageous economically but instead linked to the cosmological importance of maize. In their view, maize only increased in use alongside rapid elaboration of a social hierarchy, possibly because it was used by political officials for its ritual significance.

Food is a biological need, selected because of its availability, taste, abundance, and nutritional value. Yet these choices are often restricted and/or influenced by cultural factors, such as identity, cultural tradition, and ideology. This is important to consider even when studying small-scale societies for whom markers of social affiliation and cosmological beliefs can be difficult to discern.

An Integrated Theory in the Northern Great Lakes

The seemingly unrelated theoretical perspectives of pottery style, pottery function, and foodways can in fact be used together to effectively answer how pottery technology, pottery use, diet, and cooking habits change over time and to explore their relationship to social and environmental transformations in the precontact Northern Great Lakes. Pottery function plays an integral role in understanding cooking and cuisine, while pottery style can facilitate re-creation of ancient social environments and build interpretations of ancient foodways. Applied to the specific problem of evolving Woodland and Late Precontact lifeways in the Northern Great Lakes of North America, the multifaceted perspective can extract additional data from limited archaeological remains and bring to light new information about past human behavior.

MULTIPROXY ANALYSIS: A METHODOLOGICAL OVERVIEW

A reflection of the integrated theoretical perspective discussed above, the multiproxy methodological approach of this study applies diverse yet complementary analytic methods to pottery vessels from the Cloudman site. This includes functional and typological ceramic analysis and residue analysis, the latter including microbotanical, stable isotope, and lipid analyses. Together these methods can inform interpretations about past diet, cooking, cooking technology, technology traditions, and social relationships in the Northern Great Lakes and regions around the world.

Ceramic Taxonomic Classification: The Cloudman Site Assemblage

The Cloudman assemblage consists of a total of 202 discrete identified vessels, which served as the primary unit of analysis for this research. Branstner (1995) originally grouped and identified a total of 177 vessels, excavated between 1990 and 1994, during the initial analysis of the assemblage. Forty-nine vessels, most of them associated with the Late Late Woodland period, were categorized as "untyped" because they did not fit into established typological categories. An additional twenty-eight vessels were discovered in 1995 during a brief and limited excavation; these were sorted and grouped by vessel but never attributed to stylistic typologies (Christine Stephenson pers. comm.).

Discrete vessels were identified based on rim sherds with distinct morphology (lip shape, rim orientation, etc.), decoration, and surface treatment, along with associated body sherds. The stylistic features were then assessed and compared to established regional typological categories (e.g., Jansen 1968; McPherron 1967) and expanded to include literature from adjacent regions, particularly southern Ontario (e.g., Kenyon 1970; MacNeish 1952; Wright 1973). Those vessels already categorized by Branstner (1995) were reexamined and mostly corroborated, while previously untyped vessels were given a critical assessment (or reassessment) using the expanded literature search. The results of the taxonomic classification are detailed in chapter 5.

Functional Analysis of Cloudman Pottery

Analysis of pottery function was carried out in accordance with the standards established by Skibo (1992, 2013), with distinct vessels (rim and body sherds as grouped by Branstner [1995]) comprising the unit of analysis. Each discrete vessel in the Cloudman site pottery assemblage was evaluated for both its intended and its actual functions. Intended function was assessed through a specific set of physical characteristics. The attributes chosen as the focus for this study were selected based on the results of prior studies of morphological changes attending alteration of cooking techniques in Eastern North American (Braun 1983; Hart 2012) and on attributes that proved significant in prior studies of pottery assemblages from the Northern Great Lakes (Kooiman 2012, 2016). These properties include rim diameter, wall thickness, and temper size. Wall thickness and temper size were chosen because of their previously determined sensitivity to detecting functional change in relation to changing cooking requirements (Braun 1983; Hart 2012).

Rim diameter was chosen for its relationship to overall vessel size (Blitz 1993; Kooiman 2015b; Potter 2000) and for its standard recordation in ceramic analysis. Only rim sherds large enough to comprise 5% or more of the total rim circumference of their respective vessel were recorded, resulting in rim diameter data for 47% (94 of 202) of the total vessels. Wall thickness was measured at the lip, rim, neck, shoulder, and body, when possible, and temper size was averaged from three measurements per vessel.

Assessment of the actual function of pottery vessels is based on the presence of use-alteration traces. Each vessel was examined for exterior sooting, exterior carbonization, interior carbonization, and attrition. Exterior sooting can be difficult to distinguish from staining from contact with the burial environment or fireclouding that forms during the firing process; however, fireclouding occurs infrequently on vessels in the Northern Great Lakes. Sooting was marked as present only when it could be positively distinguished and identified. Exterior carbonization sometimes has the appearance of sooting; therefore, it was only categorized as carbonization when it was located on the rim (where sooting infrequently occurs) or in cases where there was continuity with carbonization on the interior surface. Attrition, which is rare among coastal Northern Great Lakes Woodland pottery assemblages (Kooiman 2012, 2015a), was not observed in the Cloudman assemblage.

Interior carbonization was recorded as present or absent, and its distribution patterning was also categorized. Presence was recorded only in cases where carbonization could be confidently identified. For the Cloudman pottery assemblage, the patterns could be categorized most meaningfully by the types depicted in chapter 6 (see figure 6.2): Type 1, which represents a distinct band of carbonization at or near the rim of the vessel, indicative of boiling; Type 2, in which carbonization covers a significant portion of the interior vessel wall, indicative of stewing (a long-term liquid reduction process); Type 3, which shows the presence of a thick ring of residue around the rim of the vessel with lighter carbonization along the body of the vessel, indicating both boiling and stewing processes; Type 4, in which there is definitive carbonization on the rim but the lower extent of the carbonization along the interior is unclear; and Type 5, which signifies the presence of interior carbonization with no discernible pattern. The interior carbonization pattern typology attempts to capture the full range of cooking modes employed by cooks at the Cloudman site.

Microbotanical Analysis

Microbotanical analysis has recently emerged as an increasingly common method for investigating past diet and environment. Microbotanical remains include pollen, starches, and phytoliths and may be incorporated into various forms of residue by adherence or accretion. While pollen is useful for reconstructing ancient environments, it is not typically found in contexts that can inform human food choice and consumption. Phytoliths and starches, however, can be collected from food residues adhered to artifacts such as pottery and grinding stones, connecting them directly to food processing (Pearsall and Hastorf 2011). Identifiable to plant species, phytoliths and starches can tie the processing of a specific type of plant to a ceramic vessel, providing a higher level of specificity than is possible with other types of cooking residue evidence, such as lipids or stable isotopes. Not all plants yield starches or phytoliths that preserve archaeologically, but several species routinely gathered or cultivated in the Eastern Woodlands (such as wild rice, maize, and squash) have been identified in archaeological residues (see Raviele 2010; Simon 2011). Adhered food residues typically represent the final cooking event conducted in a pottery vessel (Miller et al. 2020).

Samples for microbotanical analysis were collected from 52 discrete pottery vessels (Albert et al. 2018; Kooiman 2018). Selection of vessels for sampling was based on two criteria: presence of sufficient interior carbonized residue and the sociotemporal association of the vessel. Preserved adhered residue was present on vessels associated with all primary occupations of the site. Residue sampling was primarily restricted to the rim and neck; collection of residues from body sherds was conducted only if there was insufficient residue from rim or neck sherds of the same vessel.

Stable Isotope Analysis

Stable isotope analysis in this study focused on isotopes of the standard elements carbon and nitrogen, which enables measurement of their ratios in adhered or absorbed food residues (Evershed et al. 1999). Resultant ratios facilitate the separation of plants into three groups: legumes, non-legumous C_3 plants, and C_4/CAM plants (Hastorf and DeNiro 1985). Most plants in temperate climates are C_3 pathway plants, while tropical cultigens, such as maize, are C_4 pathway plants. This makes it possible to detect the presence of maize in human diets, especially in temperate zones such as the midwestern United States (Schoeninger 1995). Nitrogen isotope ratios can indicate whether residues were derived from terrestrial or aquatic food resources because aquatic foods have higher ^{15}N ratios than those from terrestrial environments (Ambrose 1987).

Samples for stable isotope analysis were collected from fifty discrete pottery vessels. Selection of vessels for sampling was based on two criteria: presence of sufficient interior carbonized residue and the sociotemporal association of the vessel. Samples were sent to the Illinois State Geological Survey (ISGS) for analysis.

Lipid Residue Analysis

Lipids, or fatty acids, are present in both plant and animal tissue and provide direct evidence of food processing for consumption (Malainey 2011). Absorbed lipid residues can be extracted from archaeological materials associated with cooking and food processing, such as ceramic vessel walls or cooking and grinding stones. They can be analyzed and assessed based on fatty acid composition/ratios or the presence of certain biomarkers or by measuring the stable isotope values of lipid components. Absorbed residues, including lipids, typically represent an amalgam of foods from past cooking events rather than the most recent cooking episodes (Miller et al. 2020).

A total of thirty pottery sherds was selected from the Cloudman site assemblage for lipid residue analysis, and vessels associated with each occupation period of the Cloudman site were sampled. The sample size was smaller than for the other food analyses because lipid residue analysis is destructive; pottery sherds must be destroyed for the lipids to be extracted. Selected sherds were sent to the Archaeological Residue Analysis Laboratory at Brandon University in Brandon, Manitoba, for analysis by Mary Malainey and Timothy Figol.

AMS Dating

Accelerator mass spectrometry dating allows detection of carbon-14 in small samples of organic matter. This makes it ideal for directly dating adhered pottery residues (Lovis 1990). Some have argued that in regions where freshwater fish may have been processed in ceramic vessels (such as at coastal sites in the Northern Great Lakes), AMS dating of such residue should be approached with caution. These scholars claim that cooking fish could introduce old carbon into food residues (the freshwater reservoir effect, or FRE), thereby affecting dating outcomes (see, e.g., Fischer and Heinemeier 2003; Philippssen et al. 2010). Recent studies, however, have demonstrated that the effect varies based on geographic region and is often insignificant, particularly in the Great Lakes region (Hart and Lovis 2007; Hart et al. 2013; Hart, Taché, and Lovis 2018; Heron and Craig 2015; Lovis and Hart 2015; see also Kooiman and Walder 2019 for an in-depth discussion of this issue).

Carbonized residue from a total of thirteen pottery vessels from the Cloudman site were selected for direct AMS dating. Sample selections were based on vessel type to clarify both the occupational chronology of the site and the regional ceramic chronology. The radiocarbon measurements were conducted at the Keck Carbon Cycle AMS Facility, Earth System Science Department, University of California, Irvine. A full discussion of the methods and results of the AMS dating are presented by Kooiman and Walder (2019) and Kooiman, Dunham, and Stephenson (2019).

CONCLUSION

The theoretical perspectives and methods detailed above are highly complementary and weave together a cohesive approach to studying subsistence, pottery, and cooking. Stylistic pottery analysis, functional pottery analysis, microbotanical analysis, stable isotope analysis, and lipid residue analysis are effective methods for analyzing past human diet- and technology-related behaviors and expand the interpretive potential of curated pottery assemblages. The next three chapters detail the results of these analyses and demonstrate the efficacy of multiproxy research for investigating past cuisine and culinary technology.

CHAPTER 5

Pottery Taxonomy, Chronology, and Occupational History of the Cloudman Site

Exploration of diachronic change, or change over time, requires situating units of analysis in time. Construction of an occupational history of the Cloudman site allows identification and isolation of the pottery subassemblages associated with different occupations of the site, which facilitates comparative and statistical analyses of technical properties, use-alteration traces, and chemical and microscopic food signatures. While adhered residues from pottery vessels can be directly dated using AMS radiocarbon dating, this method is cost prohibitive. Relative dating of vessels using spatiotemporal taxonomic typologies based on stylistic properties is a cost-effective and time-tested means of creating temporal groupings that facilitate examination of diachronic change. This analysis relies primarily on relative dates provided by taxonomic categorizations of pottery, although a small set of AMS-dated vessels provides absolute dates for anchoring the relative chronologies.

POTTERY TAXONOMY

Stylistic properties and taxonomic categorization of Cloudman site pottery vessels have been discussed at length by Branstner (1995). The goal of the present study is to enhance the original classifications using more recent literature and create the most accurate portrayal possible of the occupational history of the Cloudman site and the people who lived there. Many of the classifications below are a reiteration of the work done by Branstner (1995); the few points of classificatory divergence are distinguished. Appendix A presents the taxonomic classifications for each individual pottery vessel used in this study.

One challenging aspect of this task was variation in vessel completeness. Some vessels are represented by a single rim sherd (or, in some cases, a highly distinctive neck or shoulder sherd), while others are represented by dozens of sherds comprising large portions of the vessels (there are no whole vessels in the assemblage). This variation often affected taxonomic categorization. Early Late Woodland vessels generally had the most complete vessel rims and the most associated body sherds, while vessels from other time periods were often represented by small rim sherds or rim sections. The latter limited the specificity of typological classification.

TAXONOMIC CLASSIFICATION

The Cloudman assemblage consists of 202 identified, distinct minimal vessels (table 5.1; see appendix C for images of selected vessels). These vessels represent the Middle Woodland, Early Late Woodland, Late Late Woodland, and Late Precontact components of the site, with the Early Late Woodland occupation represented by the largest percentage of vessels. A few remaining vessels either possess stylistic attributes that appear transitional between time periods or lack distinctive attributes that associate them with a more specific time period.

A number of miniature vessels (n = 11) are included in the Cloudman assemblage. These include both crude, simple forms and very finely constructed pots displaying clear stylistic elements of established typological categories. Dorland (2018) determined that such "learner vessels" among Late Woodland pottery assemblages in Ontario were likely manufactured by children. Although the more ornate and accomplished vessels in the Cloudman assemblage could have been constructed by adults for special use, child potters are also able to achieve high levels of technical skill (Braun 2015; Striker, Howie, and Williamson 2017). Miniature vessels are

Table 5.1. Cloudman Pottery Vessels by Site Component

Component	Ct.	Regional Dates
Middle Woodland (MW)	35	200 BC–AD 500/600
Middle/Late Woodland (MW/LW)	7	AD 500/600–700
Early Late Woodland (ELW)	62	AD 700–1000
Middle Late Woodland (MLW)	5	AD 1000–1200
Late Late Woodland (LLW)	37	AD 1200–1400
General Late Woodland (LW)	7	AD 600–1600
Late Precontact	47	AD 1300–1500
Unknown	2	NA
Total	202	

included in vessel counts for each time period, but the miniature vessel subassemblage as a whole is also summarized and described at the end of this section.

The assemblage is described below, presented in chronological order of sociotemporal affiliations and then grouped by type. The following descriptions are not meant to be comprehensive and merely highlight the distinguishing characteristics by which the vessels were categorized. More detailed morphological and compositional details of Cloudman pottery types and vessels are provided by Branstner (1995).

Middle Woodland Ceramic Subassemblage

The Middle Woodland pottery subassemblage (n = 35) is largely homogeneous, consisting mostly of Laurel ware vessels and two North Bay vessels (table 5.2; figures C1–C5).

Laurel Ware (n = 32). Varieties of Laurel ware at the Cloudman site include Banked Linear Stamped vessels (23, 109, 110, 112, 113, 114), which are decorated with oblique stamps created by a plain tool. A single Dentate Rocker Stamped vessel (6) is distinguished by oblique dentate stamping on the interior and exterior rim with horizontal rows of dentate rocker stamping on the body. Dentate Stamped vessels (4, 12, 13, 17, 19, 20, 59) exhibit vertical, horizontal, or oblique stamping with a notched tool on the exterior rim surface. Pseudo-scallop Shell vessels (1, 2, 5, 7, 9, 10, 14, 15, 18, 22, 28, 169) are decorated along the entire upper body using push-pull stamping, a technique resulting in a pattern that resembles scallop shell stamping, and many have a single row of punctates along the rim. Laural Plain vessels (3, 91) are undecorated, while a single Laurel Trailed vessel (16) is decorated with a vertical trailed motif. The above type descriptions are based on the original definitions by Janzen (1968).

Reevaluation was consistent with Branster's (1995) classifications, except for a few cases. Vessel 30 was originally categorized as Laurel Incised, but it was instead classified as a general late Laurel vessel (see below). Vessels 39 and 144 were both originally untyped. Vessel 144 displays hallmarks of coil manufacture with a fine, sandy paste. It has a smoothed rim and oblique tool impressions on a rounded lip, which allows it to be broadly categorized as Laurel ware. Vessel 39 is a miniature vessel also classified as Laurel ware, described below with other miniature vessels.

North Bay (n = 2). The Middle Woodland subassemblage includes two North Bay vessels (131, 142). These were both originally categorized as untyped. North Bay pottery was first identified at the Heins Creek and Mero sites on the Door Peninsula of Wisconsin and is "usually thick,

Table 5.2. Middle Woodland Vessels by Type

Type	Ct.
Laurel Banked Linear Stamped	6
Laurel Dentate Rocker Stamped	1
Laurel Dentate Stamped	7
Laurel Plain	2
Laurel Pseudo-scallop Shell	13
Laurel Trailed	1
Laurel ware, untyped	2
North Bay Cordmarked	1
North Bay Linear Stamped	1
Untyped	1
Total	35

heavy, and extremely gritty" (Mason 1966, 75), distinguishing it from its more finely made Laurel counterparts. Vessel 131 is North Bay Linear Stamped, with notched tool stamping on the rim and the lip. Vessel 142 is North Bay Cordmarked, with deep vertical cordmarking on a vertical rim with a squared lip.

Untyped (n = 1). Vessel 201 is an untyped miniature vessel and is described below with the other miniature vessels.

Middle Woodland/Late Woodland Transitional Subassemblage

A small number of vessels (n = 7) appear transitional between Middle Woodland and Late Woodland types (table 5.3; figures C6, C7). Three vessels (30, 35, 170) are Late Laurel wares. Vessels 30 and 35 have broader lips than classic Laurel vessels, with straighter rim profiles than is common among Mackinac wares, exhibiting characteristics that straddle the temporal divide. Vessel 30 has a row of vertical incised lines directly below the exterior lip, a row of possible fingernail impressions on the interior rim, and incised cross-hatching on the squared lip. Vessel 170 has three rows of oblique linear stamping with cross-hatching on the body below. Vessel 35 (figure C6) has cord-wrapped stick impressions on a broad lip, a slightly everted rim, a row of double punctates (possibly made with the distal end of a phalanx of a small mammal), and cross-hatched incising over a cordmarked body. Incising is present in low quantities at many Laurel sites (Brose 1970; Janzen 1968; Stoltman 1973; Wright 1967), and some vessels exhibiting this motif are classified as Laurel Incised, a type that generally occurs late in the Laurel sequence (Stoltman 1973). Vessel 35 appears more similar to Mackinac in overall style but also displays the cross-hatched incising, more evidence in support of the late occurrence of this decorative element.

Vessels 33, 118, and 171 are untyped but possess characteristics that merge both Middle and Late Woodland features. Vessel 118 displays a thin, rounded lip, a vertical rim, and cordmarking on the exterior, defying established taxonomic categories and straddling the characteristics between typical Middle Woodland and Late Woodland wares. Vessel 171 has vertical punctate decoration on the exterior and vertical cord-wrapped stick impressions on the interior rim, exhibiting a slightly everted rim but

Table 5.3. Miscellaneous Woodland and Unknown Vessels

Temporal Affiliation	Type	Ct.
Middle/Late Woodland Transition	Late Laurel	3
	Untyped	4
	Total	7
Middle Late Woodland	Bois Blanc ware	4
	Untyped (cf. Bois Blanc ware)	1
	Total	5
General Late Woodland	Untyped, ELW/MLW	1
	Untyped (cf. O'Neil)	2
	Untyped	4
	Total	7
Unknown	Untyped	2

with a thin, rounded lip, again suggesting a time of manufacture during the Middle/Late Woodland transition and prohibiting taxonomic classification. Vessel 197 has a straight rim profile and a square, flattened lip extruded to the exterior, which was then smoothed flat over a cordmarked exterior surface. It bears a strong resemblance to North Bay Cordmarked wares but is composed of a coarser paste than is typical of Middle Woodland pottery.

The most intriguing of these transitional vessels is Vessel 33, which has a vertical rim, a flattened lip, large grit particles, a smoothed-over vertical textile impressed exterior surface, double cord-wrapped-object punctates, and a thin, folded-over flap resembling an incipient collar (figure C7). The paste, grit, and rim orientation are more in alignment with Middle Woodland manufacture, while the decorative elements are more common in the Late Woodland. Overall, the vessel most closely resembles Blackduck or Sandy Lake wares from northern Minnesota (Jill Taylor-Hollings pers. comm.). The vessel does not fit into any established typological categories but may be incipient Blackduck ware. The aforementioned vessels postdate the other Laurel types present in the assemblage, representing an ephemeral human presence at the Cloudman site after the primary Middle Woodland occupation.

Early Late Woodland Ceramic Subassemblage

The Early Late Woodland pottery vessels (n = 62) comprise 31% of the overall Cloudman assemblage, representing the largest subassemblage. The category includes Mackinac, Blackduck, and Bowerman wares (table 5.4; figures C8–C16). Although the Early Late Woodland subassemblage is slightly more stylistically diverse than the Middle Woodland subassemblage, the variation is limited.

Mackinac Ware (n = 56). Mackinac wares predominate in the Early Late Woodland assemblage. Mackinac Punctate vessels (21, 53, 80, 100, 105, 123, 139, 175) were identified by Branstner (1995), and Vessels 191 and 196/203, not included in her analysis, have also been placed in this category. Mackinac Punctate vessels have outflaring rims with exterior decoration restricted to a single or double row of punctates (McPherron 1967). A number of vessels (106, 122, 132, 137, 138, 141, 174) closely resembled Mackinac Punctate but were not complete enough for confident classification.

Table 5.4. Early Late Woodland Vessels by Type

Type	Ct.
Mackinac Banded	10
Mackinac Punctate	10
Mackinac Undecorated	2
Mackinac ware (cf. Banded)	1
Mackinac ware (cf. Punctate)	6
Mackinac ware (cf. Undecorated)	8
Mackinac ware, untyped	17
Late Mackinac ware	2
Blackduck Banded	4
Bowerman Plain v. Cordmarked	1
Untyped	1
Total	62

Branstner (1995) identified nine Mackinac Banded vessels (50, 78, 103, 108, 120, 121, 124, 172, 173). Vessel 192, which was not included in Branstner's original analysis, was also categorized as Mackinac Banded. This type is defined by complex designs in horizontal or diagonal bands of decoration bordered by rows of punctuations at the top and bottom (McPherron 1967). An additional vessel (137) closely resembled Mackinac Banded.

Mackinac Undecorated vessels, which have the everted rim and splayed lip hallmarks of Mackinac but lack exterior decoration (McPherron 1967), include Vessel 76, as identified by Branstner, and Vessel 52, originally untyped, which is a miniature vessel and is described later in this chapter. Eight vessels (116, 125, 128, 129, 147, 168, 176, 198) closely resembled Mackinac Undecorated but are not complete enough for confident classification. Another fifteen full-size vessels (8, 2, 32, 41, 46, 49, 55, 61, 72, 87, 126, 127, 130, 181) and two miniature vessels (83 and 202) were broadly categorized as Mackinac ware.

Vessels 189 and 194 represent late Mackinac ware (ca. AD 1000). Vessel 189 is relatively thin and has a lip that is an amalgamation of the thickened lip of Mackinac wares and the braced rim of Bois Blanc. The rim is almost vertical, like Bois Blanc, with a hint of Mackinac-like eversion. Vessel 194 displays the thickened lip, rim eversion, and punctates of Mackinac but has multiple bands of decoration, with a thinner and more rounded lip than is typical of Mackinac ware, suggesting a time of manufacture late in the sequence.

Blackduck Ware (n = 4). The Early Late Woodland assemblage also includes four Blackduck Banded vessels (figures C14, C15), characterized by horizontal bands of cord-wrapped stick impressions under a row of punctates (McPherron 1967). Branstner (1995) identified two Blackduck Banded vessels (81, 88) and more tentatively classified Vessel 117 as either Laurel or Blackduck. This vessel has cord-wrapped stick impressions on a broad lip and exterior decoration of a row of round punctates superior to three bands of horizontal cord-wrapped stick impressions, characteristics more closely aligned with Blackduck Banded. Vessel 193, which was not included in the 1995 analysis, clearly displays the hallmarks of Blackduck.

Bowerman Ware (n = 1). Vessel 199 (figure C16) is Bowerman Plain variety Cordmarked, with the straight rim, flat lip, and fine vertical cordmarking that are the hallmarks of the type (Hambacher 1992). This type was identified at the Skegemog Point site in northern lower Michigan and is considered generally contemporaneous with Mackinac wares (Hambacher 1992, 91).

Untyped (n = 1). Vessel 63 is a miniature vessel that appears to have been manufactured during the Early Late Woodland period but remains untyped. It is discussed below in the section on miniature vessels.

Early/Middle Late Woodland Transition (n = 1). Vessel 200 is an untyped vessel with a flared, everted rim with deeply impressed oblique cord-wrapped stick impressions on the lip, vertical cord-wrapped stick impressions on the interior rim, unusually small, round punctates on the exterior rim, and smoothed-over cordmarking on the body. These elements are an amalgamation of Mackinac and Bois Blanc characteristics, suggesting it was manufactured in the Early Late Woodland to Middle Late Woodland period (see table 5.3; figure C17).

Middle Late Woodland Ceramic Subassemblage

The initial assessment of the Cloudman site occupational history excluded a Middle Late Woodland component (Branstner 1995). Reevaluation of some of the originally untyped vessels identified a small number of vessels (n = 5) with strong affinities to Bois Blanc ware, which is associated with the Middle Late Woodland period at the Juntunen site (AD 1000–1200) (McPherron 1967).

Bois Blanc Ware (n = 5). Five vessels are categorized as or show strong affinities to Bois Blanc ware (see table 5.3; figure C18). Bois Blanc is characterized by thickened rims (by folded-over lips or by the addition of a strip or fillet), castellations, and cord-wrapped object decoration (McPherron 1967, 104). These vessels, described below, all possess the characteristic thickened rims that are the hallmark of Bois Blanc but lack cord-wrapped object impressions or apparent castellations (McPherron 1967). However, the rim morphologies are clearly Bois Blanc despite the nontraditional decorative elements.

Vessel 42 has a slightly inverted rim with a square lip, two horizontal bands of cord impressions below the lip, a fillet with oblique cord impressions, and at least one more horizontal band of cord impression below the fillet. Vessel 158 has a slightly inverted braced rim with a lip displaying widely spaced vertical linear tool impressions over a smoothed exterior rim. Vessel 215 has an inverted, wedge-shaped rim with two faint horizontal bands of cord impressions on both the interior and exterior rim surfaces and possible vertical cord-wrapped stick impressions just below the interior lip. Vessel 73 has the characteristic fillet/braced rim of Bois Blanc, the surface of which appears fabric impressed or impressed with a paddle wrapped loosely with cord, a surface treatment occasionally seen on Bois Blanc vessels (McPherron 1967, 106). A fifth vessel, Vessel 31, strongly resembles Bois Blanc ware, displaying a braced rim, but the paste and manufacture quality are poor, possibly representing an expedient vessel.

Late Late Woodland Ceramic Subassemblage

The greatest stylistic variation occurs among the Late Late Woodland ceramic subassemblage (n = 37). While the majority of the subassemblage is comprised of Juntunen ware, it also includes Traverse ware and a number of vessels of such stylistic singularity that they remain untyped (table 5.5; figures C19–C22).

Juntunen Ware (n = 24). Only three vessels (101, 102, 143) were originally categorized as Juntunen ware (Branstner 1995), but a reassessment reveals that many of the Late Late Woodland vessels that were left untyped displayed some characteristics of Juntunen ware. Furthermore, a number of vessels from the 1995 excavation, which were not included in the original report, were also identified as Juntunen vessels. Juntunen ware is characterized by the nearly universal presence of true collars and decoration of linear punctates or drag-and-jab techniques, with little to no use of cord impressions or incising (McPherron 1967, 111).

A "proto-Juntunen vessel" (Vessel 24; figure C19), likely manufactured around AD 1200, has "peaking" on the rim (an incipient castellation common among Bois Blanc) with a vertical rim shape but has a tall, thin collar and a smoothed exterior surface, which is common among later Juntunen wares. Juntunen Linear Punctate vessels (204, 205, 206, 209, 211, 212) are characterized by smoothed surfaces, true collars, and decora-

Table 5.5. Late Late Woodland Vessels by Type

Type	Ct.
Juntunen Linear Punctate	6
Juntunen Drag-and-Jab	5
Juntunen ware (cf. Jab-and-Drag)	1
Juntunen ware (cf. Linear Punctate)	2
Juntunen ware (cf. Plain)	1
Juntunen ware	8
Proto-Juntunen ware?	1
Untyped	13
Total	37

tion by closely spaced but separate punctates (McPherron 1967, 111). Juntunen Drag-and-Jab vessels (44, 45, 89, 102, 143) are distinguished by vertical rims, collars, castellations, and push-pull decorative motifs (McPherron 1967, 113). Another twelve vessels (25, 26, 47, 60, 86, 101, 115, 133, 210, 213, 214, 218) could be classified as Juntunen ware but were not complete enough for further categorization.

Untyped (n = 13). Despite the review of existing literature, thirteen vessels either remained outside of existing typological categories or did not have enough vessel material present to be properly categorized. These vessels displayed sufficient paste and morphological characteristics to conclude that they were manufactured during the Late Late Woodland period.

General Late Woodland Ceramic Vessels

Four pottery vessels (65, 85, 180, 184) show hallmarks of manufacture during the Late Woodland period, such as everted rims, cord-wrapped stick impressions, smoothing, square and flattened lips, and, in one case, brushing, but they lack visible characteristics associating them with Early, Middle, or Late Late Woodland groups (see table 5.3). Two vessels show affinity to pottery from the O'Neil site in northern lower Michigan (Lovis 1973). Vessel 152 resembles O'Neil Curvilinear, a Late Late Woodland style characterized by curved cord impressions superior to punctate decoration, and Vessel 54, a miniature vessel, closely resembles a cup from the O'Neil site (Lovis 1973). This cup is described below in the section on miniature vessels in the assemblage.

Late Precontact Ceramic Subassemblage

The final category includes pottery vessels likely manufactured after the primary Late Late Woodland Juntunen occupation (post–AD 1300), henceforth referred to as the Late Precontact occupation (n = 47). A total of thirty-seven vessels are classified as Iroquoian-style, and another ten vessels are classified as Traverse ware (table 5.6; figures C23–C29). Iroquoian-style pottery is distinguished from Woodland pottery by incised decoration techniques. Although Iroquoian pottery decorations share many of the same motifs with Juntunen ware, Juntunen motifs are created with a drag-and-jab or push-pull method of stamping, rather than incising, or cutting lines through wet clay with a sharp tool. The vessels found at the Cloudman site display many of the characteristics common to established Iroquoian typologies, such as Huron Incised, yet they diverge from their traditional descriptions too much to be classified in any of these categories. This is common among Iroquoian-style pottery found outside of the traditional Iroquoian home territories (Fox and Garrad 2004).

Eighteen pottery vessels were originally identified as "Huron"/Iroquoian, four of which were described as Algonquian/Odawa attempts to mimic Huron forms (Branstner 1995). An additional two vessels were believed to resemble Lalonde High Collar, another Iroquoian type. Re-

Table 5.6. Late Precontact Vessels

Type	Ct.
Iroquoian-style	37
Traverse Decorated v. Punctate	3
Traverse Plain v. Scalloped	5
Traverse ware	2
Total	47

assessment of these vessels confirmed their identification as Iroquoian-style. In addition, a number of vessels previously left untyped or thought to be late Juntunen wares were found to exhibit the characteristic incising or morphology of Iroquoian-style wares (see table 5.6; figures C25–C29). The origins and manufacturers of the Iroquoian-style pottery vessels at the Cloudman site are unknown (and thus their designation as "Iroquoian-style" rather than "Iroquoian"), so definitive categorization of vessels in established Iroqoian pottery typologies was avoided. A discussion of these vessels and their closest typological affinities follows.

cf. Huron Incised (n = 22). The majority of the Iroquoian-style vessels most closely resembled Huron Incised (Vessels 36, 62, 70, 74, 79, 82, 155, 156, 159, 160, 161, 163, 166, 167, 178, 179, 182, 183, 185, 186, 187). Huron Incised vessels are characterized by oblique or vertical incised line decoration on short, outflaring collars with straight or convex interior rim surfaces (MacNeish 1952, 34). This type is generally associated with Wendat-Petun groups. Vessels 167 and 182 are miniature vessels described later in the chapter.

cf. Ripley Plain (n = 3). Vessels 64, 135, and 151, previously untyped, resemble Ripley Plain. Ripley Plain is notable for its smooth surfaces and lack of decoration, and it is generally associated with the Wendat-Petun and the Neutral of southern Ontario (MacNeish 1952).

cf. Lawson Ware (n = 5). Several vessels (40/153, 136, 154, 157, 162) bear resemblance to Lawson wares. Vessel 162 displays a concave rim interior and incising on the lip that are typical of Lawson Incised (Birch and Williamson 2012; MacNeish 1952). Vessel 136 displays broadly spaced, vertical incising, resembling Lawson Incised and Huron Incised; however, it lacks both the distinct channeled or concave interior of Lawson (instead possessing a crude interior-extruded lip) and the defined collar of Huron Incised.

Vessels 40/153 and 157 lack the intact lips required for accurate typological classification, but both are collared and incised, characteristics broadly observed in Lawson wares (Macneish 1952) Vessel 154 also strongly resembles Lawson Opposed, with a thin collar and opposed oblique incising on the collar underscored by punctates.

Untyped (n = 7). Several vessels (38, 48, 68, 77, 145, 146, 188) had characteristics that associated them with Iroquoian styles of manufacture, such as incising, collars, smoothed exterior surfaces, and squared lips, but lacked enough definitive characteristics to be compared to any established typological category. Vessels 145 and 146 were originally categorized as possible late Juntunen varieties but on reexamination were found to be decorated with incising rather than the drag-and-jab method associated with Juntunen wares. Vessel 146 has opposed incising on a collarless, everted rim, with a row of punctates on the rim/shoulder margin and incised decoration on the lip. The shoulder of the vessel is cordmarked. Vessel 145 is identified from a smaller sherd lacking the shoulder and shoulder margin, but it is otherwise identical to Vessel 146 aside from the absence of lip incising.

Traverse Ware (n = 10). Most of the vessels in this category were originally categorized as "Algoma ware," a type established by Thor Conway in Ontario (Branstner 1995). However, the type was never fully described in the literature. Conway's most detailed description of the type likens it to "Dumaw Creek ware," which, along with Algoma ware, displays "scalloped lips and various modes of decoration" (Conway 1977, 21). The vagueness of this type description made it an inadequate category for type attribution. Algonquian wares with scalloped lips have been more recently categorized and described in detail by Hambacher (1992) as Traverse ware (figures C23, C24). This type is based on the assemblage from the Skegemog Point site in northern lower Michigan and is generally contemporaneous with Juntunen ware, dating to AD 1100–1550/1600 (Hambacher 1992). Therefore, all of the formerly categorized Algoma vessels have been recategorized as Traverse ware, except for Vessel 177, which was recategorized as untyped.

Five vessels (69, 75, 104, 150, 190) are categorized as Traverse Plain variety Scalloped. They are characterized by a scalloped lip, straight to everted rim profiles, and smoothed exterior surfaces (Hambacher 1992, 176). Three vessels are classified as Traverse Decorated variety Punctate (43, 56, 67). They are characterized by smooth exteriors, flat lip forms and profiles, smooth lip surfaces, and slightly everted collared rims with simple punctate exterior decoration (Hambacher 1992, 198–99). Vessels

149 and 165 were classified as Traverse ware because of their scalloped lips but were not complete enough for more specific typological attribution.

Unidentified Affiliation

Two vessels could not be confidently attributed to a specific time period or cultural affiliation (see table 5.3). Vessel 195 consists of a single rim sherd too small to display characteristics associating it with a period of manufacture. Vessel 148, however, is a unique vessel that is likely quite late in the occupational sequence of the Cloudman site but remains a stylistic anomaly. It is smoothed and peaked with a row of punctates and with at least three rows of cord impression below the rim and a very fine cording or fabric impression on a squared lip. The paste is very hard and contains a low density of temper. Its style does not fit fully with either Juntunen or Iroquoian and may represent some amalgamation of both Algonquian and Iroquoian decorative traditions.

Miniature Vessels

Branstner (1995) identified miniature vessels in the Cloudman assemblage but excluded them from the original assemblage descriptions. A total of eleven miniature vessels were identified in the Cloudman assemblage (table 5.7; figures C30–C40). Although included in the type counts and summaries above, a more detailed account of these vessels is warranted. Vessels were categorized as "miniature" if their orifice diameter was less than 10 cm.

<u>Middle Woodland</u> (n = 2). Vessels 39 and 201 display hallmarks of manufacture during the Middle Woodland period. Vessel 39 is Laurel ware, with horizontal bands of oblique stamping and a narrow, squared lip with a stamped lip. It is not as finely made as other Laurel vessels, as its interior surface is crudely smoothed, but it contains a fair amount of grit temper, suggesting that it may have been constructed for use. Vessel 201 is untyped, made of fine paste with cross-hatched incising on a thickened exterior rim with a rounded lip. It displays evidence of coil manufacture, placing it solidly in the Middle Woodland. It is a very small, shallow vessel and may be a local imitation of a Hopewellian Middle Woodland vessel more common to the south in Michigan.

Table 5.7. Miniature Vessels by Type

Component	Type	Ct.
Middle Woodland	Laurel ware	1
	Untyped, Hopewellian	1
	Subtotal	2
Early Late Woodland	Mackinac Punctate	1
	Mackinac Undecorated	1
	Mackinac ware	2
	Untyped	1
	Subtotal	5
Late Late Woodland	Untyped (cf. O'Neil cup)	1
	Subtotal	1
Late Precontact	Iroquoian-style (cf. Huron Incised)	2
	Traverse Plain v. Scalloped	1
	Subtotal	3
Total		11

Early Late Woodland (n = 5). Almost half of the miniature vessel assemblage is associated with the Early Late Woodland period. Two vessels could be attributed to specific types: Vessel 53 is Mackinac Punctate; Vessel 52 is Mackinac Undecorated. Both have the hallmark everted rims and exterior cordmarking of Mackinac ware, and both are thin-walled and very finely made. Vessel 53 also has faint staining along the top of the interior rim, suggesting it may have been used for cooking.

An additional two vessels, 83 and 202, can be generally categorized as Mackinac ware. Vessel 83 is thin-walled with an everted rim, with two rows of punctates on the exterior and one row on the interior and is overall rather crude. Vessel 202 is very fine and thin, with what appears to be fabric impressions on the exterior surface and along the exterior lip. The rim is everted, with fine, round punctates on the interior rim that were pushed through to create exterior bosses. The delicate nature of the decoration suggests it was made by a skilled juvenile or an adult potter. Vessel 63 is untyped but associated with the Early Late Woodland period because of its splayed lip with oblique cord-wrapped stick impressions and punctates on the exterior rim. However, it appears rather crudely made and lacks much visible temper.

Late Late Woodland (n = 1). Miniature vessels manufactured in the Late Late Woodland period include Vessel 54, which is 8 cm in diameter and 8 cm high with straight sides and a rounded bottom. There is no exterior surface treatment or decoration, but there are small punctates pressed downward into the anterior surface of the lip. This vessel closely resembles a cup found at the O'Neil site (Lovis 1973).

Late Precontact (n = 3). Two miniature vessels were categorized as Iroquoian-style. Vessel 167 has a very short (<1 cm), vertical collared rim with oblique incising. It is thick, crude, and heavily tempered. Vessel 182 is collared with faint vertical incising and has no visible temper. Both most closely resemble Huron Incised and may represent pots made by children. Vessel 75 is Traverse Plain variety Scalloped Lip. It has a smoothed, everted rim with cordmarking beginning at the neck, creating the neck/body zoning typical of Traverse wares (Hambacher 1992). Vessel 75 also has a ring of thick interior carbonization around the rim and was therefore used for cooking. Its manufacture and use suggest construction by a skilled potter, young or old.

AMS RADIOCARBON DATING

The diachronic nature of the research questions necessitates both absolute and relative dating of pottery from the Cloudman site. Although classification of pottery vessels in typological categories allows for the creation of a generalized chronology of occupations at the Cloudman site using relative dating, it leaves many questions. While some wares, such as Laurel, Mackinac, and Juntunen, are well dated in the immediate area of the Cloudman site, others, such as Blackduck and Traverse, are not. The chronological association of the Iroquoian-style pottery was particularly unclear. As discussed in chapter 3, Branstner (1995) initially associated Iroquoian-style wares with a Protohistoric/Contact period Odawa occupation relatively dated to around AD 1630. However, the age ranges of some of the Iroquoian types found in Ontario to which the Cloudman vessels showed affinity suggested they may be earlier, and radiocarbon dates for Iroquoian-style pottery in northern Michigan are few and far between.

The only method for establishing an accurate chronology and teasing apart the complex occupational history of the site was through the application of AMS radiocarbon dating to carbonized food residue. This was conducted using residue adhered to pottery, which permitts direct association of foods cooked in vessels to specific dates. The AMS dating results have been discussed in detail elsewhere (Kooiman and Walder 2019; Kooiman, Dunham, and Stephenson 2019) and are summarized here.

Carbonized residue was collected from thirteen vessels from the Cloudman site and submitted for AMS dating (table 5.8). Two Laurel vessels produced statistically distinct AMS dates, suggesting there were at least two different, nonoverlapping occupations by Laurel groups between AD 50 and AD 200 (Kooiman et al. 2019).

The next significant occupation is an early Woodland component characterized by Mackinac ware, which typically dates between AD 700 and AD 1000 (Lovis 2014; McPherron 1967). The dates of two Mackinac vessels and one Blackduck vessel clustered very tightly between AD 900 and AD 1000 and are statistically identical (Kooiman, Dunham, and Stephenson 2019). There also seems to have been a very brief Middle Late Woodland occupation, represented by Bois Blanc ware, which, based on a single dated vessel, dates to about AD 1150–1200 (Kooiman, Dunham, and Stephenson 2019).

The later occupations of the site were more complex. The Juntunen ware vessels yielded dates indicating an occupation by Late Late Woodland Juntunen people at the Cloudman site around AD 1200–1300 (Kooiman and Walder 2019). Traverse ware is considered another Late Late Woodland pottery tradition that is associated with northern Lower Michigan but has been found in small amounts in the Upper Peninsula of Michigan and Ontario (Hambacher 1992). Examples in the Upper Peninsula of Michigan had never been dated. A single Traverse vessel (150) yielded a date of about AD 1400 and has no overlap with the ranges

Table 5.8. AMS Dates from Carbonized Pottery Residue Samples

Vessel	Type	Calibrated Age (2 σ)	Median Age (cal)	Occupation
4	Laurel Dentate Stamped	AD 59–126[1]	AD 87[1]	Middle Woodland ca. AD 100–200
1	Laurel Pseudo-scallop Stamped	AD 80–180[1]	AD 127[1]	
193	Blackduck Banded	AD 938–87[1]	AD 946[1]	Early Late Woodland ca. AD 900–1000
103	Mackinac Banded	AD 941–97[1]	AD 968[1]	
105	Mackinac Punctate	AD 974–1031[1]	AD 1004[1]	
215	Bois Blanc ware	AD 1148–1224[1]	AD 1178[1]	Middle Late Woodland ca. AD 1150–1200
102	Juntunen Drag-and-Jab	AD 1216–75[2]	AD 1245[2]	Late Late Woodland/Juntunen ca. AD 1200–1300
205	Juntunen Linear Punctate	AD 1220–77[2]	AD 1252[2]	
146	Iroquoian-style	AD 1282–1322 or AD 1348–92[2]	AD 1354[2]	Late Precontact ca. AD 1300–1500
70	Iroquoian-style	AD 1315–56 or AD 1388–1427[2]	AD 1393[2]	
150	Traverse Plain v. Scalloped	AD 1391–1433[2]	AD 1406[2]	
162	Iroquoian-style	AD 1421–45[2]	AD 1433[2]	
179	Iroquoian-style	AD 1439–1518[2]	AD 1470[2]	

Notes:

[1]Kooiman, Dunham, and Stephenson 2019; Stuiver, Reimer, and Reimer 2017, 2018.
[2]Kooiman and Walder 2019; Stuiver, Reimer, and Reimer 2017, 2018.

for the Juntunen vessel dates (Kooiman and Walder 2019). Most interestingly, the date from the Traverse ware vessel falls squarely in between dates yielded by four sampled Iroquoian-style pottery vessels. Two Iroquoian-style vessels (146, 70) produced dates in the range of AD 1300–1400, while another two vessels (162, 179) dated to between AD 1400 and AD 1500 (Kooiman and Walder 2019).

The dates for the Iroquoian-style pottery are much earlier than anticipated, given that these vessels were found in context with European-made trade beads (Branstner 1995; Cleland 1999). However, it is likely that compaction of the sandy soil at the Cloudman site made the Late Precontact (post–AD 1300) component indistinguishable in the ground from the late seventeenth-century (post–AD 1670) Indigenous occupation of the site represented by the glass trade beads (Kooiman and Walder 2019; Walder 2018).

Instead of widely spaced Late Late Woodland and Contact period occupations, there was a sizable occupation of the Cloudman site by Juntunen groups between AD 1200 and AD 1300, while after AD 1300 the site was characterized by a series of brief occupations by groups using both Woodland (Traverse) and Iroquoian-style pottery. There is a lack of evidence for occupation of the site by pottery-making peoples post–AD 1520. The period from AD 1300 to AD 1500 is therefore referred to as the "Late Precontact" occupation because it represents a period temporally and culturally distinct from Late Late Woodland occupation characterized by Juntunen ware (Kooiman and Walder 2019).

Cloudman Site Occupation History

The AMS dates provide a greater level of specificity for the timing of the various occupations of the Cloudman site, while relative dating based on stylistic relationships of pottery vessels corroborate and enrich the occupation time line. The combined results contributed to a rich narrative of the occupational history of the Cloudman site.

The Middle Woodland occupation, the earliest known component of the site, is represented largely by Laurel ware vessels. Two Laurel vessels from the Cloudman site date between AD 50 and AD 200 and likely represent two distinct occupations (Kooiman, Dunham, and Stephenson 2019). There is little evidence to support human occupation of the site prior to the Laurel Dentate Stamped vessel, which has an AMS median age of cal AD 87. The assemblage does contain two North Bay vessels, and residues from a North Bay Plain vessel at the Winter site on the Garden Peninsula produced an AMS date with a median probability of cal BC 113, significantly earlier than the Cloudman Laurel dates. However, North Bay Cordmarked and North Bay Punctate vessels from the nearby Winter site produced median probability ages of cal AD 82 and cal AD 155, respectively (Albert et al. 2018; Lovis, Arbogast, and Monaghan 2012; Richner 1973; Stuiver, Reimer, and Reimer 2017), which are consistent with the Laurel occupations at Cloudman.

Three late Laurel ware vessels at the site, along with four other vessels that appear transitional between Middle and Late Woodland, suggest an additional, if brief, occupation sometime between cal AD 500 and 700 (Lovis 2014), although none of these vessels yielded datable material. It is unclear whether the site was occupied between AD 200 and AD 500.

A second intensive occupation of the site took place in the Early Late Woodland period. The ceramic assemblage includes both Mackinac Punctate and Mackinac Banded vessels. Mackinac Punctate was generally manufactured between AD 700 and AD 900 in the Upper Great Lakes, while Mackinac Banded commonly dates to AD 850–1000 (Lovis 2014). AMS dates from the Mackinac vessels and Blackduck Banded vessel tightly overlap and suggest a substantial occupation between AD 900 and AD 1000 (Kooiman et al. 2019). Whether this is an indication of trade, travel, or intermarriage between Blackduck ware- and Mackinac ware-producing people remains an intriguing question, since Blackduck is a nonlocal pottery type (although it is not uncommon in the Northern Great Lakes).

Only five small Bois Blanc rim sherds represent the Middle Late Woodland component of the Cloudman site, and a single dated Bois Blanc vessel places this limited and brief occupation around AD 1150–1200 (Kooiman, Dunham, and Stephenson 2019). This falls within the typical range for Bois Blanc ware, which is AD 1000 to AD 1250 (Lovis 2014; McPherron 1967).

The period between AD 1200 and AD 1500 comprises the most complex span of the Cloudman site history and includes both Late Late Woodland/Juntunen and Late Precontact occupations. Regional direct dates for Juntunen ware span between AD 1200 and AD 1500 (Lovis

2014; McHale Milner 1998; McPherron 1967). A "proto-Juntunen" vessel from around AD 1200 is the earliest of these vessels. Juntunen Linear Punctate vessels were commonly manufactured between AD 1200 and AD 1300, while Juntunen Drag-and-Jab typically dates to AD 1300 to AD 1400 (Lovis 2014). However, the two dated Juntunen vessels place the Late Late Woodland occupation of the Cloudman site firmly between AD 1200 and AD 1300.

The Late Precontact occupation of the Cloudman site is characterized by the presence of two distinct ceramic traditions: Traverse ware (n = 10), which is associated with Woodland groups in the Northern Great Lakes; and pottery vessels displaying the unique style of Iroquoian groups from southern Ontario. Traverse ware is generally contemporaneous with Juntunen ware, dating to AD 1100–1550/1600 (Hambacher 1992). A single Traverse ware vessel produced a date of around AD 1400. Further complicating the Late Precontact history of the Cloudman site, two dated Iroquoian-style vessels were likely manufactured between AD 1300 and AD 1400, preceding and statistically distinct from the Traverse vessel date. Two additional Iroquoian-style vessels postdate the Traverse vessel, representing yet another distinct occupation between AD 1400 and AD 1500. Overall, after AD 1300 the site was characterized by a series of brief occupations by migrating or traveling groups, or, as Branstner (1995) and Cleland (1999) posited, proto-Odawa traders who obtained nonlocal wares for their own use. The identities of the manufacturers and users of these vessels remain unknown.

In summary, the Cloudman site history is represented primarily by Middle Woodland (AD 50–200), Early Late Woodland (AD 900–1000), Late Late Woodland (AD 1200–1300), and Late Precontact (AD 1300–1500) occupations, punctuated by a few brief intermediary, undated occupations. Again, it is important to note that it is still unclear whether the post–AD 1400 occupants of the site would have identified as Iroquoian or whether they were Woodland groups (i.e., proto-Odawa) using Iroquoian pottery or producing Iroquoian-style pottery.

CONCLUSION

The reevaluation of the taxonomic categorization of the Cloudman pottery assemblage was largely in accordance with the original analysis conducted by Branstner (1995). The primary discrepancy between the former and present studies was in the identification and timing of the later site occupations. Iroquoian-style pottery was originally associated with an early Contact period occupation of the site (ca. AD 1630) by Odawa traders, but both relative and AMS dating indicate many of these vessels were used and disposed of at the site prior to this time, mostly between AD 1300 and AD 1500. The uncertain identity of the manufacturers and users of these wares requires further investigation.

Contextualization of the Cloudman vessels within established chronologies for regional ceramic taxonomies permitted construction of a solid occupational history of the site, supported and detailed by the set of direct AMS dates. The separation of pottery vessels into discrete temporally based subassemblages creates the framework for the rest of the analyses employed in this study, facilitating diachronic comparisons of technology, cooking, and diet. Pottery from the most intensive occupations (Middle Woodland, Early Late Woodland, Late Late Woodland, Late Precontact) identified through the work presented in this chapter serve as the primary data sets for explorations of pottery function (chapter 6) and cuisine (chapter 7) at the Cloudman site.

CHAPTER 6

Pottery Function

The establishment of a site chronology permitted a second approach to pottery analysis emphasizing vessel function. Although occasionally constructed for symbolic or ceremonial use, most ceramic vessels were made for everyday, utilitarian functions such as cooking, serving, and storage. Pottery function can be evaluated by technical properties, a vessel's characteristics chosen by the potter to suit its intended purpose, and use-alteration traces, which reveal how a vessel was used. Properties related to function can be sensitive to changes in food-processing requirements and cooking methods, reflecting diachronic alterations in pottery use and dietary habits when set against the site chronology established in the previous chapter. Synchronic variation of vessel function may signal communication of group identity, reflecting food selection and cooking styles in addition to pottery style.

This chapter evaluates both the technical and use-alteration properties of the Cloudman site pottery vessels and then discusses intended and actual ceramic function. Function is assessed synchronically, in order to explore the relationship between pottery use and identity, and diachronically, in order to answer research questions concerning pottery technology and use in relation to culinary transformations.

TECHNICAL PROPERTIES AND INTENDED FUNCTION

The three technical properties chosen as the focus of this study were temper size, rim diameter, and vessel thickness. Temper size and vessel thickness have proven sensitive measures of technical variability in relation to foodways transformations (Braun 1983; Hart 2012). Rim diameter has demonstrated variability in the Northern Great Lakes and beyond (Blitz 1993; Kooiman 2012, 2016; Potter 2000), although the significance of vessel size in relation to function is complex and unclear. Examination of vessel size in relation to other technical properties and cooking requirements could clarify its functional role among Woodland vessels; it therefore serves an exploratory purpose in this study.

Temper Size

Temper size influences the performance of a pottery vessel. Both the vessel strength and the thermal shock resistance of fired vessels increase with the reduction of temper particle size (Bronitsky and Hamer 1986). Cooking vessels are therefore expected to be constructed with smaller temper particles than serving or storage vessels because they require durability over fire. Temper size has been found to decrease over time in ancient cooking vessels from parts of the Eastern Woodlands in correlation with increased processing of starchy foods (Braun 1983), including maize (Hart 2012), because these foods require high-temperature, long-term boiling to become palatable (Wandsnider 1997). However, a previous study in the Northern Great Lakes found no significant difference in temper size between Middle Woodland vessels from the Naomikong Point site and those from the Late Woodland Sand Point site (Kooiman 2016). These sites are geographically separated by considerable distance, and the Cloudman assemblage provides an opportunity to explore the potential for diachronic temper size change at a single site.

Table 6.1 shows mean temper size among vessels associated with each component of the Cloudman site. Average temper size shows a small initial increase in the Early Late Woodland period, followed by a decrease in Late Late Woodland and Iroquoian-style vessels. A Welch's unpaired t-test, a nonparametric analysis used to compare independent samples of unequal variances and sample sizes, was used to determine the statistical relationships between the average temper size of vessels (table 6.2). The slight increase in mean temper size between Middle Woodland and Early Late Woodland vessels proved insignificant. Despite the 500-year time gap between the primary Middle Woodland occupation and the Early Late Woodland occupation at the Cloudman site, temper size remained relatively consistent.

However, in a comparatively short span of time between the Early Late Woodland and the Late Late Woodland occupations, temper underwent a statistically significant size reduction. Early Late Woodland vessel temper is significantly larger than Late Late Woodland and Late Precontact temper, and Middle Woodland temper is similarly significantly larger than Late Precontact temper. This abrupt change in temper

Table 6.1. Mean Temper Size of Pottery Vessels by Component

Component	Mean (mm)	n
Middle Woodland	1.49	33
Early Late Woodland	1.58	58
Late Late Woodland	1.35	38
Late Precontact	1.26	45

Table 6.2. Temper Size Relationships, Welch's Unpaired T-Test (significant outcomes boldfaced)

	Middle Woodland		Early Late Woodland		Late Late Woodland	
Component	p*	df	p	df	p	df
Middle Woodland	---	---	---	---	---	---
Early Late Woodland	0.2842	84	---	---	---	---
Late Late Woodland	0.0970	64	**0.0042**	93	---	---
Late Precontact	**0.0044**	57	**0.0001**	94	0.1935	74

Notes:
*two-tailed.
$\alpha = 0.05$.

size after a millennium of consistency signals a major shift in temper selection during the Late Woodland period. Following this shift, temper size remains consistently small after AD 1200.

Rim Diameter

A total of eighty-eight vessels, 43.6% of the total vessel assemblage, had rim segments sufficient in size for diameter measurements. A plot of rim diameters shows a roughly normal distribution (figure 6.1), with an overall mean of 19.27 cm. The average rim diameter for Middle Woodland vessels was 17 cm, smaller than the averages for Early Late Woodland, Late Late Woodland, and Late Precontact vessels (table 6.3). A Welch's t-test confirmed that Middle Woodland rim diameters were significantly smaller than Early Late Woodland rim diameters (table 6.4). Meanwhile, Early Late Woodland, Late Late Woodland, and Late Precontact subassemblages were almost statistically identical. The results demonstrate a significant increase in orifice diameter during the Middle Woodland/Late Woodland transition.

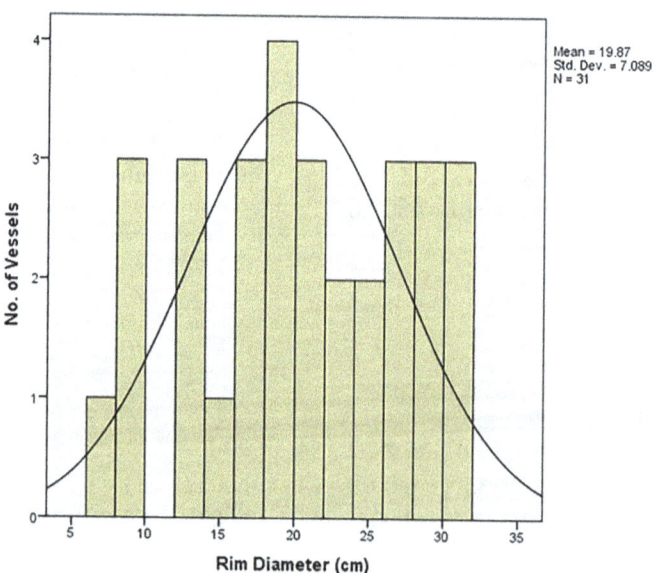

Figure 6.1. Rim diameter frequencies of the Cloudman pottery assemblage.

Table 6.3. Mean Rim Diameter of Pottery Vessels by Component

Component	Mean (cm)	n
Middle Woodland	17	16
Early Late Woodland	20	41
Late Late Woodland	20	13
Late Precontact	19	18

Table 6.4. Rim Diameter Relationships, Welch's Unpaired T-Test (significant outcomes boldfaced)

	Middle Woodland		Early Late Woodland		Late Late Woodland	
Component	p*	df	p	df	p	df
Middle Woodland	---	---	---	---	---	---
Early Late Woodland	**0.0448**	**30**	---	---	---	---
Late Late Woodland	0.2375	20	0.7359	18	---	---
Late Precontact	0.3235	30	0.9216	33	0.7081	23

Notes:
*two-tailed.
α = 0.05.

Vessel orifice (rim) diameter is an aspect of pottery morphology that is not fully understood. Rim diameter is often used as a proxy for vessel volume/size, but only a handful of studies in North America have demonstrated the relationship between the two measures (Blitz 1993; Parker and Kennedy 2010; Potter 2000; Shapiro 1984). Statistical relationships between rim diameter and vessel volume in Late Woodland vessels from the Upper Great Lakes have been demonstrated previously (Kooiman 2015b), although a similar examination of Middle Woodland and Iroquoian-style/Late Precontact vessels has not been carried out. While the overall morphologies of these three categories of ceramic vessel differ, the disparities are not drastic enough to preclude using rim diameter as a proxy for size/volume for Middle Woodland and Late Precontact vessels.

Still, the significance of vessel volume/size is largely unknown and probably varies through space and time. Size may be related to utilitarian function (Kobayashi 1994; Rice 1987, 299), social function (Blitz 1993; Potter 2000), and/or household size (Nelson 1981; Tani 1994; Turner and Lofgren 1966). The pottery assemblage from the Laurel Middle Woodland site of Naomikong Point was statistically significantly smaller than Late Woodland vessels from the Sand Point site; however, at Sand Point, Late Woodland vessels from habitation contexts were significantly smaller than vessels from mound contexts at the site and statistically equivalent to the Middle Woodland vessels from Naomikong Point (Kooiman 2016). Ethnoarchaeological studies have also shown that there is a clear size distinction between daily cooking pots and ceremonial cooking pots (Kobayashi 1994). Therefore, context of use (utilitarian vs. ceremonial) may be one reason for size variation among pottery vessels in the Northern Great Lakes.

A burial mound is present at the Cloudman site, but it was excavated in the early twentieth century and the whereabouts of associated artifacts are unknown (Branstner 1995). All of the measured pottery vessels derived from excavations within the primary habitation zone, and the function of the site appears mostly undifferentiated between the components (aside from a feature containing a dog burial; see details in chapter 3). Pottery vessels from surface collections, which could potentially be refuse from mound looting, were not included in this analysis. Therefore, the relationship between vessel size and context of use at the Cloudman site cannot be assessed, although it could be a factor in the diachronic size variation among the assemblage. The increase in vessel size over time could also be linked to several other factors: new cooking techniques may have been better accommodated by larger vessels, increased group size may have necessitated larger vessels to accommodate feeding more people, or decreased mobility may have allowed for greater energy investment in manufacturing larger vessels that no longer needed to be carried from site to site. At present, the reason for diachronic vessel orifice/vessel size variation remains unclear.

Vessel Thickness

Pottery vessel wall thickness was measured on the lip, neck, shoulder, and body of eligible vessels from the Cloudman site (table 6.5). Lip thickness increases, as expected, from the narrow-lipped Middle Woodland vessels to the splayed-lip Early Late Woodland vessels and then decreases slightly with the collared, squared-lipped Late Late Woodland and Iroquoian-style vessels. Shoulder thickness varies greatly through time, initially decreasing from the Middle Woodland to the Early Late Woodland, then increasing in the Late Late Woodland and decreasing among Iroquoian-style vessels, which had the thinnest average shoulders overall.

Neck thickness steadily increases through time, likely correlated with the proliferation of collared wares after AD 1200. Collars, which are created by doubling over the top edge of the rim or by adding an additional ring of clay to the uppermost portion of the rim, are common among Juntunen and Iroquoian-style pottery vessels. Although neck thickness was measured below collars, the need for structural support of the collar would manifest in thicker vessel necks.

Body thickness is the most important characteristic of a ceramic cooking vessel when assessing the relationship between thickness and vessel function. This is because the body is the most important portion of the vessel for heating effectiveness as this is where the heat source is applied (rather than above the shoulder). Body thickness was expected to decrease over time, along with the predicted increased use of starchy foods, which require more intensive cooking to be made edibile. However, while body thickness decreases from the Middle Woodland to the Early Late Woodland, it increases slightly among Late Late Woodland vessels and again among Late Precontact vessels. These latter periods were hypothesized as the times when starchy foods would be most important at

Table 6.5. Vessel Wall Thickness by Component

Component	Lip Mean (mm)	n	Neck Mean (mm)	n	Shoulder Mean (mm)	n	Body Mean (mm)	n
Middle Woodland	4.43	35	6.1	33	6.79	9	7.4	6
Early Late Woodland	8.51	61	6.36	57	6.43	25	6.11	9
Late Late Woodland	7.38	37	8.23	37	8.24	16	6.7	7
Late Precontact	6.88	39	7.43	35	6.21	10	9.12	4

the Cloudman site, running counter to predictions that vessel wall thickness would steadily decrease over time.

Statistical analysis was used to determine whether the differences in observed body thickness variations between subassemblages were significant (table 6.6). A Welch's t-test was employed to examine the relationships between analytic subsets. The results show no statistically significant differences in body thickness over time. This outcome may have been affected by the small sample sizes for body thickness: few vessels were complete enough to include these portions for measurement. Temporal attribution of body sherds not associated with identified vessels is a dubious task since most body sherds do not display decorations that can be connected to a time period or typology. Therefore, most body sherds in the Cloudman assemblage are not associated with specific vessels or taxonomic categories.

Overall, these results of vessel thickness measurements do not follow predicted trends of thinning over time. The lack of body sherds associated with identified vessels, which were the focus of this study, affected a true assessment of vessel thickness of the areas that would be most influenced by a potter's actions to improve heating effectiveness. The relationship between neck and shoulder thickness to overall vessel thickness should be a topic of future inquiry.

Table 6.6. Body Thickness Relationships, Welch's Unpaired T-Test

Component	Middle Woodland		Early Late Woodland		Late Late Woodland	
	p^*	df	p	df	p	df
Middle Woodland	---	---	---	---	---	---
Early Late Woodland	0.4722	9	---	---	---	---
Late Late Woodland	0.8712	9	0.3491	9	---	---
Late Precontact	0.6965	7	0.2323	5	0.5879	7

Notes:
*two-tailed.
α = 0.05.

Synchronic Technical Variation

Technical properties within each component subassemblage were investigated to assess synchronic variability. Contemporaneous taxonomic types could represent separate social groups with distinct stylistic traditions. Functional variability could mirror stylistic variability, signifying different pottery construction traditions and perhaps even different functional requirements if culinary habits vary according to group identity. Rim diameter and temper of pottery vessels (averaged from three measurements per vessel) from each typological category were compared to investigate the question of synchronic intended function variability. Comparisons of body thickness were left out because of the small sample sizes. Only types comprising large portions of their respective subassemblages were chosen for comparison; other types with small sample sizes are excluded from the discussion below.

Three major distinct pottery types were present in the Middle Woodland subassamblage (table 6.7). Variation in technical properties

Table 6.7. Technical Properties of Pottery Vessels by Type/Ware

Component	Pottery Type	Rim Radius Mean (cm)	n	Temper Size Mean (mm)	n
Middle Woodland	Laurel Banked Linear Stamped	22	2	1.5	6
	Laurel Dentate Stamped	19.5	4	1.41	7
	Laurel Pseudo-scallop Shell	15	5	1.46	13
Early Late Woodland	Blackduck Banded	22.5	4	1.37	4
	Mackinac Banded	20	8	1.82	11
	Mackinac Punctate	21.1	10	1.56	15
Late Late Woodland	Juntunen Drag-and-Jab	28	2	1.58	4
	Juntunen Linear Punctate	21	4	1.39	6
Late Precontact	Traverse ware	16	4	1.29	10
	Iroquoian-style	20	14	1.26	35

among the types was low. This is unsurprising given that all three types are variations of Laurel ware. Relationships of these properties between types were assessed using Welch's t-test, which revealed no statistical differences. Pottery construction techniques appear consistent across all Middle Woodland taxonomic types.

Variation in technical properties slightly increases between types in the Early Late Woodland subassemblage. AMS dates from a Mackinac Banded vessel and a Blackduck Banded vessel revealed extremely close contemporaneity (see table 5.8), although Mackinac is a local ware and Blackduck has a broader distribution and is more common to regions north of the Upper Peninsula. Most apparent is the difference in mean temper size, with Blackduck temper smaller on average than Mackinac Banded. However, this difference was not statistically significant. Mackinac Punctate ware, which generally predates but also temporally overlaps with Mackinac Banded, had a smaller mean temper size. However, comparisons of physical properties between various Early Late Woodland types demonstrated no statistically significant differences.

Late Late Woodland vessels consist primarily of Juntunen ware, including Drag-and-Jab and Linear Punctate (see table 6.7). These two wares are generally contemporaneous but differ in style. However, rim diameter and temper size of Drag-and-Jab and Linear Punctate vessels are not statistically distinct. Given that the AMS dates associated with both vessel types were statistically identical, it is no surprise that physical properties beyond style did not vary among the different Juntunen ware categories.

Finally, Iroquoian-style vessels were compared against Traverse ware vessels to investigate potential variation during the Late Precontact period (see table 6.7). These two ceramic traditions are so stylistically distinct that it was predicted that the greatest synchronic variation would occur between them. Temper size was statistically identical between the two subassemblages, demonstrating that overall, temper size decreased among even vastly different stylistic traditions after AD 1300. At first glance, it would appear that Traverse ware vessels are much smaller than their Iroquoian-style counterparts based on their different average rim diameters (16 cm vs. 20 cm). However, this difference is not statistically significant, perhaps a result of the small sample size for Traverse ware vessels (n = 4).

Overall, technical variation within each component was low. Middle Woodland vessels are, as predicted, particularly consistent, but technical variability also remained low among later pottery subassemblages, even among the drastically different stylistic types of the Late Precontact period. Although the small sample sizes available for most of these comparisons may have affected the statistical analyses, there is an apparent synchronic consistency in the construction of pottery vessels at the Cloudman site, regardless of decoration and style.

Intended Function Summary

Middle Woodland pottery vessels were overall the most technologically distinct among the Cloudman assemblage. Middle Woodland pots were generally small and thin, with large temper particles relative to thickness. Although vessel size significantly increased during the subsequent Early Late Woodland period, thickness and temper size of vessels associated with this time remained relatively consistent with Middle Woodland vessel properties. Late Late Woodland potters continued to construct larger but thicker pots, with significantly smaller temper particles. Late Precontact vessels, although displaying very different decorative techniques from their Juntunen predecessors, retained many of the same technical properties of Late Late Woodland vessels. Late Woodland and Late Precontact potters preferred larger vessels, although the functional advantage of greater vessel volume is still unclear. The differences observed between Algonquian and Iroquoian pottery vessels in the northeastern United States by Chilton (1998), including larger, thinner, and more homogeneous Iroquoian vessels, were not observed among the Cloudman vessels. Without further investigation of paste composition, physical characteristics do not inform differences in Woodland versus Iroquoian-style vessel manufacturing traditions, aside from their decorative style.

After AD 1200, there is clear evidence for intentional use of significantly smaller temper particles, a decision that could reflect new food processing requirements that entailed more intensive (longer and/or higher-temperature) cooking techniques. Unlike temper size, vessel body thickness did not follow the predicted trend of thinning over time. In fact, there seems to be an inverse relationship between temper size and thickness, where decreases in temper particle size are accompanied by an

Table 6.8. Comparison of Mean Temper Size and Mean Body Thickness of Pottery Vessels by Component

Component	Mean Body Thickness (mm)	Mean Temper Size (mm)
Middle Woodland	7.40	1.49
Early Late Woodland	6.11	1.58
Late Late Woodland	6.70	1.35
Late Precontact	9.12	1.26

increase in body thickness, and vice versa (table 6.8), an intriguing trend that warrants further exploration. The diachronic trends in technical variation contrasts with the synchronic consistency of the same properties, suggesting that contemporary social groups did not enact social identity through these pottery construction techniques.

USE-ALTERATION TRACES AND ACTUAL FUNCTION

The functions fulfilled by a pottery vessel in the past can be accessed through use-alterations traces, or the physical and chemical changes that indicate the various processes in which the vessel was involved throughout its life history (Schiffer and Skibo 1987, 1997). Use-alteration traces include exterior sooting, exterior carbonization, interior carbonization, attrition, and absorbed residues (see chapter 4 for definitions). Sooting and carbonization are direct evidence of a vessel's use over fire, meaning a vessel with either of these traces was probably involved in cooking. Attrition involves removal of the pottery surface through various physical and chemical processes; however, this was not detected in any of the Cloudman pottery assemblage and is not discussed further here.

The Cloudman pottery assemblage was assessed for the presence of exterior sooting, exterior carbonization, and interior carbonization. Patterning of interior carbonization was also categorized and recorded to identify distinct cooking techniques. Presence and patterning of use-alteration traces are compared both diachronically and synchronically to identify trends and changes in pottery use at the Cloudman site. Together, these data provide insight into the actual function of Cloudman pottery vessels.

Exterior Sooting

Sooting on the exterior of a pottery vessel forms when smoke from a fire adheres to the ceramic surface and is an important indication of a vessel's involvement in cooking. Sooting most commonly forms around the bottom and lower sides of a vessel, where smoke from the fire contacts the vessel surface (Skibo 1992, 2013). Only 10% of identified vessels from the Cloudman site displayed exterior sooting (table 6.9). Sooting was most frequent on Early Late Woodland vessels, the component yielding the largest vessel portions. As previously discussed, vessels from other components are often represented only by rim or upper body sherds, where exterior sooting is unlikely to be present. Therefore, sooting is probably underrepresented among the identified vessels in the Cloudman assemblage, which overall have few associated body sherds and even fewer basal sherds. While a review of body sherds not associated with identified vessels would likely reveal a higher frequency of sooting at the site, it would be difficult to associate these sherds with a specific occupation and therefore would not contribute to the study of diachronic pottery function.

Table 6.9. Frequency of Use-Alteration Traces by Component

Component	Exterior Sooting		Exterior Carbonization		Interior Carbonization	
	Ct.	%	Ct.	%	Ct.	%
Middle Woodland	0	0.0	2	5.7	16	45.7
Middle/Late Woodland	0	0.0	1	14.3	4	57.1
Early Late Woodland	14	22.6	10	16.1	34	54.8
Middle Late Woodland	1	20.0	0	0.0	3	60.0
Late Late Woodland	1	2.6	8	21.1	22	57.9
Late Precontact	5	10.9	10	21.7	26	56.5
Total	21	10.4	31	15.3	106	53.0

Exterior Carbonization

Burned food residue on the exterior surface of a pottery vessel is another indicator of a pottery vessel's involvement in cooking. Foodstuffs burned onto the outside of a cooking pot can be the result of pouring or spilling or boiling over. Exterior carbonization was positively identified on approximately 15% of all identified vessels (see table 6.9). Exterior carbonization is most likely to appear on the upper portions of a vessel and is, therefore, likely not underrepresented. However, only a small proportion of cooking events would be expected to result in exterior carbonization, so frequencies observed within the Cloudman assemblage align with expectations.

Interior Carbonization

Food residue burned onto the vessel's interior surface is the most important evidence of the vessel's involvement in cooking. The mere presence of interior carbonization is direct proof that resource processing took place within the vessel, and the patterning (discussed below) and microbotanical/chemical composition (see chapter 7) of the residue is vital to reconstructing cooking and food selection habits.

Over half of all identified vessels from the Cloudman site displayed interior carbonization (see table 6.9). Interior carbonization is consistently present through time, occurring on 45% to 60% of vessels from each component. This demonstrates that a high proportion of vessels, throughout all occupations, was involved in resource processing.

Despite its relatively high frequency, interior carbonization is still likely to be underrepresented in the assemblage. Differential preservation of residues on pottery surfaces is evident on vessels with portions that refit together; in many cases, one sherd is stained with carbonization, while an adjacent sherd is not (as has also been observed in other Northern Great Lakes pottery assemblages). Discrepancies could result from variations in postdepositional taphonomic processes (where parts of the same vessels were exposed to different environments or events after disposal) or archaeological laboratory processing (overeager artifact scrubbing). Ancient pottery cleaning habits may also affect the preservation of adhered interior residues, as some vessels may have been cleaned prior to breakage/disposal while others were not. Some vessels may never have been used. The fail rate of firing pottery in open fire can be as high as 100% (Rice 1987, 173), so vessels without use-alteration traces may have broken during manufacture, causing overrepresentation of vessels lacking carbonization. While it is also plausible that pots lacking visible interior residues were used as storage vessels, cooking appears to be the primary function of pottery vessels during all occupations of the Cloudman site.

Habitual Cooking Behaviors

Vessels with interior carbonization were further categorized based on the patterning of residue along the vessel wall. Carbonization location and patterning inform interpretations of past cooking habits and methods and are rooted in ethnoarchaeological observations among modern-day societies using locally made ceramic cookware (see Kobayashi 1994; Skibo 1994). Both the level at which vessels are filled and the patterning of the interior carbonization are useful indicators of cooking traditions, such as habitual vessel use and modes of cooking.

<u>Vessel Fill Levels</u>. The presence of carbonization on the uppermost portions of the interior surface is almost ubiquitous among Cloudman site pottery vessels. In many cases, residue extended all the way to the lip; in others, there was a half- to one-inch buffer between the residue line and the lip. This pattern indicates high fill levels during cooking. This is consistent with patterning found in other Northern Great Lakes sites (Kooiman 2012, 2016) and stands in contrast to habits found in other regions of the world, where cooking pots are often filled two-thirds to prevent boiling over (Kobayashi 1994; Skibo and Blinman 1999), a costly mistake that would waste food and douse the hearth fire.

Several ethnographic sources note that organic skin or birchbark vessels can be placed directly over the fire without burning as long as they are kept full (Densmore 1979; Wallis and Wallis 1955; Waugh 1973), potentially representing a habitual behavior extended to pottery vessels, which were adopted in the region after millennia of cooking in organic vessels. In this case, boil-overs may not have been as costly a mistake as in other regions, such as Colorado (see Skibo and Blinman 1999), where population density is higher and access to wood resources is more limited than in the Northern Great Lakes.

Considering that many vessels in the Cloudman assemblage are represented solely by rim sherds, it is possible that fill lines along the shoulder of the vessel are present but not observable in the sample. However, defined fill lines at the vessel shoulder were not observed in any of the partial vessels in the assemblage.

Interior Carbonization Patterns. Although cooks at the Cloudman site consistently filled vessels to the top during the cooking process, the cooking techniques employed were varied. Figure 6.2 illustrates the five patterns observed in the Cloudman assemblage, which signify different modes of cooking. Pattern 1 (figures 6.2a, 6.3) represents residue restricted to a distinct ring around the rim of the vessel. This pattern is consistent with boiling, a wet-cooking mode in which the aqueous nature of the vessel contents prevent adherence of food particles to the ceramic surface, except at the water line, where both small starchy and fatty food particles accumulate and burn in this high-temperature zone (Skibo 1992, 2013). Pattern 2 (figures 6.2b, 6.4) represents residue distributed over most or all of the interior surface of the pot, which most likely indicates stewing, a long-term liquid reduction process. Stewing gradually removes much of the water from the food mix, allowing more food particles to come into contact with the vessel wall and become charred when exposure is prolonged. Dry mode cooking techniques, such as parching or roasting, can also leave thick residue deposits across the vessel surface, although this is usually restricted to either the very bottom or one side of the pot (Skibo 1992, 2013). Roasting often takes place with a vessel placed on its side, and neither interior carbonization nor exterior sooting patterns observed in the Cloudman assemblage are consistent with this behavior. However, given the lack of complete vessels from the Cloudman site, it cannot be stated that pottery vessels were never used for roasting or parching, although this pattern was not observed at other Northern Great Lakes sites with more complete or partially reconstructed vessels (Kooiman 2012, 2016).

Interior carbonization Pattern 3 (figures 6.2c, 6.5) represents a ring of thick carbonization around the rim with a thinner layer of residue covering the remaining interior surface, indicative of a single vessel involved in both boiling and stewing of foods. Vessels displaying only one type of carbonization pattern could signify the designation of vessels for specific purposes (e.g., boiling pots vs. stew pots) or that stewing events may have simply obscured evidence of prior boiling episodes. Vessels could also

Figure 6.2. Interior carbonization patterns for the Cloudman site (20CH6) pottery assemblage. Courtesy of Erin Beachey.

Figure 6.3. Interior carbonization Pattern 1 (boiling).

Figure 6.4. Interior carbonization Pattern 2 (stewing).

Figure 6.5. Interior carbonization Pattern 3 (boiling + stewing).

have been washed and scrubbed between uses, the pattern present archaeologically representing only the last mode of cooking for which the pot was used. The newly observed Pattern 3, however, is a clear indicator of multiple stages of cooking in a single event or multiple cooking events taking place in the same vessel: one or more intensive boiling episodes resulting in thick residue deposition, distinct from thinner residues representing less intensive prior or subsequent stewing events.

Pattern 4 (figure 6.2d) was used to categorize cases in which interior carbonization is visible along the rim of the vessel while the extent of the residue below the rim is indeterminate. This pattern could represent either boiling or stewing. In most cases there is not enough of the rim present to determine whether the residue distribution distinctly stops at or near the base of the rim (boiling) or continues farther down the side of the interior vessel surface (stewing). Pattern 5 (figure 6.2e) represents patchy interior carbonization on the vessel surface with no discernible pattern.

Table 6.10 shows the frequency of each interior carbonization pattern by component. The most frequent pattern among all subsets is Pattern 4, largely due to the fragmentary nature of the assemblage, which precludes proper assessment of the distributional extent of residues on many vessels, especially those represented by small rim sherds. Unfortunately, Pattern 4 tells us very little about past cooking behaviors, and this is also the case with Pattern 5. Subsequent discussion therefore focuses on Patterns 1 through 3 (table 6.11; figure 6.6), which more clearly represent specific cooking behaviors.

Table 6.10. Interior Carbonization Pattern Frequency by Component

Pattern Category	Middle Woodland Ct.	Middle Woodland %	Early Late Woodland Ct.	Early Late Woodland %	Late Late Woodland Ct.	Late Late Woodland %	Late Precontact Ct.	Late Precontact %	Totals Ct.	Totals %
1	2	13	8	24	6	26	4	16	20	21
2	5	31	4	12	4	17	3	12	16	16
3	0	0	4	12	2	9	6	24	12	12
4	4	25	14	41	9	39	10	40	37	38
5	5	31	4	12	2	9	2	8	13	13
Total	16	100	34	100	23	100	25	100	98	100

Among Middle Woodland vessels, Pattern 2 (stewing) is the most frequent interior carbonization pattern. This is consistent with prior assessments of Middle Woodland cooking, where stewing predominates and boiling is less frequently represented (Kooiman 2012, 2016). However, the fragmentary nature of the Middle Woodland vessels resulted in a small sample size (n = 7) of vessels with clear carbonization patterns, which is small enough to skew the results. However, Pattern 3 was not observed among Middle Woodland vessels, and clear signatures for boiling were observed in only two vessels.

Table 6.11. Primary Interior Carbonization Pattern Frequency by Component

Pattern Category	Middle Woodland		Early Late Woodland		Late Late Woodland		Late Precontact	
	Ct.	%	Ct.	%	Ct.	%	Ct.	%
1	2	29	8	50	6	50	4	31
2	5	71	4	25	4	33	3	23
3	0	0	4	25	2	17	6	46
Total	7	100	16	100	12	100	13	100

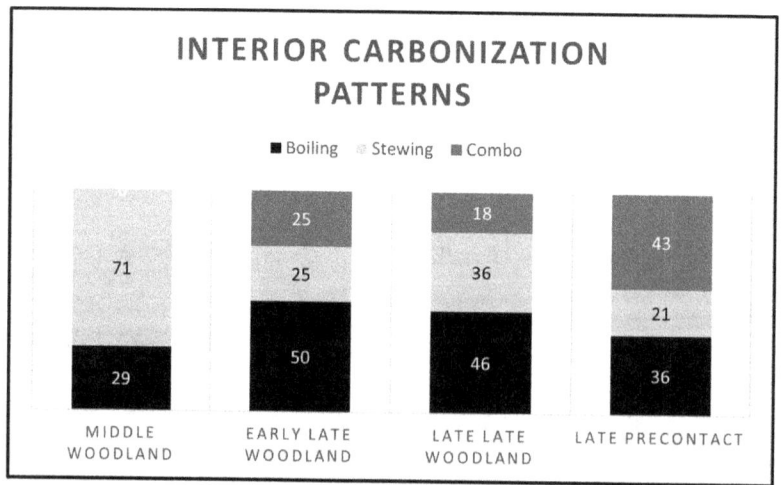

Figure 6.6. Proportions of interior carbonization patterns by component (percentages of total analyzed vessels displayed).

Pattern 2 (stewing) is much less frequent among the Early Late Woodland, Late Late Woodland, and Late Precontact components, in which Patterns 1 (boiling) and 3 (boiling + stewing) predominate. These two cooking methods increased in frequency at the outset of the Late Woodland and continued until the Late Precontact period. As previously observed at other sites in the Northern Great Lakes (Albert et al. 2018; Kooiman 2016), boiling seems to have become a more popular (or more visible) cooking technique during the later periods, although stewing habits continue through all occupations. By the Late Precontact occupation, Pattern 3, or boiling + stewing, becomes the predominant cooking mode.

To assess the statistical significance of patterns suggested in the raw frequencies, the data were subjected to a Kruskal-Wallis test. Kruskal-Wallis is a nonparametric, one-way analysis of variance by ranks that evaluates whether k independent samples are from different populations (Siegel 1956). The results of the Kruskal-Wallis show no significant differences in the distributions of interior carbonization patterns between component assemblages (table 6.12), although the small sample sizes likely affected this outcome. The evidence is still indicative of an overall shift in cooking behaviors after AD 500.

<u>Synchronic Variation of Interior Carbonization Patterns</u>. Variability of cooking styles between contemporary pottery types could indicate distinct culinary traditions associated with social or cultural identity. As with

Table 6.12. Interior Carbonization Pattern Relationships, Kruskal-Wallis

Component	Middle Woodland (p^*)	Early Late Woodland (p)	Late Late Woodland (p)
Middle Woodland	---	---	---
Early Late Woodland	0.094	---	---
Late Late Woodland	0.241	0.829	---
Late Precontact	0.061	0.466	0.300

Notes:
*two-tailed.
$\alpha = 0.05$, df = 2.

synchronic variation of technical properties (see above), assessment of synchronic variation of interior carbonization patterns is limited by small sample sizes. Table 6.13 shows the proportions of vessels within the major typological categories from each occupation exhibiting interior carbonization Patterns 1, 2, and 3. The most drastic differences are apparent among the Middle Woodland and Late Precontact assemblages. In the Middle Woodland, two-thirds of the Laurel Banked Linear Stamped vessels with clearly patterned interior carbonization exhibited Pattern 1 (boiling), whereas Pattern 2 (stewing) was the only pattern present among Laurel Dentate Stamped and Laurel Pseudo-scallop Shell vessels.

During the Late Precontact occupation, users of Traverse ware stewed or boiled and stewed (Patterns 2 and 3) rather than just boiled their food, while users of Iroquoian-style vessels appear to have favored boiling or boiling + stewing (Patterns 1 and 3). This could reflect different culinary traditions between the users of these stylistically very different vessels; however, the samples sizes are too small for statistical analysis and meaningful interpretations about specialized vessel use. Fewer differences between types are apparent in Early Late Woodland and Late Late Woodland subassemblages. Overall, conclusions about synchronic variation in cooking and pottery use are limited.

Table 6.13. Interior Carbonization Pattern Frequency by Type/Ware

Component	Pottery Type	n	Pattern 1 Ct.	%	Pattern 2 Ct.	%	Pattern 3 Ct.	%
Middle Woodland	Laurel Banked Linear Stamped	3	2	66.7	1	33.3	0	0
	Laurel Dentate Stamped	1	0	0	1	100	0	0
	Laurel Pseudo-scallop Shell	2	0	0	2	100	0	0
Early Late Woodland	Blackduck Banded	1	0	0	0	0	1	100
	Mackinac Banded	4	2	50	1	25	1	25
	Mackinac Punctate	5	3	60	1	20	1	20
Late Late Woodland	Juntunen Drag-and-Jab	2	1	50	1	50	0	0
	Juntunen Linear Punctate	2	0	0	1	50	1	50
Late Precontact	Traverse ware	3	0	0	1	33.3	2	67.7
	Iroquoian-style	10	4	40	2	20	4	40

Actual Function Summary

Use-alteration traces present on the Cloudman site pottery vessels allow several insights into the actual function of ancient pottery. Over half of all vessels contained interior carbonization, strong evidence that the primary function of pottery at the Cloudman site was cooking. Although the proportion of the assemblage with exterior sooting, another good indicator of cooking function, is low, this may be the result of the low frequency of identified vessels with associated body sherds, where sooting is most likely to occur. As with other Woodland vessels found throughout the Northern Great Lakes, cooking vessels at the Cloudman site were filled nearly to the top, a routine potentially carried over from cooking with organic vessels.

Interior carbonization patterns, while not significantly different between subassemblages, still change in accordance with previous observations of cooking change in the Middle and Late Woodland periods (Kooiman 2012, 2016). Clear boiling signatures are proportionally low in the Middle Woodland, a period during which there is also a complete absence of clear evidence that the same vessels were employed in both boiling and stewing. Larger proportions of Early Late Woodland, Late Late Woodland, and Iroquoian-style vessels displayed boiling and dual-use patterns. Changes in patterning frequencies among Cloudman pottery vessels supports the hypothesis that cooking styles changed over time, and that boiling became an increasingly important means of food processing during the Late Woodland/Late Precontact period.

As with technical properties, synchronic variation between distinct types within the same analytic subsets was low. Sample sizes were too small for detectable or meaningful distinctions. The matter of differential pottery use based on group identity will require more data from multiple sites to draw more meaningful conclusions.

DISCUSSION

Results of the functional analysis of pottery from the Cloudman site demonstrate the tension between tradition and innovation among Woodland and Late Prehistoric peoples. Pottery construction, pottery use, and cooking methods were altered to suit new needs and new generations, albeit slowly and subtly. Middle Woodland vessels were relatively small, with large temper in relation to thickness. Early Late Woodland pots maintained thicknesses similar to their Middle Woodland predecessors but gained in overall size and volume. The upper portions of Late Late Woodland vessels grew thicker, while grit temper particles became significantly smaller. The same properties also characterize Iroquoian-style vessels from the Late Precontact component.

Vessel size variation could be associated with several factors. Middle Woodland groups were the first to use pottery vessels, despite being generally mobile and having a malleable social structure (Brose and Hambacher 1999). Their mobile nature may have constrained the construction of vessels to sizes manageable during travel, although this may not have been an issue if pots were being transported via canoe. As attraction and attachment to "persistent places," or locales repeatedly occupied and used for more focused and intensive extraction of food and other resources, increased throughout the Late Woodland period (see Dunham 2014, 2017), vessels may have been constructed for in situ use and stored for future use at the site. This would have given potters the freedom to make larger pots. If, as Cleland (1982) claimed, occupation of coastal aggregation sites increased in size and duration during the Late Woodland, the larger vessel size could also have grown according to needs. The Early Late Woodland vessels assemblage is the largest at Cloudman (n = 49), suggesting either the presence of larger groups or more prolonged occupations after AD 900.

Potters continued to construct larger vessels after AD 1200, but they also began incorporating significantly smaller temper particles into ceramic pastes. Smaller temper is one of many technical characteristics that improve both impact resistance and thermal shock resistance (Bronitsky and Hamer 1986), the latter integral for maintaining vessel integrity during heat-intensive and/or long-term cooking events. Smaller temper particles also provide greater green phase (pre-firing) ceramic strength (Chu 1968; Rice 1987, 362), facilitating the often more complex decorations and collars common to late Late Woodland Juntunen vessels and Iroquoian-style vessels. Thinner vessel walls allow for greater heating effectiveness during cooking and also improve thermal shock resistance. Body thickness would be the most important factor in heating effectiveness and shock resistance, and an underrepresentation of body sherds among the identified Cloudman vessels affected the sample size for effectively assessing the evolution of this characteristic through time.

Changes in cooking techniques are apparent if subtle. Middle Woodland vessels were less frequently engaged in boiling-only cooking events, and signs of using Middle Woodland vessels for both boiling and stewing are completely absent. Clear signatures for boiling increase in relative frequency among Early Late Woodland vessels and remain consistent throughout subsequent occupations of the site, while a cooking behavior combining both boiling and stewing appeared in the Early Late Woodland and became most frequent during the Late Precontact occupation of the Cloudman site. Synchronic variation of both technical properties and use-alteration traces was also limited because of small sample sizes. A regionwide survey of Northern Great Lakes pottery assemblages would be required to obtain sufficient data.

CONCLUSION

The evolution of pottery technology and use at the Cloudman site both aligns and contrasts with outlined expectations. The greatest distinctions are observed between Middle Woodland and Late Woodland/Late Precontact pottery. Although vessel size was not predicted to change, Middle Woodland vessels were smaller, with vessel size increasing in size in the Early Late Woodland and remaining consistent thereafter. These smaller vessels were employed in stewing more frequently than in boiling, a cooking style that, as predicted, increases in frequency through time. Although boiling becomes more frequent and vessel size increases around the same time, it is presently unclear whether these two factors are connected by intentional choice to fulfill a particular function or whether both are the result of greater social and behavioral changes occurring at the outset of the Late Woodland period. A significant decrease in temper size, which has been associated with increased processing and consumption of starchy foods, including maize, does not appear in vessels until after AD 1200, centuries after the observed changes in both vessel size and cooking habits.

Technological variability of pottery is often associated with changes in subsistence, as processing needs change in relation to food types. The next chapter addresses questions of subsistence and cooking at the Cloudman site and discusses pottery residue composition. The combination of lipid residue, stable isotope, and microbotanical analyses provides direct evidence of foods cooked in pottery vessels, allowing closer associations between dietary, technological, and cooking style changes.

CHAPTER 7

Diet and Cuisine at the Cloudman Site

Holistic depictions of past food choice and processing techniques derived from multiple lines of archaeological evidence allow for reconstructions of ancient cuisine and a nuanced view of past identity and adaptive decision making. Archaeological food residues, both adhered and absorbed, link specific foods directly to processing tools and techniques, informing interpretations of synchronic and diachronic variation in food choice and cooking. This chapter reviews diet and cooking behaviors at the Cloudman site using stable isotope, lipid residue, and microbotanical analyses of adhered and absorbed food residues associated with ceramic cooking vessels. The results are used to assess the degree of diachronic dietary change, especially in relation to hypotheses arguing for intensified use of aquatic, wild starchy, and/or domesticated resources in the Northern Great Lakes throughout the Woodland period. Food choice in relation to possible group identity is also discussed.

CARBON AND NITROGEN STABLE ISOTOPE ANALYSIS

Intensified exploitation of both fish and maize at coastal sites but primarily autumn season coastal sites during the Late Woodland period have been proposed by Cleland (1982) and O'Shea (2003), respectively.

Nitrogen and carbon stable isotope ratios have been used to identify aquatic resources and maize in carbonized food residues (e.g., Craig et al. 2013; Hart, Thompson, and Brumbach 2003; Lovis 1990; Morton and Schwarcz 2004; Taché and Craig 2015). Stable isotope analysis is thus well suited for informing questions about diachronic variation in aquatic and terrestrial fauna, trophic levels, and maize exploitation. Carbonized food residue was collected from the interior rims of fifty identified vessels, selected from all periods of occupation of the Cloudman site. The samples were sent to the Illinois State Geological Survey Prairie Research Institute for analysis of bulk stable isotope values of $\delta^{15}N$ and $\delta^{13}C$.

Nitrogen Isotopes

Stable isotope analysis of Cloudman site residue samples revealed consistently enriched $\delta^{15}N$ values (figure 7.1), with a mean of 11.69‰ (Kooiman 2018). $\delta^{15}N$ values higher than 9‰ are associated with processing aquatic resources (i.e., fish or aquatic plants), as observed in experimental cooking residues (Craig et al. 2007; Craig et al. 2013; Morton and Schwarcz 2004). Only residues from two vessels (88, a Blackduck Banded vessel, and 179, an Iroquoian-style vessel) fell below this threshold.

Potential contamination of the soil from nitrogen-rich fertilizers was considered a possible factor in these results, but an interview with Gary Cloudman, whose family has owned the land surrounding the Cloudman site for over one hundred years, revealed that intensive agriculture has never taken place on the property. Stratigraphic profiles from excavation corroborate this account, demonstrating the lack of a plow zone (Ap horizon) at the site (Branstner 1995). The high nitrogen levels in the Cloudman pottery residues are therefore likely associated with foods processed in the vessels. Aquatic resources produce higher $\delta^{15}N$ values than terrestrial resources (Schwarcz and Schoeninger 1991; Shoeninger 1985). The enriched nitrogen isotope signatures from the Cloudman samples appear indicative of aquatic resources, such as fish or aquatic plants.

Carbon Isotopes

The presence of maize may be detected in food residues using carbon isotope ratios (Hastorf and DeNiro 1985). Current standards interpret $\delta^{13}C$

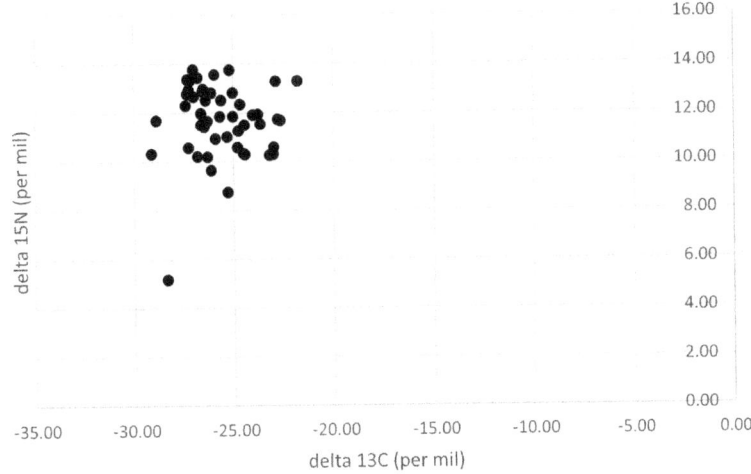

Figure 7.1. Plot of δ15N/δ13C values of Cloudman pottery residues.

values above -17.4‰ as indicative of the presence of maize in adhered food residues (Katzenberg and Pfeiffer 1995). The average $\delta^{13}C$ values for residues associated with vessels from all components of the Cloudman sites are well below that threshold (-25.65‰) (Kooiman 2018). The carbon enrichment of the Cloudman pottery residue samples are therefore not high enough to indicate intensive maize processing. The results do not entirely preclude the presence of maize in pottery residues, however; Hart et al. (2007) found that maize may be underrepresented in carbon isotope signatures depending on the ratio of maize in the cooking mix and the types of food with which maize is cooked.

Diachronic Nitrogen and Carbon Isotope Trends

Overall both carbon and nitrogen stable isotope values of the Cloudman samples display considerable consistency at the site through time. The carbon and nitrogen isotope values derived from pottery residues demonstrate no statistically significant differences between occupations (Kooiman 2018). The consistency of the nitrogen isotope values demonstrates that acquisition, processing, and consumption of aquatic resources were important activities throughout the 1,400-year occupational history of the Cloudman site.

LIPID RESIDUE ANALYSIS

Detection of a wide array of both plants and animals processed in pottery cooking vessels is best attained by lipid analysis of absorbed food residues. Sherds from a total of thirty vessels were submitted to the Archaeological Residue Analysis Laboratory at Brandon University in Brandon, Manitoba, for lipid residue analysis (Kooiman 2018; Malainey and Figol 2018).

Nut lipids were prevalent in residues associated with all occupations of the site (figure 7.2). There is a slight decrease in the frequency of vessels used for nut processing over time, but these differences are not statistically significant (Kooiman 2018).

Frequencies of the remaining food/content categories are relatively consistent across the pottery assemblages of all components, suggesting relative dietary consistency through time. Signatures for large herbivores (such as white-tailed deer) are relatively infrequent, appearing in residue from only three vessels. Moderate high fat foods were only clearly detectable in a single Middle Woodland vessel. This signature is indicative of medium-sized mammals (Malainey and Figol 2018). Animals of this category consumed by Historic period Ojibwe and Iroquoian groups include beaver, porcupine, skunk, woodchuck, muskrat, and hare (Hilger

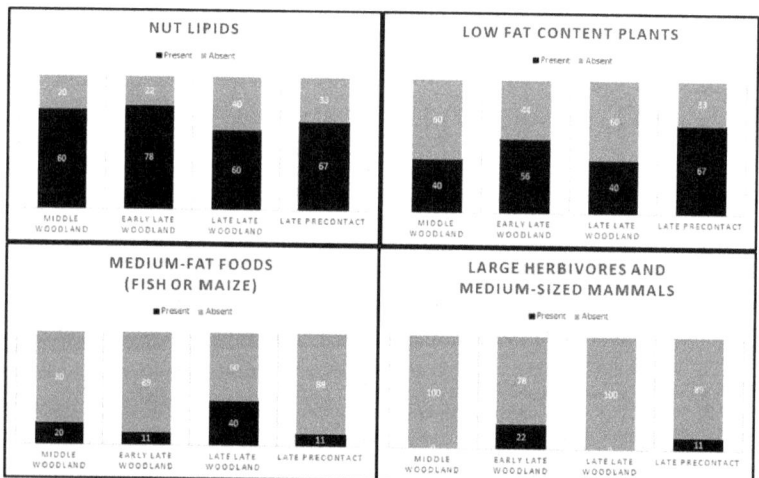

Figure 7.2. Frequencies of lipid residue food categories by component (percentages of total sampled vessels displayed).

1959; Rogers 1962; Waugh 1973). Medium fat content foods include maize and fish. These were identified in low frequencies in samples from each component (see figure 7.2), detected in only 17% of vessels sampled. The category "low fat content plants" includes berries, roots, and greens, as well as wild rice, and these foods were commonly cooked in pottery vessels at the Cloudman site throughout all occupations.

The sole nonfood category apparent in the lipid signatures is conifer product. Probable or possible conifer product appears in eight total vessels. Signatures for conifer product are completely absent from Middle Woodland vessels and appear minimally in every other subset. Pine resin may have been applied to the interior of the vessel to reduce permeability, as observed in precontact pottery from New York (Reber and Hart 2008) and among modern pottery-producing societies with low-fired, unglazed wares (Aronson, Skibo, and Stark 1994; Kobayashi 1994; Skibo 2013).

The results of the lipid residue analysis reveal that nut processing was very important at the Cloudman site during all occupations. Various low fat content plants were also important components of the Cloudman residents' diets. Terrestrial mammals and medium fat content foods, such as fish and maize, were present in lipid signatures but infrequent, indicating that it may have been more common to cook animal protein without the use of pottery vessels. Animal and plant products were routinely cooked in the same vessels, so it does not appear that there were food-specific cooking functions for ceramic cooking pots at the Cloudman site.

MICROBOTANICAL ANALYSIS

Although limited to the identification of only certain plants, microbotanical analysis provides the greatest degree of specificity of all the food identification methods used in this study, allowing classification at the species level. Adhered food residues sampled from fifty-two Cloudman pottery vessels were subjected to microbotanical analysis (Albert, Kooiman, and Lovis 2018; Kooiman 2018). Analysis was conducted by Rebecca Albert.

Phytoliths from maize, wild rice, and squash and starches from maize and squash were identified in the Cloudman samples (Albert, Kooiman, and Lovis 2018; Kooiman 2018, 158). All three food groups were represented in vessels associated with nearly all components, processed and consumed at the site consistently or periodically throughout the entire 1,500-year occupational history of the site (figure 7.3). The results underscore the deep historical importance of these foodstuffs to Indigenous groups in the Northern Great Lakes and distinguish the Cloudman site as an important exploitation or processing locale for all three resources.

The frequency at which maize, wild rice, and squash are present in pottery residues varies between components (see figure 7.3). Contrary to expectations, the frequency of maize is reduced during the Late Late Woodland period. Present in 42% of Middle Woodland vessel residues, it occurs in only 32% of Early Late Woodland residues and 25% of Late Late Woodland samples (Albert, Kooiman, and Lovis 2018; Kooiman 2018). Although there is evidence of moderate maize consumption among Late Late Woodland populations in lower Michigan (Brandt 1996; Muhammad 2010) and casual maize consumption by Late Late Woodland occupants of the nearby Juntunen site (Brandt 1996), maize does not seem to have been an important component of the diet at the Cloudman site at this time. Perhaps more surprisingly, maize is least common during the Late Precontact period, a time when this food was increasingly important to many groups in Eastern North America, including the neighboring Wendat-Petun (Iroquoian) groups. However, among Late Precon-

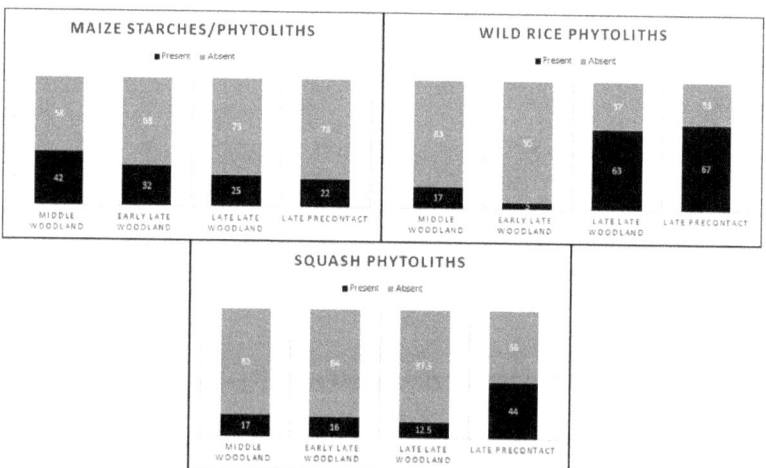

Figure 7.3. Microbotanical frequencies of maize, wild rice, and squash by component (percentages of total sampled vessels displayed).

tact vessels, maize is associated with Iroquoian-style vessels and is absent from Traverse ware vessels, which are associated with Woodland peoples (Kooiman 2018).

Conversely, the frequency of both squash and wild rice increases through time. Wild rice underwent the greatest change in frequency, represented in only 5% of Early Late Woodland samples but present in half or over half of the Late Late Woodland and Late Precontact samples. This sudden increase in wild rice exploitation in the Late Late Woodland supports previous findings in the Northern Great Lakes (Dunham 2014). Squash is present in low levels throughout all occupations, until a notable spike during the Late Precontact period.

Cluster analysis was used to explore associations between vessels with similar microbotanical content. Jaccard's coefficient of association was applied to the data to evaluate within-group similarity (Kooiman 2018, 166). The resultant clusters were distinct and showed diachronic trends of resource exploitation and cooking, particularly when the groupings are displayed with corresponding interior carbonization patterns (table 7.1). Cluster 1 consists of vessels with residues containing only maize microbotanical remains. These include only Middle Woodland vessels with interior carbonization patterns representing stewing and Early Late Woodland vessels with interior carbonization patterns indicative of boiling. This supports the observation that maize may have been more important at the Cloudman site during the Middle and Early Late Woodland periods than in later occupations.

Within Cluster 1, there is an apparent diachronic shift in the way that maize is cooked. Among Middle Woodland vessels, maize processing is associated with stewing; it may have been used primarily as flour or meal added to soups and stews to thicken them. In the Early Late Woodland, the vessels used for processing maize show signatures for boiling, suggesting that cooks at this time may have begun engaging in nixtamalization, a processing technique in which maize is boiled with hard wood ash, breaking down the pericarp and improving grain palatability (Lovis et al. 2011). This process can also mask maize signatures in stable isotope assays, potentially explaining the lack of $\delta^{13}C$ enrichment of Cloudman samples (Lovis et al. 2011).

Cluster 2 includes vessels with residues containing only wild rice phytoliths, which is restricted to Late Late Woodland Juntunen and Late

Table 7.1. Vessel Clusters by Microbotanical Species Content (Jaccard's Coefficient)

	Vessel	Period	Type	Maize	Wild Rice	Squash	IC Pattern
Cluster 1	4	MW	Laurel Dentate Stamped	1	0	0	2
	109	MW	Laurel Banked Linear Stamped	1	0	0	2
	120	ELW	Mackinac Banded	1	0	0	1
	122	ELW	Mackinac ware (cf. Punctate)	1	0	0	1
	173	ELW	Mackinac Banded	1	0	0	1
	174	ELW	Mackinac ware (cf. Punctate)	1	0	0	1
Cluster 2	101	LLW	Juntunen ware	0	1	0	2
	204	LLW	Juntunen Linear Punctate	0	1	0	2
	146	LP	Iroquoian-style	0	1	0	3
	162	LP	Iroquoian-style	0	1	0	3
Cluster 3	23	MW	Laurel Banked Linear Stamped	0	0	1	1
	76	ELW	Mackinac Undecorated	0	0	1	3
	105	ELW	Mackinac Punctate	0	0	1	3
	75	LP	Traverse Plain v. Scalloped (mini)	0	0	1	3
Cluster 4	5	MW	Laurel Pseudo-scallop Shell	1	1	0	2
	8	ELW	Mackinac ware	1	1	0	2
Cluster 5	40	LP	Iroquoian-style	1	1	1	2
	70	LP	Iroquoian-style	1	1	1	3

Precontact/Iroquoian-style vessels, additional evidence for the increased importance of wild rice to the subsistence regime at the Cloudman site after AD 1200. As in Cluster 1, there is an associated diachronic shift in wild rice cooking styles. Among Late Late Woodland vessels, only stewing was employed in the processing of the rice (and other contents). Wild rice is edible either when it is barely just cooked or when it has been boiled extensively (Hart and Lovis 2013), so this suggests a possible change in wild rice processing habits. Users of Iroquoian-style vessels, on the other hand, processed food mixes containing wild rice through a combination boiling + stewing method.

Cluster 3 includes vessels involved in the processing of squash, and Cluster 4 represents vessels associated with both maize and wild rice.

There are no obvious diachronic trends within these clusters aside from the emergence of a culinary tradition combining maize and wild rice, a nutritionally complementary food mix that emerged in the Middle Woodland, in accordance with previous observations (Boyd et al. 2014; Hart and Lovis 2013; Raviele 2010). This combination seems associated with stewing (Cluster 4), while the processing of squash is associated with boiling + stewing practices throughout the later occupations (Cluster 3).

Cluster 5 may be connected to an important historical culinary development. This cluster includes the only vessels with microbotanical evidence for maize, wild rice, and squash together. The traditional Three Sisters subsistence regime characteristic of Iroquoian groups is composed of maize, squash, and beans and is believed to have emerged after AD 1300 (Bamann et al. 1992; Hart 2008; Kuhn and Funk 2000). Boyd et al. (2014) found that in areas where wild rice was available, beans tended to be less important because the two foods are nutritionally similar. The use of maize, squash, and wild rice together in vessels dating to after AD 1300 signals the emergence of the Three Sisters culinary tradition at the Cloudman site with the opportunistic substitution of local wild rice for beans.

DISCUSSION

The application of three different analytic methods for evaluating foods cooked in ancient pottery provides a robust depiction of precontact Indigenous cuisine. In total, residues from sixty-two vessels were subjected to one, two, or all three dietary analyses (see appendix B). Residues from only five vessels lacked any identifiable foods remains, while another fourteen vessels yielded evidence for only one food category (Kooiman 2018). This fact attests to the strength of using these methods collaboratively, but more important, it demonstrates that Woodland and Late Precontact cooking vessels were multipurpose, used to cook a variety of foods either in sequential cooking episodes or together in the form of multi-ingredient soups and stews. Miller et al. (2020) found that adhered residues represent food cooked in the final episode (or final few episodes) of cooking in the use history of a vessel, while absorbed residues represent an accumulation of foods cooked in earlier cooking events. The results here suggest that foods represented by microbotanical remains and stable isotopes (maize, wild rice, squash, and aquatic resources) were often cooked together in those final cooking events, and absorbed lipid residues demonstrate that many vessels were used for cooking a variety of animal foodstuffs during the course of their use life. Pottery vessels at the Cloudman site were multipurpose and accommodated the cooking of a variety of recipes and dishes.

Important ingredients for Cloudman site cuisine include acorns/nuts, aquatic resources, maize, wild rice, and squash, in addition to various wild plants and terrestrial animals. Exploitation of acorns and aquatic resources appears intensive and consistent throughout the occupational history of the site, while the intensity of maize, wild rice, and squash consumption varied over time.

Food Selection at the Cloudman Site

Together, analyses of chemical and microscopic food remains revealed a wide variety of foods chosen and consumed by the occupants of the Cloudman site. Lipid residue analysis revealed that nuts were a popular food throughout all occupations of the site. Ethnographic accounts of Ojibwe groups consistently report the use of acorns and rarely refer to other types of nuts (Densmore 1979; Hilger 1959). Densmore (2005, 307) lists hazelnut (*Corylus americana*) in a table of plants used as foods but does not discuss them further in her text, as she does acorns. Hazelnut, butternut/white walnut (*Juglans cinerea*), and acorn are referenced by Yarnell (1964, 63, 67) as nuts consumed by the Ojibwe. Acorns are the only nut mentioned by Tooker (1991, 62) as a common food among the Wendat/Huron, and Waugh (1973, 123) describes Iroquois utilization of a variety of nuts (e.g., hickory, walnut, butternut, hazelnut, beechnut, chestnut) but emphasizes acorns.

Acorns and hazelnuts are the most common nuts in the eastern Upper Peninsula (Comer et al. 1995; Dunham 2009, 2014; Voss and Resnicek 2012). Macrobotanical remains from select features at Cloudman reveal that acorn remains account for 84% of total nut specimens and 75% of total nut weight (Egan-Bruhy 2007), but small amounts of hazelnut and butternut were also present. Maps of presettlement vegetation on Drummond Island show that beech–sugar maple–hemlock forest, where acorn-producing oaks (of the beech family) would have been abundant, are present within reasonable distance of the Cloudman site (Comer et al. 1995; Comer and Albert 1997). These evidences suggest that the decomposed nut oil in the lipid residues most likely represent acorns, although other nuts, particularly hazelnut, may have contributed to the signatures. Either the Cloudman site was a very important acorn/nut processing locale or processed acorns/nuts were an overall integral component of Woodland cuisine.

Low fat content plants were more common in the lipid residues signatures. These include berries, roots, greens, and wild grains. Berries found in macrobotanical remains at the Cloudman site include hawthorn, strawberry, cherry, wild plum, raspberry, elderberry, and grape (Egan-Bruhy 2007). Other berries and fruits commonly used by Historic period Ojibwe groups include juneberry, bearberry, cranberry, currant, blackberry, and blueberry (Densmore 2005, 307). Roots common in Ojibwe diets were wild ginger, wild bean, Jerusalem artichoke, and bugleweed, as well as aquatic roots like arrowhead and bulrush (Densmore 2005, 307). Leaves of aster, creeping snowberry, wintergreen, and hemlock were also used (Densmore 2005, 307). Low fat content plants would also include wild rice, which was recovered in the macrobotanical remains from Late Woodland features at the site (Egan-Bruhy 2007). However, wild rice cannot be distinguished from other low fat content foods in lipid residue analysis and requires other methods of detection.

The inhabitants of the Cloudman site were hunter-gatherers, although the lipid residue analysis showed that only a few vessels from each component were used to cook meat. While Ojibwe cooks sometimes boiled meat, spit roasting was also common (Densmore 1979; Hilger 1959; Rogers 1962); these may have been the primary methods of meat processing at the Cloudman site. Medium fat content foods include fish and maize, although these foods were limited in their representation in the lipid residues, despite the coastal setting of the site, which would make it ideal for both fishing and horticulture.

The stable isotope analysis provides little clarification on the matters of maize and fish. Elevated $\delta^{15}N$ values suggest that aquatic resources were commonly processed in vessels throughout the history of the Cloudman site. The location of the site and the high proportion of faunal remains derived from fish (Cooper 1996) suggest that the Cloudman site was used as a base for fishing activities. However, previous research found that habitual processing of fish in pottery vessels across the Northern Great Lakes was not common (Kooiman 2016; Lovis and Hart 2015; Malainey and Figol 2015; Skibo, Malainey, and Kooiman 2016), although others have argued the opposite (Taché and Craig 2015).

Aquatic plants can also yield high $\delta^{15}N$ values, although these values vary widely according to geographic location (Chappuis et al. 2017; Cloern, Canuel, and Harris 2002; Milligan, Pretzlaw, and Humphries 2010). Aquatic plants may also have contributed to the $\delta^{15}N$ enrichment of the Cloudman samples, although no aquatic plant remains were present in the microbotanical assemblage at the site aside from a single wild rice seed (Egan-Bruhy 2007). Microbotanical evidence of wild rice was also found in Cloudman pottery vessels, although the $\delta^{15}N$ values associated with this plant are not yet known. Further exploration of isotope values for aquatic plants in the Northern Great Lakes is required to clarify future isotopic interpretations.

The $\delta^{13}C$ values were not high enough to confirm the processing of maize in pottery vessels at the Cloudman site. However, as Hart et al. (2007) note, maize can be underrepresented in carbon isotope signatures, depending on the cooking method and cooking mixes in which the maize is processed. This appears to be the case among the Cloudman samples. Microbotanical analysis revealed that maize was, in fact, cooked in pottery vessels at the site.

Altogether, the occupants of the Cloudman site had broad, varied diets that included nuts, aquatic resources, various wild plants, terrestrial mammals, maize, wild rice, and squash. The contributions of the microscopic and chemical analyses of food residue, alongside existing faunal and macrobotancial data, provide an in-depth picture of Woodland and Late Precontact diet in the Northern Great Lakes.

Seasonality at the Cloudman Site

Cumulative results of the three dietary analyses provide a wealth of information about subsistence at the Cloudman site. The food categories most frequently identified at the site were aquatic resources, nuts/acorns, wild rice, squash, and maize. As discussed in chapter 3, both spring- and fall-spawning fish species were identified in faunal remains from features associated with the later components of the site (Cooper 1996), although spring-spawning fish were more common. Archaeological plant remains indicate intensive use of the site during the late summer and fall. Hazelnut, butternut, and acorn were all present in the macrobotanical remains (Egan-Bruhy 2007), and nut lipids featured prominently in lipid signatures from a majority of vessels sampled. Hazelnut is harvested in August and September, acorn in September and October, and butternut in October (Yarnell 1964). Wild rice is harvested in late August or early September (Hilger 1959, 147; Vennum 1988). Maize and squash are also harvested in the fall.

Foods represented in pottery residues suggest intensive fall occupation of the Cloudman site. Residents lived there from late August until November, using the site as a central residential locale from which logistical forays for hunting, fishing, and gathering activities could be conducted. Small-scale horticulture involving cultivation of maize and squash may also have taken place at the site. This does not preclude a spring occupation, as many species of fish and animals could be acquired in the spring, and nuts, maize, and wild rice are all easily stored for spring consumption, and crops would require planting at this time.

Early Use of Domesticates and Wild Rice at the Cloudman Site

The presence of maize, squash, and wild rice at the site from the outset of occupation (ca. AD 100) is a significant discovery. Maize has been reported in the Upper Peninsula of Michigan by cal 200 BC (Albert et al. 2018); in Minnesota, central New York, and southern Quebec, by cal 300 BC (Burchill and Boyd 2015; Hart, Brumbach and Lusteck 2007; St-Pierre and Thompson 2015); and in the Saginaw drainage of lower Michigan, by AD 1 (Raviele 2010). At the Cloudman site, maize starch was encountered in residues from Vessel 4, a Laurel Dentate Stamped vessel that produced an AMS date of cal AD 60–125, yet another line of evidence supporting the early use of maize in the Northern Great Lakes region.

The microbotanical results also offer some of the earliest evidence for regional exploitation of wild rice and squash. Although neither plant was detected in either of the Middle Woodland vessels subjected to AMS dating, they occur in vessels of the same taxonomic types. A wild rice phytolith was detected in Vessel 5, identified as a Laurel Pseudo-scallop

Shell vessel and in a similar vessel dated to cal AD 80–214. Athough Vessel 5 was not directly dated, a similar vessel (1) was dated to cal AD 80–180. Squash phytoliths were identified in residue from Vessel 12; a nearly identical vessel (4) produced an associated AMS date of cal AD 60–125.

Although wild rice appears in the paleoecological record in northeastern Minnesota by 7000 BC and in northwestern Ontario by 4100 BC (Boyd et al. 2013; Huber 2001), evidence for widespread human exploitation of wild rice is not apparent until the Middle Woodland period, when archaeobotanical remains appear at sites from Minnesota to Ontario (Arzigian 2000; Boyd and Surette 2010; Boyd et al. 2014; Burchill and Boyd 2015; Hart and Lovis 2013; Surette 2008). Wild rice seeds from the Laurel Big Rice Lake site in northeastern Minnesota have been dated to as early as cal 172 BC (1σ) (Valppu 2000, 36). In the lower peninsula of Michigan, at the Schultz site in the Saginaw basin, wild rice remains were found in association with materials dated to cal AD 90–383 (1σ) (Lovis et al. 2001). Few other early contexts for wild rice in the region have been directly dated. The dates from the Cloudman site are therefore among the earliest for wild rice in the Northern Great Lakes.

Squash was an unexpected component of the food mixes at the Cloudman site. Archaeological squash remains have been found in Pennsylvania dating to cal 5064–4336 BC (2σ), in lower Michigan dating to around cal 2300 BC (Monaghan, Lovis, and Egan-Bruhy 2006), in southeastern Minnesota from 580 BC (Perkl 1998), and in the central Mississippi River valley around AD 434–613/681–889 (Hart, Brumbach, and Lusteck 2007). Squash has rarely been encountered in the Northern Great Lakes. Cucurbit microbotanicals were found in residues from Vessel 12, a Laurel Dentate Stamped vessel. Another Laurel Dentate Stamped vessel (4) produced an AMS date of cal AD 60–125, providing some of the only and earliest evidence for squash exploitation in the Upper Peninsula of Michigan.

Diet and Environment at the Cloudman Site

The previous chapter highlighted changing cooking habits through time at the Cloudman site observed through patterns of interior carbonization on cooking pots. The increased use of boiling at the outset of the Late Woodland Period (post–AD 600) is a trend observed at Cloudman and at other Woodland sites in the Northern Great Lakes (Albert et al. 2018;

Kooiman 2016, 2018). One explanation was that cooking methods changed in response to changing dietary food staples, so microscopic and chemical analysis of these same food residues was required to test this hypothesis.

The results of the lipid residue and stable isotope analyses were largely consistent through time. Residents of the Cloudman site depended on dietary staples such as nuts, low-fat plants, and aquatic resources over the course of the site's 1,500-year history. The microbotanical remains, however, tell a different story. Squash was present in low frequencies in pottery residues from the three earliest components of the Cloudman site. A spike in squash cooking and consumption in the Late Precontact period signals a spike in the importance of this food after AD 1300.

Maize was most frequent in residues from Middle Woodland cooking vessels and steadily decreased in overall frequency in each subsequent period. The intensification of maize at coastal sites during the Northern Great Lakes Late Late Woodland period has been proposed by O'Shea (2003), but evidence from the Cloudman site does not support this hypothesis at the local level. Several studies have found evidence of moderate maize consumption in Late Late Woodland diets in the Upper Great Lakes (Brandt 1996; Muhammad 2010), so the data may signal a possible change in the use of maize at the Cloudman site rather than a macroregional dietary shift.

Conversely, the presence of wild rice microbotanicals in pottery residues increases in frequency over time. Although present in the Middle Woodland samples, it is not as abundant as maize during the same period of occupation. Wild rice microbotanicals all but disappear in the Early Late Woodland period, occurring in only 5% of samples. Among pottery vessels constructed after AD 1200, the frequency of wild rice in residues dramatically increases: it is present in half of the Late Late Woodland samples and over 71% of the Late Precontact samples. The Cloudman site is located at the mouth of the Potagannissing River and downriver from contemporary wild rice patches, and although the antiquity of these patches is unknown, the microbotanical remains indicate that wild rice has grown in the area for some time and was consumed by local populations.

The Early Late Woodland period occupation of the Cloudman site occurred at the outset of the Medieval Climatic Optimum (AD 900–1000), a warm period during which lake levels dropped, causing riverine fluctuation and flooding (Lovis, Arbogast, and Monaghan 2012; Monaghan and Lovis 2005). Wild rice is very sensitive to climate and water levels (Boyd et al. 2013; Vennum 1988), so water-level fluctuations may have disrupted local rice beds, and the warmer climate would have been conducive to maize horticulture. The end of the Medieval Climatic Optimum brought cooler weather and caused higher lake levels and streams grading to higher elevations, thereby reducing riverine fluctuations and allowing stable aquatic environments required for the reestablishment of productive wild rice beds (Lovis, Arbogast, and Monaghan 2012; Monaghan and Lovis 2005). The Late Late Woodland occupation of the Cloudman site took place after the amelioration of the Medieval Climatic Optimum. Located along a river with modern-day wild rice beds, the site may have served as a base locale for logistical forays to exploit the renewed abundance of this resource. At the same time, it may not have remained an ideal locale for maize cultivation because of the cooler weather, or the expense of energy invested in growing maize or acquiring it through social relationships may have been too great.

Occupants of the site after AD 1300 continued to slightly intensify their use of wild rice and decrease their consumption of maize. The beginning of this Late Precontact occupation of the Cloudman site coincides with the outset of the Little Ice Age, which prolonged the trend of cooler average temperatures following the end of the Medieval Climatic Optimum. Even though the cooler climate may have dampened local attempts at growing maize, evidence for maize is associated with Iroquoian-style pottery. Iroquoian identity is closely tied to maize, and the users of these pots, whether Iroquoian or not, may have had access to maize grown in southern Ontario through trade or interaction networks. Ultimately, more environmental and climatological data at the local level are needed to fully understand possible relationships between subsistence and environment at the Cloudman site and across the Northern Great Lakes.

Diet and Identity

Culinary trends associated with social identity were not clear from the results of the dietary data. The consistency in chemical food signatures (lipids and stable isotopes) associated with cooking pots were relatively consistent within each site occupation and between them, regardless of pottery style. Greater variation was observed in the plant species identifiable in the microscopic food remains, particularly wild rice and maize.

The focus on wild rice exploitation and the apparent disappearance of maize beginning in the Late Late Woodland period (post–AD 1200) may signal a shift in local food-related identities at a time of increased group localization and identity, as indicated by the proliferation of distinct pottery styles during the Late Late Woodland period (McHale Milner 1991, 1998; O'Shea and McHale Milner 2002). While a shifting environment and/or climate may have affected the ability of Cloudman site residents to effectively grow maize at this time, its availability and/or appeal may also have changed in the altering social landscape. Wild rice is closely related to modern Ojibwe identity (Densmore 1979, 2005; Scott 1996; Vennum 1988), so as a locally abundant resource, Late Late Woodland groups may have begun to base both their subsistence and their identity in this sacred food.

Maize microbotanicals appear again in residues associated with cooking vessels from the Late Precontact period (post–AD 1300). Although present in only 22% of residue samples from this component, those containing evidence of maize were associated only with Iroquoian-style vessels, not with Traverse ware vessels. The presence of microscopic maize remains in Iroquoian-style vessel residues is unsurprising given the centrality of maize in Iroquoian diets (Tooker 1991), although it is still unknown whether these vessels were used by Iroquoian groups or by Late Woodland/proto-Odawa groups.

However, even among the Iroquoian vessels, wild rice was more common than maize. Wild rice is not mentioned in ethnohistorical accounts of Iroquoian (Huron/Wendat) groups (Tooker 1991; Waugh 1973), nor is it generally associated with the Odawa (Scott 1996; Smith 1996). Wild rice must have been abundant enough at the site for it to become an important resource for all local groups using the site after AD 1200. Furthermore, the only vessels in which maize, wild rice, and squash were found together were Iroquoian-style ones. This could be a local variety of the Three Sisters food tradition that later formed the foundation of Iroquoian cuisine, which, although important to modern Anishinaabe/Algonquian groups, has been historically more closely associated with Iroquoian peoples and is the strongest evidence for cuisine-related identity at the Cloudman site.

Cooking and Cuisine

Inferences about ancient cuisine can be drawn when the dietary data are compared to pottery function, particularly interior carbonization patterns, which vary according to cooking methods. In the Middle Woodland, maize is associated with stewing, while in the Early Late Woodland, it is associated with boiling. This could represent a switch from using maize meal or green corn stews on the initial incorporation of maize into the local diet and the later adoption of a processing technique known as nixtamalization, in which maize is boiled in an alkali solution, removing toxins and the hard outer pericarp and rendering the kernels more palatable and nutritious (Lovis et al. 2011). Nixtamalization is practiced across the Americas and may be a behavior learned from interactions with other groups.

Squash and wild rice are associated with stewing or boiling + stewing patterns. Squash would not necessarily require boiling, but anyone who has cooked winter squash in a stew knows it breaks down and acts almost as a thickening agent, so its association with interior carbonization Pattern 3 (boiling + stewing) comes as no surprise. Wild rice, although requiring boiling to be made edible, is cooked via a water-reduction process, wherein the final product contains very little water. Although cooking wild rice begins as wet-mode cooking (boiling), it ends as semidry-mode cooking, producing a carbonization pattern resembling stewing (Pattern 2), the pattern with which wild rice was associated (see table 7.1). Boiling + stewing is the most frequent cooking pattern observed during the Late Precontact period, when wild rice and squash exploitation is also at its height.

CONCLUSION

Results of microbotanical and chemical (stable isotope and lipid residue) analyses of adhered and absorbed food residues from ancient pottery contribute rich insight into the dietary and culinary habits of groups occupying the Cloudman site. Nuts (mostly acorns) and aquatic resources were important dietary staples of people living at the site throughout all periods of occupation. Maize, wild rice, and squash were also consumed throughout the occupational history of the site, although with varying intensity. Maize was most frequent in residues among Middle Woodland pottery vessels and gradually reduced in frequency throughout all subsequent occupations. A near-inverse trend is observed with wild rice, which increases in frequency through time, possibly supplanting maize as an important starchy component of the diet, particularly after AD 1200. It is not known whether external social relationships, environmental change, or culinary preferences changed, although the environmental effects of the Medieval Climatic Optimum after AD 900 may have affected resource abundance and selection.

These results support Dunham's (2014) finding that exploitation of starchy foods, particularly wild rice and acorns, was intensified in the eastern Upper Peninsula of Michigan in the Late Late Woodland period. If Cloudman is considered representative of the larger region, there is little evidence to support widespread intensive maize agriculture among Northern Great Lakes coastal sites during the Late Late Woodland period. There is also no clear evidence in support of an increased reliance on deep-water spawning fish during the Late Woodland period. Although the exploitation of aquatic resources appears consistent at the Cloudman site throughout its occupational history, the data are not fine grained enough for evaluation of the relative dietary proportion of these resources at any given time.

The combined use of multiple types of archaeological dietary data has substantially increased our understanding of culinary habits of people who lived at the Cloudman site. It can, however, be further enhanced by examining ethnographic and ethnohistorical accounts of food selection and cooking. The next chapter reviews observed culinary traditions of historic Native American groups living in the Upper Great Lakes region and discusses them in context with the outcomes of the archaeological data, comparisons that will deepen and strengthen interpretations of past cuisine.

CHAPTER 8

Ethnographic and Ethnohistorical Accounts of Diet and Cooking

Interpretations of archaeological data can be supported and enhanced by comparisons with traditions and practices of historic or modern peoples by forming analogical connections between culinary behavior and its physical (i.e., archaeological) manifestations. This chapter reviews ethnographic and ethnohistorical accounts of Ojibwe and Iroquoian culinary practices and discusses dietary and cooking data from the Cloudman site in the context of observed Indigenous traditions. The ethnographic information can highlight food preparation methods and recipes and, together with the archaeological data, can be used to reconstruct ancient Northern Great Lakes cuisine.

Ethnographic analogy as a method for interpreting archaeological data has limitations and is approached here with recognition of its limits and biases (Johnson 2010). As the archaeological evidence demonstrates, diet and cooking are not static behaviors and are instead subject to change over time, although subsistence behaviors are also often conservative, with certain culinary traditions remaining constant through long stretches of time (Twiss 2012). Historic period lifeways of Indigenous communities in the Great Lakes may therefore resemble those of precontact groups inhabiting the same locations and environment. These accounts also capture Native American life only after contact with Europeans and subsequently cannot fully reflect precontact lifeways, whether explicitly acknowledged by the ethnographer (e.g., Rogers 1962) or not (e.g., Densmore 1979; Hilger 1959). For example, most of the groups no longer manufactured or used pottery at the time of observation, which prevents analogous observation of cooking habits, as metal cooking pots have performance characteristics and ranges of functions different from their ceramic predecessors. Access to local, traditional foods may have been limited to communities inhabiting reserve lands, while the introduction of Western (Euro-American) foods after and during contact with Europeans would also have impacted local foodways. Historical and ethnographic accounts are likewise biased, both in the information recorded by the observers and in the ways in which the information is conveyed.

Despite these concerns, ethnographic data is informative when carefully examined in context with archaeological data. Ethnographic and ethnohistorical accounts of the Historic period Algonquian and Iroquoian groups provide additional details and support the archaeological data. Accounts of Ojibwe (Baraga 1976; Densmore 1979, 2005; Hilger 1959; Rogers 1962; Vennum 1988), Wendat (Huron) (Tooker 1991), and Iroquois (Waugh 1973) lifeways were used to examine and summarize general culinary habits and behaviors. Culinary habits as inferred from the archaeological data are compared to and reassessed in context with behaviors observed in the ethnographic and ethnohistorical sources.

ACORNS

The lipid analysis of absorbed pottery residue suggests that nut processing was a regular if not important function of pottery vessels at the Cloudman site. Among some Ojibwe groups, acorns of white oak (red oak was considered too bitter) were "boiled in hulls, cooled, hulled, and dried in the sun, [and] when needed they were crushed or pounded to meal, boiled with meat, and served as thick soup" (Hilger 1959, 145). Densmore (2005) reported that other Ojibwe groups had an affinity for *Quercus macrocarpa*, or burr oak, which produces large acorns. These were gathered in late fall and buried for use in winter or spring, but they were also cooked for immediate consumption, when they were roasted in ashes, boiled and mashed or boiled, split open, and "eaten like a vegetable" (Densmore 2005, 320).

According to Waugh (1973, 123), hickory nuts were the most esteemed nuts among Historic period Iroquoian groups, but they also routinely consumed walnut, butternut, hazelnut, beechnut, and chestnut. Acorns were also popular, prepared by "first boiling them in lye made from ashes, in order to take from them their excessive bitterness" (122–23). Nut meats were "pounded, boiled slowly in water, and the oil skimmed off into a bowl," the oil then mixed with a variety of foods, used in ceremonial foods of the False Face society, or used as mosquito repellent (Waugh 1973, 124). Nut meats were also ground, sifted, and added to corn soup to "make it rich" (Waugh 1973, 90, 124). Tooker (1991, 62) mentions that among the Huron, acorns were boiled several times to "take away the bitter taste" and then consumed.

Although acorns are never referred to as primary staples of either the Ojibwe or the Iroquois/Huron, their ubiquity in lipid signatures and macrobotanical remains demonstrates their importance to the occupants of the Cloudman site. Acorns were cooked and eaten independently but also added to soups and stews as a thickener. As Hilger (1959) noted, acorns were boiled to leech the tannins before they were stored or consumed, so the Cloudman site may have served as a seasonal residential locale to which parties of gatherers brought acorns for large-scale processing and/or consumption.

MAIZE

According to the microbotanical evidence, there is a long history of maize consumption at the Cloudman site. The Ojibwe considered maize a primary food staple, which they roasted in the husks, parched in hot kettles, dried and boiled, or incorporated in soup (Densmore 1979, 39; Densmore 2005, 319). Maize was also boiled in its shucks prior to ripening, then braided and hung to dry; the dried maize was then ground into meal and used primarily for thickening soups, although it was occasionally made into breads (Hilger 1959, 145). The Ojibwe also made hominy by boiling maize in hardwood ashes (nixtamalization), rinsing, and boiling again, removing the indigestible outer pericarp of the maize kernels (Densmore 2005, 319).

Iroquoian groups developed a maize-centric cuisine over the course of several centuries, resulting in over forty methods of corn preparation

(Waugh 1973). The Huron (Wendat) preferred boiling maize to roasting it and commonly used it as the primary ingredient in soups, which constituted many of their meals (Tooker 1991, 68). Waugh (1973) lists pages upon pages of Iroquoian maize preparations. Maize was routinely nixtamalized, rinsed, hulled, and pounded into a flour. Corn bread was common and was boiled rather than baked; the resulting broth was then used to make corn soup (Waugh 1973, 84).

Both maize nixtamalization and cooking processes are enhanced by extensive boiling, the preferred cooking method for the grain. During nixtamalization, maize would have been the sole content of a pottery vessel, but in all other preparations, corn was cooked with other ingredients, most commonly in soups and stews. Of the sixteen total vessels from the Cloudman site associated with residues containing maize microbotanical remains, maize always co-occurs with another food or food group (Kooiman 2018). This tradition of cooking maize primarily with other foods may have extended back to its earliest incorporation into the Northern Great Lakes subsistence regime.

SQUASH

The persistent and consistent presence of squash was the most unexpected result of the food residue analyses at the Cloudman site. This is not because squash was unimportant for Indigenous groups historically but because the antiquity of its use in the Northern Great Lakes is relatively unknown and rarely discussed. Squash and pumpkins were in common use by 1847, when Frederick Baraga recorded them as one of the few crops grown by the L'Anse Ojibwe in the western Upper Peninsula of Michigan. The Ojibwe ate pumpkins and squash fresh, or they dried them for use later in the winter (Densmore 1979, 2005; Hilger 1959). When consumed fresh, they were generally baked in coals (Hilger 1959, 144). Neither Hilger nor Densmore mentions boiling fresh squash. Squash was cut into strips to dry, and dried squash and pumpkin were boiled with meat or maple sugar (Densmore 2005, 319; Hilger 159, 144). If dried squash were boiled, it might gradually break down and act as a thickening agent, potentially resulting in the dual boiling + stewing interior carbonization patterns associated with squash phytoliths in Cloudman cooking vessels.

Iroquoian peoples incorporated squash into a more complex cuisine. They, too, dried, boiled, or baked squash and pumpkins in coals (Tooker 1991, 71; Waugh 1973, 114). Squash or pumpkin and corn were "frequently combined in the preparation of food" (Waugh 1973, 87), including corn and squash or pumpkin bread (into which berries were also mixed), dried pumpkin hominy porridge, and a sort of boiled pudding made of pumpkin or squash and hominy. Squash microbotanical remains were most common among Late Precontact vessels, present in both Iroquoian-style and Traverse ware vessels, suggesting the growing popularity of this foodstuff after AD 1300.

Like maize and wild rice, squash was never the sole foodstuff cooked in the sampled vessels from the Cloudman site. Although squash has long been associated with maize as two of the Three Sisters, it is not found in context with maize except in two Iroquoian-style vessels, possibly marking the development of a new culinary identity after AD 1300.

WILD RICE

Wild rice, or manoomin, has long been a primary dietary staple of Ojibwe groups of the Northern Great Lakes. An ideologically and ceremonially important food, it has transformed into a marker of Ojibwe identity (Vennum 1988) and has even been used to distinguish their cuisine from those of neighboring Odawa groups in archaeological studies (Scott 1996). Densmore (1979, 2005), Hilger (1959), and Vennum (1988) all identify wild rice as the primary staple of the Ojibwe diet.

Following harvest, wild rice was dried. Both Hilger and Densmore discuss the two primary methods of drying: air or fire drying or parching. Hilger (1959, 14) claims the divide in practices can be attributed to technology: prior to European contact, wild rice was routinely spread on sheets of birchbark to dry in the sun, while after contact it was instead parched in metal kettles. Densmore does not link parching to metal kettles but does comment that drying has greater antiquity than parching.

> The second [method] is undoubtedly the oldest process, and produced what was known as "hard rice." This was greenish black in color, much darker than parched rice and requiring longer to cook. This rice could be kept indefinitely, and could be used for seed. In

preparing "hard rice," a frame was made similar to that on which berries were dried. It was covered by a layer of hay on which the rice, either on stalks or in the husk, was spread to a depth of about 3 inches. A slow fire was kept burning beneath the frame. In this manner the rice was dried as vegetables or berries are dried. (2005, 315)

After drying or parching, which loosened the husks, the rice was pounded and stored in birchbark makuks (Densmore 1979, 148). To prepare it for consumption, wild rice was boiled in water or broth (Densmore 1979, 39) or boiled in soups (Hilger 1959, 148). It was also boiled in water and eaten "with or without maple sugar" or boiled with meat (Densmore 2005, 319). Sometimes meat or fish broth was poured over fresh parched rice and allowed to "steam" until softened, while so-called hard rice was stored with dried blueberries in the winter and cooked together in the spring (Densmore 2005, 319).

Some historical accounts record Contact period groups preparing wild rice in the form of a gruel, which required a greater liquid-to-rice ratio than nonglutinous (fluffy) rice (Vennum 1988, 47). Rice was also "used to thicken broths including venison, bear, fish, and wildfowl," cooked into a breadlike paste, or pounded into flour (48). Wild rice is cited by Vennum (1988) as being incorporated into a variety of stews with venison, small game, duck, or tassimanonny, a dish of boiled wild rice, corn, and fish.

Wild rice is not mentioned in ethnohistorical accounts of the Iroquoian groups, suggesting it was not a primary resource for these groups after European contact, but it is also not generally perceived of as an Iroquoian food staple, despite the fact that it grows regularly throughout traditional Iroquois territory (Boyd et al. 2013; Terrell et al. 1997). The high proportion of Iroquoian-style vessels containing traces of wild rice implies opportunistic foraging habits of the users of these vessels (be they Iroquoian or not). Considering the possible proximity of the Cloudman site to wild rice stands, occupants of the site, despite their cultural identity, opportunistically exploited this local and seasonally abundant resource.

Like maize, wild rice phytoliths were only identified in vessels containing signatures for other foods. Although not entirely clear, ethnographic accounts seem to indicate that wild rice was sometimes cooked independently, as we cook rice today. At the Cloudman site, rice may have been cooked with other foods or processed in alternating cooking events with other foods. However, adhered residues generally represent only the last cooking event in a vessel's use history (Miller et al. 2020), and microbotanical remains are derived from adhered carbonized food residues. Wild rice is frequently found in context with microbotanical remains of maize and squash in the Cloudman pottery residues, suggesting these foods were cooked together. Pottery vessels, then, were not constructed specifically for rice cooking, as is seen in other societies (see Kobayashi 1994; Skibo 1994), but instead were all-purpose cooking pots. Regardless, wild rice requires long-term boiling to become palatable, necessitating cooking vessels with sufficient heating effectiveness and thermal shock resistance to withstand these processing demands. Late Late Woodland and Late Precontact pottery from the Cloudman site with small temper particles would be technologically ideal for rice processing.

AQUATIC RESOURCES

The high ratios of N isotopes derived from the adhered pottery residues suggest that aquatic resources were frequently processed in ceramic cooking vessels at the Cloudman site. It is unclear if this represents aquatic plants or fish or both. Previous ethnographic surveys of Ojibwe, Cree, Innu, and Iroquoian ethnographic and ethnohistorical literature concluded that boiling was among the least common methods of fish preparation (Kooiman 2012, 2016; Lovis and Hart 2015), explaining the lack of fish lipids in previous sampling of pottery from other Woodland sites on the south shore of Lake Superior (Malainey and Figol 2015; Skibo, Malainey, and Drake 2009). One of the earliest accounts of Ojibwe life, from Rev. Frederick Baraga in 1847, claims that the L'Anse Chippewa of the Upper Peninsula "have no particular skill in boiling fish" (Baraga 1976, 64). In *Chippewa Customs*, Densmore (1979, 42) notes that fish were either eaten fresh or stored by drying or freezing. When eaten fresh, the fish were commonly spit roasted, fried, or flaked and packed with sugar.

However, fish were occasionally processed in cooking pots. Occasionally, "the head of fresh fish, especially suckers, were boiled and greatly liked," and "fresh fish were boiled and the broth used"; when dried or smoked fish were needed for food, they were also boiled (Densmore 1979, 42). Hilger notes in *Chippewa Child Life and Its Cultural Background* that both fresh and smoked fish were important in early Chippewa diets, but that meat, fish and fowl "were boiled with cultivated vegetables, such as beans, corn, squash, and pumpkin, and with native ones, such as wild rice, wild potatoes, and tips of certain plants" (1959, 144). The Round Lake Ojibwe in northern Ontario mostly dried or smoked fish, but "fish head and intestine provide oil; boiled in water, oil rises to surface and skimmed off with a wood spoon" (Rogers 1962, C49). Species of fish other than whitefish were infrequently used as food (Rogers 1962, C47–C48), indicating the taste preference for the high-trophic-level species reflected in the stable isotope values of pottery residues at the Cloudman site.

Iroquoian groups also relied heavily on fish and processed them with a variety of cooking techniques. F. W. Waugh (1973, 136) recounts how early explorers encountered "great kettles of Indian corn soup . . . with dried eels and other fish boiled in it." Among the preparations for fish observed directly by Waugh are boiled fish, fish soup, and fish and potato soup, although fish were also fried, roasted, and dried (137). Among the Huron of Ontario, fish was commonly dried in the sun or smoked but was also used "as a relish for their soup, especially in the winter," and the "biggest and fattest fish" were boiled to extract the fat (Tooker 1991, 64). According to these sources, boiling fish was practiced among the Ojibwe and the Iroquois of the Historic period and therefore cannot be precluded.

Aquatic plants may also have contributed to the high $\delta^{15}N$ values detected in the stable isotope analysis of the Cloudman pottery residues. Those consumed by the Ojibwe include wild rice, arrowhead root, bulrush (cattail), and hog peanut (Densmore 1979, 2005; Yarnell 1964). The Iroquois were known to consume marsh marigold, watercress, yellow pond-lily roots, and skunk cabbage (Waugh 1973). Aside from wild rice, aquatic plants were exploited and consumed but do not appear to have been a significant component of indigenous diet in the Great Lakes region. While they may have been available on Drummond Island prior to contact, none of these species were present in the macrobotanical remains from the Cloudman site (Egan-Bruhy 2007). The ethnographic sources inform but do not clarify why Cloudman pottery residues displayed high $\delta^{15}N$ values.

OTHER FOODS

Also integral to the Ojibwe and Iroquoian diets were meat, berries, some vegetables, and maple sugar, although the degree to which these foods could be distinguished in the food residues is variable. Lipid signatures for large herbivores and medium-sized mammals were present in a few vessels (Malainey and Figol 2018). Most vegetables or greens (including aquatic plants) and berries would be considered low fat content plants but cannot be identified to a more specific level. A unique chemical signature for maple sugar has not yet been identified by archaeological chemists. Nonetheless, these foods were all important components of Ojibwe and Iroquoian diets and may have been incorporated into the cuisine of pre-contact Cloudman site occupants.

The Ojibwe prepared meat in much the same way as fish: it was boiled; cut in pieces and spit roasted on the fire; or cut in thin slices, dried in the sun or smoked over a low fire, and stored for later use, when it was typically boiled (Densmore 1979, 43; Hilger 1959, 148). Fresh meat was often cooked with green vegetables, dried berries, and/or wild rice (Hilger 1959, 148). Moose meat and rabbit bones were boiled to render fat and grease (Densmore 1979, 44). The Iroquois employed similar yet slightly different methods of cooking meat. Large game was boiled twice, then removed from the pot and fried in grease (Waugh 1973, 134). Meat and bones of bear, raccoon, and porcupine were rendered for their grease, which was retained for medicinal purposes. Meat was also spit roasted or dried and rehydrated by boiling (Waugh 1973, 134). Nonmammal species consumed by Iroquoian groups include frogs, snakes, and turtles (Waugh 1973, 138).

Berries were integral to Ojibwe and Iroquoian diets. They were regionally abundant (Baraga 1976, 10) and added flavor to many dishes. Berries were eaten fresh but also extensively collected and dried, then boiled with other foods (Densmore 1979, 40; Hilger 1959, 144; Waugh 1973, 126). Fresh berries were also boiled down and spread into little patches on birchbark sheets, leaving storable and transportable concentrated berry cakes that could be eaten raw or easily added to a pot of food (Densmore 1979, 127; Rogers 1962, C52; Waugh 1973, 127). Among the Iroquois, dried berries were often incorporated into cornbread (Waugh

1973, 80). Blackberries and thimbleberries were combined with maple sugar and used in longhouse ceremonies (Waugh 1973, 145).

Vegetables are not emphasized in the ethnographic literature but played an important role in ancient diet nonetheless (Yarnell 1964). Roots, bark, and lichen are referred to as Ojibwe starvation foods by Baraga (1976, 65), and Rogers (1962, C47) claims the collection of vegetal foods is of "limited importance" among the Round Lake Ojibwe. However, a wide array of vegetables is mentioned in other sources. Milkweed flower, woodbine bark, and white pine moss are "unusual vegetable foods" of the Ojibwe, according to Densmore (1979, 40). Milkweed shoots and tips of ferns were boiled and flavored with grease by the Lac Courte Oreilles Ojibwe (Hilger 1959, 146). Wild potatoes were eaten by both the Ojibwe and the Iroquois and were typically boiled (Densmore 2005, 319; Waugh 1973, 119). The Iroquois extensively used the vegetal parts of various trees and shrubs, which were "cooked like spinach" (Waugh 1973, 117). They also used roots such as pepper root, burdock, and artichoke, which were boiled or fried, and bark was pounded and made into bread (Waugh 1973, 118–20). A number of other vegetable foods present in archaeological and ethnographic records associated with Indigenous diets in the Upper Great Lakes are detailed by Yarnell (1964).

Maple sugar was an important component of the historical Ojibwe diet. It served as one of the primary food seasonings, used with fruits, vegetables, cereals (including wild rice), and fish (Densmore 1979, 123). It was also considered a snack, as "all forms of the sugars were extensively eaten as a delicacy" (Densmore 1979, 39). Even various Iroquoian groups enjoyed maple sugar, adding it to hominy to make "parched corn meal" or sometimes even fermenting the sap for use as an intoxicant (Waugh 1973, 141, 147).

Unfortunately, standard lipid residue, stable isotope, or microbotanical analysis cannot distinguish maple sugar in pottery residues as unique chemical signatures have not yet been identified. The antiquity of maple sugaring has been hotly debated (Holman 1984; Holman and Egan 1985; Mason 1986; Mason and Holman 2000), so the timing of its incorporation into regional cuisine is unclear. Many of the foodstuffs present in the residues are late summer/early fall foods, suggesting the Cloudman site was used extensively in the fall, while maple sap is collected in the spring. Still, faunal and macrobotanical remains indicate some spring occupation of the site (Cooper 1996; Egan-Bruhy 2007), so some occupations may have taken place during sugaring season. Maple sugar is also easily storable, and, as an important flavoring agent and source of carbohydrates, it may have been brought to the site for consumption during the fall. Even if pottery vessels at Cloudman were not involved in maple sap processing, maple sugar may have been incorporated into recipes and meals cooked in the pots, leaving chemical signatures in the residues. Biomolecular analysis of organic residues may be a line of future study for detecting maple sugar in archaeological pottery (see McGovern and Hall 2016).

COOKING AND CUISINE

The historical focus of archaeological investigations into foodways has been the individual components of diet. Cuisine, or food culture, encompasses not only food choice but also food combinations and cooking styles (Twiss 2012). Patterning of carbonized food residues on Cloudman pottery vessels (and pottery from other sites in the Northern Great Lakes) shows some degree of diachronic variation, suggesting a change in cooking styles over time (see chapter 6). Microbotanical analysis revealed a diachronic shift in maize and wild rice processing, yet connections between transformations of diet and cooking styles remain speculative. The archaeological food residues also prove that different types of foods were routinely cooked in the same vessels, but they cannot provide clear recipes or dishes made and consumed by ancient peoples. Ethnographic observations of cooking behaviors, coupled with actualistic experiments, can inform and enhance inferential connections between diet and cuisine.

Among both the Ojibwe and the Iroquois, the following are specified as foods that are habitually boiled: corn, squash/pumpkin, fish, berries, meat, acorns, wild potatoes, roots, greens, and maple sap. Wild rice was also boiled by the Ojibwe. Among the Round Lake Ojibwe, "all food is prepared basically in one of two ways, either boiling or roasted on a spit beside a fire; boiling is more common and practically all species of mammal, bird, and fish are cooked in this way" (Rogers 1962, C53). The ubiquity of boiling as a cooking practice among postcontact Ojibwe and Iroquois/Huron appears rooted in cooking traditions extending back to the Middle Woodland period and popularized at the beginning of the Late Woodland period.

"Stewing" was only mentioned as a cooking technique by Vennum (1988) in his discussion of wild rice preparations, although several other sources mention adding ingredients such as acorn flour, pumpkin blossoms, and corn silk to soups as "thickening agents" (Densmore 1979; Hilger 1959; Waugh 1973). Stewing, a cooking process involving water-content reduction, was practiced at the Cloudman site throughout its occupational history, but it was most commonly employed during the Middle Woodland occupation.

Groups with distinct cultural identities and traditions may consume the same foods as other groups but maintain unique methods of food preparation. For the Ojibwe, "a typical meal comprised meat or fish, broth, rice with maple sugar, and dried berries prepared in some way" (Densmore 1979, 40). Meat and fish were "boiled with cultivated vegetables, such as beans, corn, squash, and pumpkin, and with native ones, such as wild rice, wild potatoes, and tips of certain plants" (Hilger 1959, 144). Foods were boiled, often multiple types together, but it is not clear if food was extracted from the cooking water and served or if components of each dish were served together as soups. Stews incorporating wild rice were common (Vennum 1988).

Among the Iroquois, "a very large proportion of . . . foods were evidently of liquid nature—[there are] numerous references to soups and broths made from ripe and unripe corn, beans, squashes, meats, and other materials" (Waugh 1973, 79). Corn soup was particularly common, and modern iterations tend to be rather aqueous. There are reports of "great kettles of Indian corn soup, or thin hominy, with . . . fish boiled in it" (Waugh 1973, 136).

However, another Iroquoian dish, sagamité, could be characterized as a stew or thick soup made by "pounding two or three handfuls of raw pounded [corn] meal which had not had the hull removed; put in an earthen pot full of water, boiled very clear and stirred to prevent meal from sticking to the pot and burning; if available a small quantity of fish . . . or meat was added, sometimes pumpkin, too. If fish had been added, it was taken out and pounded very fine, without removing the bones, scales or entrails, and put back into the pot" (Tooker 1991, 68). In this process, maize was first boiled, then other foods, such as squash or pumpkin and pounded fish, were added, which would thicken the soup. Sagamité preparation could result in the combined interior carbonization pattern (Pattern 3) indicative of both boiling and stewing, which was slightly more prevalent among the Late Precontact (including Iroquoian-style) pottery than among Late Late Woodland Juntunen vessels (see table 6.10).

Both Ojibwe and Iroquoian cuisines included varieties of boiled foods and dishes. Although foods can be boiled in organic containers by either adding hot stones to the contents or by filling containers full and putting them directly over the fire (Densmore 1979; Holman and Egan 1985; Speth 2015; Wallis and Wallis 1955; Waugh 1973), the advent of pottery at the outset of the of the Woodland period would have facilitated greater incorporation of boiling into everyday culinary routines. The eventual adoption of metal cooking pots by Native American groups following the establishment of trade with Europeans may have led to an increase in boiling practices in the Historic period, resulting in possible overrepresentation of the cooking method in the ethnographic record. Nevertheless, interior carbonization patterns present in the Cloudman pottery assemblage demonstrates that boiling practices were employed as early as the Middle Woodland period and became increasingly common through time.

Stewing, or long-term, low-heat cooking, was employed by the Ojibwe for certain preparations of wild rice and squash, which could result in interior carbonization patterns corresponding to stewing or boiling and stewing. In Middle, Early Late, and Late Late Woodland vessels, wild rice phytoliths are associated only with stewing interior carbonization patterns (see table 7.1). Among Iroquoian-style pottery vessels, wild rice is associated with the dual boiling + stewing pattern.

Ojibwe and Iroquoian cuisines share many similarities while remaining distinct. Soup was a common dish among the Iroquois; Ojibwe cooks boiled food and consumed their meals with broth—ethnographers only occasionally refer to their dishes as "soups"—and wild rice stews were popular. Overall, cooking styles appear similar. The Iroquois diet centered on maize, while wild rice was more important to the Ojibwe. However, maize was less frequent and wild rice more frequent in residues from Late Precontact vessels (including Iroquoian-style pots) than among Late Late Woodland vessels (see figure 7.3). If the users of Iroquoian-style pottery were indeed Iroquoian, they did not always adhere to ethnographically defined culinary practices.

The Three Sisters culinary tradition—maize, beans, and squash—may be represented at the Cloudman site, with wild rice serving as a substitute for beans. Maize, wild rice, and squash co-occur in residues only from Iroquoian-style vessels, possibly representing a local expression of Three Sisters cuisine. However, because the identity of the people using the Iroquoian-style vessels at the Cloudman site is still unclear, such an interpretation is merely speculative since the Ojibwe and other Woodland/Algonquian groups also routinely consumed these foods. The cumulative data leave firm identification of the users of the Iroquoian-style pottery elusive. Future study is required to determine if these vessels were at the Cloudman site as a result of travel, trade, or intergroup marriage.

CONCLUSION

The ethnographic and ethnohistorical records largely support the archaeological data for the food types selected and modes of cooking employed at the Cloudman site. Most of the primary food staples consumed by post-European contact Ojibwe and Iroquoian groups were represented in the pottery food residues, with the exception of maple sugar, which is not detectable by means of conventional residue analyses. Common cooking methods, particularly boiling, reflect interior carbonization patterns encountered in the ceramic cooking vessels, particularly those from later occupations of the site. Stewing as a primary cooking technique may have gradually fallen out of favor with Northern Great Lakes cooks over time and was likewise a less common cooking method observed by ethnographers. Culinary distinctions are apparent between historic Ojibwe and Iroquois, although these differences cannot definitively distinguish the ethnic identities of the groups that occupied the Cloudman site.

Overall, the ethnographic and ethnohistorical evidence supports and enhances interpretations of the archaeological data presented in this study. Historic Ojibwe and Iroquoian resource selection closely parallels the archaeological food remains and chemical signatures discovered at the Cloudman site. Firsthand observations of Indigenous preparations of the same suite of resources have proved a useful tool for connecting cooking styles with specific foodstuffs and food mixes. Reinforced by these data, interpretations of the results of this study can be reviewed and final conclusions summarized.

CHAPTER 9

Culinary and Technological Tradition and Change at the Cloudman Site

The pottery assemblage from the Cloudman site has produced a robust body of data about precontact Northern Great Lakes Indigenous pottery technology, pottery use, and cuisine. Application of a novel combination of taxonomic categorization and functional analysis of pottery in tandem with vessel-specific AMS dating, stable isotope analysis, lipid residue analysis, and microbotanical analysis of food residues associated with pottery yielded an incredible array of new information about Woodland and Late Precontact peoples and how they interacted with their natural and social environments. This is the largest sample subjected to this range of analytic approaches in the Great Lakes region, and the results, enhanced by ethnographic analogy, inform local site history and long-standing regional questions in the Northern Great Lakes.

CONTEXT AND CHRONOLOGY OF THE CLOUDMAN SITE

The occupational history of the Cloudman site was established through the taxonomic classification of pottery vessels and AMS dating of adhered pottery residues. Diachronic comparisons of the ceramic technical and use-alteration properties and outcomes of dietary analyses could not have been achieved without an established chronological framework. Initial taxonomic classifications of the Cloudman assemblage by Branstner (1995) were revisited and refined with new data. Middle Woodland, Early Late Woodland, Late Late Woodland, and Late Precontact (including Traverse and Iroquoian-style) pottery types represented the most substantial portions of the site's ceramic assemblage. Small subassemblages from the Middle Woodland/Late Woodland transition and the Middle Late Woodland period were identified but represented small, ephemeral occupations.

The taxonomic identifications left some questions unanswered, such as the timing of the appearance of nonlocal wares, such as Blackduck, Iroquoian-style, and Traverse, at the site. AMS dating allowed further refinement and clarification of the occupational history of the site. The earliest occupation is represented by Laurel Middle Woodland pottery. AMS radiocarbon dates of carbonized food residues from two Laurel vessels anchor the Middle Woodland occupation to approximately AD 50–200 (Kooiman 2018; Kooiman, Dunham, and Stephenson 2019). The Early Late Woodland occupation (ca. AD 900–1000) is represented by AMS dates from local Mackinac and nonlocal Blackduck vessels. An ephemeral Middle Late Woodland (Bois Blanc) occupation dating to about AD 1150 immediately precedes the Late Late Woodland occupation, which is represented by Juntunen ware vessels dating between AD 1200 and AD 1300 (Kooiman 2018; Kooiman, Dunham, and Stephenson 2019; Kooiman and Walder 2019).

Iroquoian-style pottery vessels, alongside European-made glass trade beads, found at the site were originally considered part of a Protohistoric/Contact period Odawa occupation of the site around AD 1630. A separate study found that the beads likely date to after AD 1670, while AMS dates of carbonized residues suggest the Iroquoian-style vessels at the Cloudman site were used between AD 1300 and AD 1500 (Kooiman and Walder 2019). Traverse ware vessels, a Late Woodland type that is stylistically distinct from both Juntunen and Iroquoian-style wares, dated to about AD 1400 (Kooiman and Walder 2019). The category "Late Precontact" was created to describe all pottery associated with the post-Juntunen component of the site, which, while temporally distinct from the Late Late Woodland occupation, is nonetheless characterized by a complex series of occupations, perhaps by diverse groups (Kooiman and Walder 2019).

POTTERY TECHNOLOGY IN THE NORTHERN GREAT LAKES

If regional reliance on starchy foods increased during the Late Woodland period, as proposed by Dunham (2014), it was predicted that there would be changes in pottery vessel thickness and temper size to accommodate new food processing needs, specifically, intensive boiling to make foods like acorn, wild rice, and maize palatable and digestible. Tethered dietary and technological changes have been observed elsewhere in the Eastern Woodlands (Braun 1983; Hart 2012). Observed technical changes include thinner pottery walls to increase heating effectiveness and/or temper size reduction to improve thermal shock resistance.

Temper size proved the most significant and informative technical property of the Cloudman pottery vessels. Particle size remained relatively consistent among Middle Woodland and Early Late Woodland pottery but was significantly reduced among Late Late Woodland and Late Precontact vessels. Decreased temper size can improve the overall strength of a vessel, a property appealing to potters constructing the collared wares characteristic of both Late Late Woodland and Iroquoian societies, but, more important, it increases thermal shock resistance, a trait required for vessels employed in intensive and/or long-term cooking episodes required for processing starchy foods such as wild rice, acorns, and maize.

Contrary to expectations, average vessel wall thickness did not follow the trend of decreasing thickness over time. Body thickness would be the most sensitive indicator of technical decisions to increase heating effectiveness, but sample sizes for body thickness were small because of the low incidence of body sherds that could be confidently associated with identified vessels. Based on the limited data, there actually appears to be an inverse relationship between body thickness and temper size, a subject worth closer investigation in the future.

Prior diachronic studies of ceramic technology have not included vessel size as a factor, and its use in the study was largely exploratory. Using rim diameter as a proxy for size, Middle Woodland vessels were found to be significantly smaller than those constructed after AD 700. Since people in the Middle Woodland period were more mobile and may have traveled in smaller groups (Brose and Hambacher 1999), the diminutive vessel size may be connected to group size or the need for more transportable vessels. If later occupations included larger aggregates of people and their durations of stay were more prolonged, construction of larger vessels would have been warranted. The increase in vessel size also co-occurs with the proliferation of boiling signatures, so vessel capacity may also be associated with some aspect of cooking effectiveness, although the connection is unclear at present and requires experimental work for clarification. Vessel size may also be related to context of use, as other studies have indicated that larger vessels may be used in ritual contexts (Blitz 1993; Kooiman 2016; Potter 2000). The Cloudman site contains a mound and a dog burial, which may mark it as a ceremonial aggregation site (Howey and O'Shea 2006; O'Shea and McHale Milner 2002; Smith 1996). Larger vessels may have been used to feed large amounts of people attending ritual gatherings at important locales between group territories.

COOKING AT THE CLOUDMAN SITE

Pottery use and cooking at the Cloudman site is characterized by both consistency and change. Pottery vessels from all occupations were primarily involved in cooking over fire, evidenced by high frequencies of vessels with interior carbonization across all subassemblages. Distribution of interior carbonization patterns also demonstrated that pots from all time periods were routinely filled to the top during the cooking process, a culinary habit seen at Woodland sites across the Upper Peninsula of Michigan (Kooiman 2012, 2015a, 2016).

Interior carbonization patterning, however, varied over time, representing alterations in cooking behaviors. Patterns indicative of stewing were most frequent among the Middle Woodland pottery assemblage, while boiling patterns increased in frequency among Early Late Woodland, Late Late Woodland, and Late Precontact subassamblages. This corroborates previously observed trends among Woodland pottery assemblages in the Northern Great Lakes (Albert et al. 2018; Kooiman 2012, 2016).

An interior carbonization pattern not previously observed in the Northern Great Lakes is present within the Early Late Woodland, Late

Late Woodland, and Late Precontact pottery assemblages (see figures 6.2, 6.5). This pattern represents distinct signatures for both boiling and stewing in the same vessel. It was not observed in any Middle Woodland vessels and is therefore a cooking habit apparently adopted by Northern Great Lakes peoples sometime after AD 600, and it becomes especially common during the Late Precontact period (post–AD 1300) at the Cloudman site. The boiling + stewing pattern could indicate boiling of starchy foods followed by water-reduction cooking (as with cooking rice) or later incorporation of other foods (such as squash or ground meal) to create a thick soup or stew. The overall increase in the frequency in boiling and boiling + stewing patterns, when contextualized with data from other sites in the Northern Great Lakes, signals a shift in cooking styles following the end of the Middle Woodland period. Boiling became a more common cooking technique, and while stewing was still employed, it diminished in importance.

DIET AND ENVIRONMENT IN THE NORTHERN GREAT LAKES

Results of lipid residue and stable isotope analyses revealed that some aspects of diet remained consistent throughout the occupational history of the Cloudman site. Lipid residue analysis revealed that a majority (67%) of ceramic cooking vessels sampled from all components were involved in nut processing. Based on the proximity of the Cloudman site to precontact oak stands (Comer et al. 1995; Comer and Albert 1997), the prevalence of acorns in microbotanical remains at the site (Egan-Bruhy 2007), and a preference for acorns among historic Ojibwe groups (Densmore 1979; Hilger 1959; Yarnell 1964), the nut lipids most likely represent acorns (although hazlenut and butternut were also probably consumed at the site).

Stable isotope analysis of Cloudman pottery residues yielded high $\delta^{15}N$ values, representing aquatic resources, either fish or plants. While consumption of fish at the Cloudman site was expected, the processing of fish in pottery vessels was not predicted based on the absence of fish lipids in absorbed pottery residues from other sites in the Northern Great Lakes (Kooiman 2016; Malainey and Figol 2015; Skibo, Malainey, and

Drake 2009). Enriched $\delta^{15}N$ values were encountered in 96% of sampled vessels from the Cloudman assemblage, including vessels from all occupations (Kooiman 2018). Although not the most common method of cooking fish, boiling is chronicled in several ethnographic and ethnohistorical sources, which demonstrates that fish may have contributed to the $\delta^{15}N$ values. Aquatic plants, including wild rice, may also have contributed to the nitrogen enrichment of the pottery residues. Whether floral or faunal, aquatic resources were consistently processed in pottery vessels at the Cloudman site throughout all occupations.

Analysis of microscopic plant remains (phytoliths and starches) yielded several important results. First, in conjunction with AMS dating, it provided evidence of some of the earliest dated remains of wild rice and squash in the Northern Great Lakes. Microscopic remains of both foods were encountered in carbonized food residues of Laurel Middle Woodland pottery vessels that were either directly dated or adhered to vessels of the same taxonomic type as those with directly dated residues. Very few remains, either macroscopic or microscopic, of either wild rice or squash have been found in archaeological contexts in the region. The Cloudman site had one of the only preserved wild rice seeds found in the Northern Great Lakes, although it is associated with the Late Woodland occupation. The presence of these foods in the region as early as AD 100 is important for understanding the spread and use of domesticates and wild cultivated foods in North America.

The microbotanical remains also revealed diachronic disparities in foods processed in ceramic vessels (Albert, Kooiman, and Lovis 2018; Kooiman 2018). Maize was present at highest frequencies in adhered food residues in Middle Woodland vessels but decreased steadily in subsequent occupations. Conversely, wild rice increased in frequency over time. All but absent in the Early Late Woodland, wild rice is present in half or more than half of all Late Late Woodland and Late Precontact pottery residues sampled. Squash is present in very low frequencies during the earliest three components but became a more important food source after AD 1300. Differences in microbotanical frequencies between the Early Late Woodland and Late Late Woodland signal an important shift in subsistence habits between AD 1000 and AD 1200.

These shifts in resource selection could be associated with the Medieval Climatic Optimum (AD 900–1000), which caused both an overall warmer climate and lower lake levels, contributing to increased riverine fluctuations and flooding episodes that could destabilize established wild rice beds (Lovis et al. 2001; Lovis, Arbogast, and Monaghan 2012; Monaghan and Lovis 2005). Higher temperatures would have increased the productivity of horticultural efforts while water level fluctuations adversely affected the availability of wild rice during the Early Late Woodland occupation of the Cloudman site. Climatological cooling concurrent with the Late Late Woodland period may have inhibited productivity of maize horticulture, and restabilization of riverine environments would have facilitated regrowth of wild rice beds, causing a reversal in resource availability and selection (Lovis, Arbogast, and Monaghan 2012). The large increase in the frequency of squash microremains associated with the Late Precontact occupation, identified in pottery residues derived from both Iroquoian-style and Traverse ware vessels, could represent the arrival and local adoption of *Curcurbita pepo* ssp. *pepo*. This is a large-seeded squash variety domesticated in Mexico that spread across Eastern North America after AD 1000 (Simon 2011; B. D. Smith 2006).

Previous studies argued that exploitation of deep-water, fall-spawning fish (Cleland 1982), maize (O'Shea 2003), and wild rice and acorns (Dunham 2014) intensified in the Late Woodland period, particularly after AD 1200. Results of this study support the increased importance of wild rice but do not support the increased importance of maize at the Cloudman site during the Late Late Woodland period. The results presented here also indicate consistent exploitation of aquatic resources and nuts/acorns from AD 100 to AD 1500. Increased intensification of aquatic resources, including fish, during the Late Woodland is neither supported nor refuted by data from the Cloudman site. Nut lipids are present in over half of all samples during all time periods, indicating that acorns and other nuts were consistently important resources at the Cloudman site throughout all occupations.

SUBSISTENCE, STYLE, AND SOCIAL IDENTITY

Synchronic variation of technology and diet was difficult to assess given the limited size of the Cloudman assemblage, although some observations about identity can be made. As hypothesized, the number of distinct taxonomic pottery types increased over the span of the Woodland occupations. The Middle Woodland subassemblage was dominated by Laurel wares; only two non-Laurel vessels are associated with the Middle Woodland occupation. The Early Late Woodland pottery assemblage was only slightly more varied, comprised primarily of Mackinac wares but also including Blackduck ware, which is common to the north, and Bowerman ware, which is local to the northern lower peninsula of Michigan. The Late Late Woodland assemblage, while consisting largely of Juntunen ware, also comprised a number of vessels with Late Late Woodland characteristics but without fitting into any established stylistic taxonomic categories. This supports the narrative that the social fluidity of Middle Woodland groups was gradually replaced with increased social localization of Late Woodland groups, with socially distinct groups (using distinct pottery types) interacting at seasonal aggregation sites, including Cloudman, during the Late Woodland period (Brose and Hambacher 1999; Carroll 2013; Cleland 1982; Dorothy 1978; McHale Milner 1998; McPherron 1967).

Cuisine also provides clues about social identity. According to ethnographic information, maize was commonly consumed by both historic Ojibwe and Iroquoian groups, although it was much more central to Iroquoian cuisine. Based on observed frequencies of starches and phytoliths, maize was least common during the Late Precontact occupation of the site, although only Iroquoian-style vessels were associated with evidence for maize; it was absent from residues associated with Traverse vessels. Users of the Iroquoian-style cooking pots may not have been Iroquoian, but they appear to have had a cuisine distinct from groups cooking in Traverse ware vessels.

Wild rice was considered a staple food among the Ojibwe, although it does not seem to have been a staple among groups at the Cloudman site until the Late Late Woodland period, capturing the possible emergence of wild rice as a crucial resource for local peoples. Wild rice was not reported in reviewed ethnographic sources as a component of either Historic period Iroquoian (Tooker 1991; Waugh 1973) or Odawa cuisine (Scott 1996). The presence of wild rice in food residues adhered to Iroquoian-style pottery poses an intriguing question about the identity of the users of these vessels. Whoever the occupants of the site after AD 1300 may have been, they were opportunistically exploiting a locally abundant resource that may not have been part of their traditional cuisine. Residues from Iroquoian-style vessels also yielded a unique combination of maize, wild rice, and squash microbotanicals not observed in residues associated with earlier occupations or among roughly contemporary Traverse ware vessels, possibly reflecting a local variant of the Three Sisters cuisine, which was at the heart of Iroquoian identity.

THE CLOUDMAN SITE: A NARRATIVE THROUGH TIME

Data derived from ceramic taxonomic classifications, pottery function analysis, dietary analyses, and ethnographic analogy successfully informed the discrete archaeological queries posed in this study, but when evaluated together, they create a dynamic narrative of life at the Cloudman site. Middle Woodland Laurel peoples occupied the Cloudman site on at least two separate occasions between AD 50 and AD 200. The highly mobile, socially fluid Middle Woodland groups made small pottery vessels that served the primary function of stewing foods. Pottery vessel size may have been restricted to facilitate mobility and transportability, to feed smaller groups of people, or to fulfill other cooking-related requirements. Diet consisted of aquatic resources, nuts/acorns, various wild animal and plant foods, including wild rice, and cultivated food such as maize and squash. While boiling was employed as a cooking method at this time, it was not as prevalent as stewing, a habit observed at other Middle Woodland sites in the eastern Upper Peninsula of Michigan (Albert et al. 2018; Kooiman 2012, 2016). Maize macrobotanicals are associated with stewing patterns of adhered food residues; maize at this time may have been incorporated into the diet primarily as a ground meal added to soups as a thickening agent or in a green, unripened state. Peoples inhabited the site after the primary Middle Woodland occupations, as represented by a few Late Laurel vessels (ca. AD 500–700), although use-alteration traces and food residues reflect general continuity with prior food-related behaviors.

At the outset of the Early Late Woodland period, pottery vessels grew larger and were employed more frequently for boiling food than for stewing. The increase in vessel size concurrent with the proliferation of boiling practices, so expanded volume may have provided a functional advantage for this method of cooking. The variety of foods cooked during this period did not significantly differ from those processed and consumed during the Middle Woodland, so the impetus for transforming cooking habits lies elsewhere. Among Early Late Woodland vessels, maize microbotanicals are associated with interior carbonization patterns for boiling, potentially representing the emergence of nixtamalization (boiling whole kernels in alkaline solutions) as a maize processing method in this region. Despite the increase in boiling practices, temper particle size did not decrease as would be expected, since this characteristic would help prevent cooking vessels from breaking during the higher cooking temperatures required for intensive boiling.

During the Late Late Woodland period, distinct social groups, including Juntunen people and groups using unique, uncategorized pottery styles, aggregated at the site for intensive seasonal resource extraction. Potters selected temper particles that were significantly smaller than observed in earlier pottery. This technical choice, which improves increased thermal shock resistance, may have been related to requirements for vessel durability during prolonged high-temperature cooking events. Frequency of wild rice phytoliths in carbonized residues increases during this same period. Wild rice requires long-term cooking to be made palatable and would require vessels built to withstand prolonged use over fire.

People occupying the Cloudman site during the Late Late Woodland period continued to manufacture large vessels (relative to Middle Woodland pottery). The larger vessels may reflect larger groups gathering at "persistent places," locales repeatedly visited for extended occupations to exploit abundant nearby resources (Schlanger 1992; Thompson 2010), a trend observed among Late Woodland sites in the eastern Upper Peninsula of Michigan (Dunham 2014). The new social and settlement patterns accommodated manufacture and use of less transportable materials, such as larger cooking pots, that could be stored at a site for future use, a practice known as "locale provisioning" (Lovis, Donahue, and Holman 2005).

Larger pottery vessels have also been associated with ceremonial contexts in the Northern Great Lakes (Kooiman 2016) and elsewhere in Eastern North America (Blitz 1993; Potter 2000). The Cloudman site includes a burial mound that could have played a ceremonial function in the lives of the local group. The mound has been tentatively characterized as Middle Woodland (Branstner 1995, 21; Demers 1991), but a similar mound at the nearby Juntunen site, a significant Late Woodland site with a smaller Middle Woodland component, contained both Middle and

Late Woodland burials and materials (McPherron 1967). The pottery excavated from the mound at the Cloudman site during an amateur excavation was described as having "geometric designs" (Branstner 1995, 19), which could refer to the motifs common to Juntunen ware vessels. Woodland mounds were spaces for community bonding for members of different residential communities (Chivis 2016), and Late Late Woodland mound sites in the Northern Great Lakes have been interpreted as meeting places for social, economic, and ritual interaction between dispersed groups at this time (Howey and O'Shea 2006; Howey, Palace, and McMichael 2016; O'Shea and McHale Milner 2002). Drummond Island is located on a thoroughfare between modern-day southeastern Ontario and the Upper Peninsula of Michigan, and the Cloudman site may have been an ideal locale for dispersed groups to gather not only for intensive resource extraction but for ceremonial purposes as well. If the mound dates to the Late Woodland, then the use of the site as a gathering place for larger groups may also explain the larger vessels as well as the proliferation of uncategorized pottery types, which may represent nonlocal groups.

Maize continues to decrease in ubiquity in Late Late Woodland pottery residues. The amelioration of the Medieval Climatic Optimum at this time would have led to a cooler climate with riverine stabilization, a reversal that would have decreased maize productivity while creating an advantageous growing environment for wild rice on Drummond Island (Lovis, Arbogast, and Monaghan 2012; Monaghan and Lovis 2005). A new local abundance of wild rice may have undercut the value of maize output given the energy required to cultivate the crop. The Late Late Woodland period also signals a time of greater social localization (McHale Milner 1991, 1998; O'Shea and McHale Milner 2002). Distinct group identities manifested in pottery style may also have been expressed in food selection, representing a conscious choice by Late Late Woodland Cloudman occupants to exploit and associate themselves with locally abundant wild rice. Microbotanical remains and lipid residues provide evidence for selection of wild rice in lieu of maize by Late Late Woodland occupants of the Cloudman site.

The Late Precontact component of the Cloudman site (ca. AD 1300–1500) is characterized by a series of brief occupations by users of both nonlocal Woodland (Traverse) and Iroquoian-style pottery vessels. As in the Late Late Woodland, pottery vessels were relatively large and with small temper particles. The users of these vessels were most likely to both boil and stew foods in the same pottery vessels. Evidence for maize appears in residue associated with Iroquoian-style pottery, although not with Traverse pottery, and squash in general becomes more common in association with both stylistic types. Despite the onset of the Little Ice Age after AD 1300, which would have prolonged local conditions not conducive to maize cultivation, users of Iroquoian-style vessels still incorporated maize into their diet. If they were Iroquoian travelers, then they may have carried maize with them as they journeyed to the Cloudman site. If they were Woodland groups, they may have received maize through trade with Iroquoian neighbors. The cumulative subsistence choices made by these people may better inform identity-related culinary choice. Iroquoian-style vessels are the only ones in which wild rice, maize, and squash microbotanical remains co-occur in pottery residues, perhaps reflecting a local variation of the Three Sisters (maize, squash, and beans) Iroquoian cuisine (Bamann et al. 1992; Hart 2008; Kuhn and Funk 2000). This culinary tradition may have been maintained by traveling parties or by Iroquioan women marrying into Woodland groups. However, Woodland peoples may also have received these foodstuffs through trade.

Late Precontact vessels, both Iroquoian-style and Traverse, continued to be constructed with larger capacities. Given the presence of diverse pottery styles at the site from this period as well as the dog burial, which are thought to mark sites of exchange during the Late Precontact and Historic periods in the Northern Great Lakes (Smith 1996), Cloudman may have continued to serve as a meeting place for dispersed groups after AD 1300. The AMS dates for Late Precontact vessels are spaced with little to no statistical overlap, suggesting a series of more ephemeral occupations of the site over time. The Cloudman site may have served as a temporary encampment for exchange rather than as a site for seasonal aggregation and intensive resource procurement during this period.

THE CLOUDMAN LEGACY: NEW QUESTIONS AND DIRECTIONS

This study lays the groundwork for future research by revealing aspects of the archaeological record requiring additional clarification. Among these issues is the disentanglement of the social environment of Drummond

Island after AD 1300. The Cloudman site occupies a unique geographic crossroads between the Upper Peninsula of Michigan, traditionally occupied by Woodland Algonquian groups, and southwestern Ontario, the territory of Iroquoian groups such as the Wendat, Petun, and Neutral (Trigger 1976). The presence of Iroquoian or Iroquoian-style pottery in areas outside of southwestern Ontario is commonly interpreted as the result of trade between local Algonquian groups and the Iroquoians rather than the result of Iroquoian occupation of these sites (Fox and Garrad 2004; Guindon 2009). Such is the case at the Cloudman site, where the use of Iroquoian-style pottery was attributed to Odawa traders occupying the site around AD 1630 (Branstner 1995; Cleland 1999). However, residues from all four Iroquoian-style pottery vessels sampled dated between AD 1300 and AD 1500 (Kooiman and Walder 2019), demonstrating an earlier presence of Iroquoian-style wares at the site than previously believed. Residue from a single Traverse vessel, which was used by Woodland groups, yielded a date that fell amid those from Iroquoian-style vessels, revealing an intriguing and potentially complex social environment in the eastern Upper Peninsula of Michigan after AD 1300. Juntunen wares continued to be manufactured and used at other sites in the region after this time as well, although it does not appear that Juntunen groups returned to Cloudman during the Late Precontact occupation sequence of the site.

While cuisine can be used to investigate identity, the Cloudman assemblage was not large enough to provide definitive insights about the relationship between cuisine and identity. The results presented here do hint at some possible trends that may be used to distinguish identity based on cuisine in the future. Foods and food mixes cooked in Iroquoian-style vessels appear somewhat distinct from those cooked in pottery produced by Woodland groups (Juntunen and Traverse). This would not be the case if Iroquoian-style pottery vessels were present in the Northern Great Lakes as a result of trade but would instead indicate the movement of people, either through group travel or intermarriage. A regional survey of pottery and food residue contents of common local ceramic taxonomic types common between AD 1200 and AD 1600 would facilitate more accurate examination of food choice and cuisine in relation to group identity. Clay and temper sourcing of Late Late Woodland and Late Precontact vessels may also provide insight as to where the pots were manufactured and whether they were manufactured in the same place, which may also help clarify the nature of economic and social interactions at the site after AD 1200.

The differences found in resource selection over time also warrants further investigation. Maize remains steadily decrease in frequency over time at the Cloudman site. Wild rice, conversely, becomes much more prevalent after AD 1000. These changes may coincide with broader climatological and environmental phenomena, specifically, the Medieval Climatic Optimum. Regional paleoenvironmental surveys could evaluate the degree to which the local climate and vegetation may have been affected and delineate the timing of such changes. If the climate was cooler and the hydrological conditions for productive wild rice patches were right, this may suggest that dietary changes were part of an adaptive process of innovative local groups. If not, then social factors, such as new settlement patterns or social interactions, may have played a larger role in shaping cuisine through time.

Experimental archaeology could help answer lingering questions related to cooking techniques, pottery function, and interpretations of dietary analyses. Experiments testing the heating efficacy and other cooking-related capabilities of vessels of varying size and capacity could allow further insight into the function of vessel size in food processing. Controlled testing of the stable isotope values of aquatic plants could also improve the interpretive strength of this method for investigating diet through chemical analysis of carbonized food residues.

BEYOND CLOUDMAN: A NEW METHODOLOGICAL APPROACH

Many aspects of the experiences and choices of the residents of the Cloudman site were brought alive using a multiproxy, multidimensional approach to pottery analysis. This study employed a combination of methods, from conventional taxonomic pottery classification to the increasingly popular functional pottery analysis to the cutting-edge field of chemical and microscopic analysis of adhered and absorbed residues associated with ceramic cooking vessels. Along with AMS radiocarbon dating, these methods have facilitated the reconstruction of diet, cooking, and technology through time at the Cloudman site and provided glimpses into the possible natural and social environments that shaped and were shaped by the occupants of the site. The conclusions drawn from this study were also based on a pottery assemblage excavated decades ago and did not require any new, costly excavations, only reevaluation of curated materials. Ultimately, this book underlines the strength of this multifaceted, collaborative approach that can be used to understand the lives of past peoples at sites across the world.

CONCLUSION

A decades-long debate about the nature of Woodland settlement and subsistence has persisted in Northern Great Lakes archaeological research, and this study has brought new data to light. Archaeological remains from the Cloudman site revealed the deep historical importance of fish, acorns, maize, wild rice, and squash to groups occupying the Northern Great Lakes. Fluctuations in the intensity of wild rice and maize exploitation and variations in cooking methods and pottery technology reflect adaptive reactions to changes in the natural and/or social environments, reinforcing both the maintenance of food traditions and the adaptability and dynamism of human response to social and environmental change.

This study has also demonstrated the efficacy of a multiproxy approach to pottery and culinary research. Taxonomic and functional pottery analyses intertwine time, identity, and pottery use patterns, resulting in a deeper understanding of ancient social and human-environment relationships. The collaborative application of lipid residue, stable isotope, and microbotanical analysis, further informed by macrobotanical information and ethnographic research, to a large pottery assemblage culminated in a comprehensive picture of ancient diet and cooking and serves as a model for future research initiatives exploring past foodways in contexts across the world.

APPENDIX A

Cloudman Pottery Data

Cloudman Pottery Data

Vessel	Period	Final Type	Dates	Original Type (Branstner 1995)
1	MW	Laurel Pseudo-scallop Shell	cal AD 80–180 (AMS)	Laurel Pseudo-scallop Shell
2	MW	Laurel Pseudo-scallop Shell	AD 50–200	Laurel Pseudo-scallop Shell
3	MW	Laurel Plain	AD 50–200	Laurel Plain
4	MW	Laurel Dentate Stamped	AD 50–200	Laurel Dentate Stamped
5	MW	Laurel Pseudo-scallop Shell	AD 50–200	Laurel Pseudo-scallop Shell
6	MW	Laurel Dentate Rocker Stamped	AD 50–200	Dentate Rocker Stamped
7	MW	Laurel Pseudo-scallop Shell	AD 50–200	Laurel Pseudo-scallop Shell
8	ELW	Mackinac ware	AD 900–1000	Mackinac Phase/untyped
9	MW	Laurel Pseudo-scallop Shell (oblique)	AD 50–200	Laurel Oblique/Pseudo-scallop Shell variety
10	MW	Laurel Pseudo-scallop Shell	AD 50–200	Laurel Pseudo-scallop Shell
11	MW	Laurel Pseudo-scallop Shell (oblique)	AD 50–200	Laurel Oblique/Pseudo-scallop Shell variety
12	MW	Laurel Dentate Stamped (oblique)	AD 50–200	Laurel Oblique/Dentate Stamped
13	MW	Laurel Dentate Stamped	AD 60–125	Laurel Dentate Stamped
14	MW	Laurel Pseudo-scallop Shell	AD 50–200	Laurel Pseudo-scallop Shell
15	MW	Laurel Pseudo-scallop Shell (oblique)	AD 50–200	Laurel Oblique/Pseudo-scallop Shell variety
16	MW	Laurel Trailed	AD 50–200	Laurel Trailed
17	MW	Laurel Dentate Stamped (oblique)	AD 60–125	Laurel Oblique/Dentate Stamped
18	MW	Laurel Pseudo-scallop Shell	AD 50–200	Laurel Pseudo-scallop Shell
19	MW	Laurel Dentate Stamped (oblique)	AD 60–125	Laurel Oblique/Dentate Stamped
20	MW	Laurel Dentate Stamped (oblique)	AD 60–125	Laurel Oblique/Dentate Stamped
21	ELW	Mackinac Punctate	AD 900–1000	Mackinac Punctate
22	MW	Laurel Pseudo-scallop Shell	AD 50–200	Laurel Pseudo-scallop Shell
23	MW	Laurel Banked Linear Stamped	AD 50–200	Laurel Banked Linear Stamped
24	LLW	"proto-Juntunen" ware (plain)	AD 1200	untyped
25	LLW	Juntunen ware	AD 1200–1300	untyped
26	LLW	Juntunen ware	AD 1200–1300	untyped

Cloudman Pottery Data (*cont.*)

Vessel	Period	Final Type	Dates	Original Type (Branstner 1995)
27	LLW	untyped	AD 1200–1600	untyped
28	MW	Laurel Pseudo-scallop Shell	AD 50–200	Laurel Pseudo-scallop Shell
29	ELW	Mackinac ware	AD 900–1000	Mackinac Phase/untyped
30	MW/LW	Late Laurel (cf. Laurel Incised)	AD 500–700	Laurel Incised
31	MLW	cf. Bois Blanc ware (expedient?)	AD 1100–1200	untyped
32	ELW	Mackinac ware	AD 900–1000	Mackinac Phase/untyped
33	MW/LW	untyped (incipient Blackduck? MN type)	AD 500–700?	untyped
34	ELW	Mackinac ware	AD 900–1000	Mackinac Phase/untyped
35	MW/LW	Late Laurel (cross-hatched, cf. Laurel Incised)	AD 500–700	Cross-hatched/Impressed lip
36	LP	Iroquoian-style (cf. Huron Incised)	AD 1300–1500	Huron Incised
37	LLW	untyped	NA	untyped
38	LP	Iroquoian-style (untyped)	AD 1300–1500	untyped
39	MW	Laurel ware (mini)	AD 50–200	untyped
40/153	LP	Iroquoian-style (cf. Lawson ware)	AD 1300–1500	untyped/chevron; cf. Lalonde High Collar
41	ELW	Mackinac ware	AD 900–1000	Mackinac Phase/untyped
42	MLW	Bois Blanc ware	AD 1150–1200	untyped
43	LLW	Traverse Decorated v. Punctate	AD 1400–1450	cf. Algoma ware/scalloped lip
44	LLW	Juntunen Drag-and-Jab	AD 1200–1300	untyped
45	LLW	Juntunen Drag-and-Jab	AD 1200–1300	untyped
46	ELW	Mackinac ware	AD 900–1000	Mackinac Phase/untyped
47	LLW	Juntunen ware	AD 1200–1300	untyped
48	LP	Iroquoian-style (untyped)	AD 1300–1500	untyped
49	ELW	Mackinac ware	AD 900–1000	Mackinac Phase/untyped
50	ELW	Mackinac Banded	AD 900–1000	Mackinac Banded
52	ELW	Mackinac Undecorated (mini)	AD 900–1000	untyped
53	ELW	Mackinac Punctate (mini)	AD 900–1000	Mackinac Punctate

Cloudman Pottery Data (*cont.*)

Vessel	Period	Final Type	Dates	Original Type (Branstner 1995)
54	LW	untyped (cf. O'Neil site cup)	AD 1200–1600	untyped
55	ELW	Mackinac ware	AD 900–1000	Mackinac Phase/untyped?
56	LP	Traverse Decorated v. Punctate	AD 1400–1450	cf. Algoma ware/scalloped lip
57	LLW	untyped (cf. Juntunen ware)	AD 1200–1400	untyped
58	LLW	untyped	AD 1200–1600	untyped
59	MW	Laurel Dentate Stamped (oblique)	AD 50–200	Laurel Oblique/Dentate Stamped
60	LLW	Juntunen ware	AD 1200–1300	untyped
61	ELW	Mackinac ware	AD 900–1000	Mackinac Phase/untyped
62	LP	Iroquoian-style (cf. Huron Incised)	AD 1300–1500	Huron Incised
63	ELW	untyped (mini)	AD 800–1000	untyped
64	LP	Iroquoian-style (cf. Ripley Plain)	AD 1300–1500	untyped
65	LW	untyped (brushed)	NA	untyped
67	LP	Traverse Decorated v. Punctate	AD 1400–1450	cf. Algoma ware/scalloped lip
68	LP	Iroquoian-style (untyped)	AD 1300–1500	untyped
69	LP	Traverse Plain v. Scalloped	AD 1400–1450	cf. Algoma ware/scalloped lip
70	LP	Iroquoian-style (cf. Huron Incised)	cal AD 1315–1427 (AMS)	Huron Incised
71	LLW	untyped	AD 1200–1600	untyped
72	ELW	Mackinac ware	AD 900–1000	Mackinac Phase/untyped
73	MLW	Bois Blanc ware	AD 1150–1200	untyped
74	LP	Iroquoian-style (cf. Huron Incised)	AD 1300–1500	Huron Incised
75	LP	Traverse Plain v. Scalloped (mini)	AD 1400–1450	cf. Algoma ware
76	ELW	Mackinac Undecorated	AD 900–1000	Mackinac Undecorated
77	LP	Iroquoian-style (untyped)	AD 1300–1500	untyped
78	ELW	Mackinac Banded	AD 900–1000	Mackinac Banded
79	LP	Iroquoian-style (cf. Huron Incised)	AD 1300–1500	Huron Incised
80	ELW	Mackinac Punctate	AD 900–1000	Mackinac Punctate

Cloudman Pottery Data (*cont.*)

Vessel	Period	Final Type	Dates	Original Type (Branstner 1995)
81	ELW	Blackduck Banded	AD 900–1000	Blackduck Banded
82	LP	Iroquoian-style (cf. Huron Incised)	AD 1300–1500	untyped
83	ELW	Mackinac ware (mini)	AD 900–1000	Mackinac Phase
85	LW	untyped	NA	untyped
86	LLW	Juntunen ware (cf. Plain)	AD 1200–1300	untyped
87	ELW	Mackinac ware	AD 900–1000	Mackinac Phase/untyped
88	ELW	Blackduck Banded	AD 900–1000	Blackduck Banded
89	LLW	Juntunen Drag-and-Jab	AD 1200–1300	untyped
90	LLW	untyped	NA	untyped
91	MW	Laurel Plain	AD 50–200	Laurel Plain
100	ELW	Mackinac Punctate	AD 900–1000	Mackinac Punctate
101	LLW	Juntunen ware	AD 1200–1300	jab-drag/cw object; untyped
102	LLW	Juntunen Drag-and-Jab	cal AD 1216–75 (AMS)	jab-drag; untyped
103	ELW	Mackinac Banded	cal AD 941–97 (AMS)	Mackinac Banded
104	LP	Traverse Plain v. Scalloped	AD 1100–1550/1600	cf. Algoma ware/scalloped lip
105	ELW	Mackinac Punctate	cal AD 974–1031 (AMS)	Mackinac Punctate
106	ELW	Mackinac ware (cf. Punctate)	AD 900–1000	Mackinac Phase/untyped/punctate
108	ELW	Mackinac Banded	AD 900–1000	Mackinac Banded
109	MW	Laurel Banked Linear Stamped	AD 50–200	Laurel Banked Linear Stamped
110	MW	Laurel Banked Linear Stamped	AD 50–200	Laurel Banked Linear Stamped
112	MW	Laurel Banked Linear Stamped	AD 50–200	Laurel Banked Linear Stamped
113	MW	Laurel Banked Linear Stamped	AD 50–200	Laurel Banked Linear Stamped/Incised?
114	MW	Laurel Banked Linear Stamped	AD 50–200	Laurel Banked Linear Stamped?
115	LLW	Juntunen ware	AD 1200–1300	Cross-hatched/Impressed lip
116	ELW	Mackinac ware (cf. Undecorated)	AD 900–1000	Mackinac Phase/undecorated
117	ELW	Blackduck Banded	AD 900–1000	similar to Laurel and Blackduck banded

164   Appendix A

Cloudman Pottery Data (*cont.*)

Vessel	Period	Final Type	Dates	Original Type (Branstner 1995)
118	MW/LW	untyped (cordmarked/undecorated)	AD 500–700?	Cordmarked/undecorated
120	ELW	Mackinac Banded	AD 900–1000	Mackinac Banded
121	ELW	Mackinac Banded	AD 900–1000	Mackinac Banded
122	ELW	Mackinac ware (cf. Punctate)	AD 900–1000	Mackinac Phase/punctate?
123	ELW	Mackinac Punctate	AD 900–1000	Mackinac Punctate?
124	ELW	Mackinac Banded	AD 900–1000	Mackinac Banded?
125	ELW	Mackinac ware (cf. Undecorated)	AD 900–1000	Mackinac Phase/undecorated?
126	ELW	Mackinac ware	AD 900–1000	Mackinac Phase/untyped
127	ELW	Mackinac ware	AD 900–1000	Mackinac Phase/untyped
128	ELW	Mackinac ware (cf. Undecorated)	AD 900–1000	Mackinac Phase/undecorated
129	ELW	Mackinac ware (cf. Undecorated)	AD 900–1000	Mackinac Phase/prob. Undecorated
130	ELW	Mackinac ware	AD 900–1000	Mackinac Phase/untyped
131	MW	North Bay Linear Stamp	AD 100–300	untyped
132	ELW	Mackinac ware (cf. Punctate)	AD 900–1000	Mackinac Phase/punctate?
133	LLW	Juntunen ware	AD 1200–1300	untyped
134	LLW	untyped	NA	untyped
135	LP	Iroquoian-style (cf. Ripley Plain)	AD 1300–1500	untyped
136	LP	Iroquoian-style (cf. Lawson ware)	AD 1300–1500	untyped
137	ELW	Mackinac ware (cf. Banded)	AD 900–1000	Mackinac Phase/banded
138	ELW	Mackinac ware (cf. Punctate)	AD 900–1000	Mackinac Phase/punctate
139	ELW	Mackinac Punctate	AD 900–1000	Mackinac Punctate
140	LLW	untyped	NA	untyped
141	ELW	Mackinac ware (cf. Punctate)	AD 900–1000	Mackinac Phase/M. Punctate?
142	MW	North Bay Cordmarked	AD 100–300	untyped
143	LLW	Juntunen Drag-and-Jab	AD 1200–1300	Juntunen Phase/jab-drag
144	MW	Laurel ware	AD 50–200	untyped

Cloudman Pottery Data (*cont.*)

Vessel	Period	Final Type	Dates	Original Type (Branstner 1995)
145	LP	Iroquoian-style	AD 1300–1500	Juntunen Phase/late?
146	LP	Iroquoian-style	cal AD 1282–1392 (AMS)	Juntunen Phase/late?/chevron
147	ELW	Mackinac ware (cf. Undecorated)	AD 900–1000	Mackinac Phase/undecorated
148	NA	untyped (late, peaked, smoothed, punctates)	NA	untyped
149	LP	Traverse ware	AD 1400–1450	cf. Algoma ware/scalloped lip
150	LP	Traverse Plain v. Scalloped	cal AD 1391–1433 (AMS)	untyped
151	LP	Iroquoian-style (cf. Ripley Plain)	AD 1300–1500	untyped
152	LW	cf. O'Neil Curvilinear	AD 1200–1600?	untyped
154	LP	Iroquoian-style (cf. Lawson ware)	AD 1300–1500	untyped
155	LP	Iroquoian-style (cf. Huron Incised)	AD 1300–1500	"imitation" Huron incised
156	LP	Iroquoian-style (cf. Huron Incised)	AD 1300–1500	Huron Incised
157	LP	Iroquoian-style (cf. Lawson Opposed)	AD 1300–1500	untyped/chevron; cf. Lalonde High Collar
158	MLW	Bois Blanc ware (cf. Braced Rim)	AD 1150–1200	untyped
159	LP	Iroquoian-style (cf. Huron Incised)	AD 1300–1500	"imitation" Huron incised
160	LP	Iroquoian-style (cf. Huron Incised)	AD 1300–1500	Huron Incised
161	LP	Iroquoian-style (cf. Huron Incised)	AD 1300–1500	Huron Incised
162	LP	Iroquoian-style (cf. Lawson Incised)	cal AD 1421–45 (AMS)	Huron Incised
163	LP	Iroquoian-style (cf. Huron Incised)	AD 1300–1500	Huron Incised
164	LP	Iroquoian-style (cf. Huron Incised)	AD 1300–1500	Huron Incised
165	LP	Traverse ware	AD 1400–1450	cf. Algoma ware/scalloped lip
166	LP	Iroquoian-style (cf. Huron Incised)	AD 1300–1500	similar to Huron Incised
167	LP	Iroquoian-style (cf. Huron Incised) (mini)	AD 1300–1500	Huron Incised
168	ELW	Mackinac Ware (cf. Undecorated)	AD 900–1000	Mackinac Phase/undecorated
169	MW	Laurel Pseudo-scallop Shell	AD 50–200	Laurel Pseudo-scallop Shell
170	MW/LW	Late Laurel (cf. Laurel Incised)	AD 500–700	cross-hatched/linear stamped/incised
171	MW/LW	untyped (vertical punctate)	AD 500–700?	vertical punctate

Appendix A 165

Cloudman Pottery Data (*cont.*)

Vessel	Period	Final Type	Dates	Original Type (Branstner 1995)
172	ELW	Mackinac Banded	AD 900–1000	Mackinac Banded
173	ELW	Mackinac Banded	AD 900–1000	Mackinac Banded
174	ELW	Mackinac ware (cf. Punctate)	AD 900–1000	Mackinac Phase/punctate
175	ELW	Mackinac Punctate	AD 900–1000	Mackinac Punctate
176	ELW	Mackinac ware (cf. Undecorated)	AD 900–1000	Mackinac Phase/undecorated?
177	LLW	untyped	AD 1200–1600	cf. Algoma ware/scalloped lip
178	LP	Iroquoian-style (cf. Huron Incised)	AD 1300–1500	Huron Incised
179	LP	Iroquoian-style (cf. Huron Incised)	cal AD 1439–1518 (AMS)	similar to Huron incised
180	LW	untyped	NA	untyped
181	ELW	Mackinac ware	AD 900–1000	Mackinac Phase/untyped
182	LP	Iroquoian-style (cf. Huron Incised) (mini)	AD 1300–1500	Huron Incised
183	LP	Iroquoian-style (cf. Huron Incised)	AD 1300–1500	Huron Incised
184	LW	untyped	NA	untyped
185	LP	Iroquoian-style (cf. Huron Incised)	AD 1300–1500	Huron Incised
186	LP	Iroquoian-style (cf. Huron Incised)	AD 1300–1500	Huron Incised
187	LP	Iroquoian-style (cf. Huron Incised)	AD 1300–1500	Huron Incised
188	LP	Iroquoian-style (untyped)	AD 1300–1500	untyped
189	ELW	Late Mackinac ware	AD 1000	pseudo-collared/exterior beveled lip
190	LP	Traverse Plain v. Scalloped	AD 1400–1450	cf. Algoma ware/poss. shell tempered
191	ELW	Mackinac Punctate	AD 900–1000	Mackinac????
192	ELW	Mackinac Banded	AD 900–1000	Mackinac Banded?
193	ELW	Blackduck Banded	cal AD 938–87 (AMS)	NA
194	ELW	Late Mackinac ware	AD 1000	Mackinac Banded?
195	NA	untyped, unknown time period	NA	NA
196/203	ELW	Mackinac Punctate	AD 900–1000	NA
197	MW/LW	untyped	AD 500?	NA

Cloudman Pottery Data (*cont.*)

Vessel	Period	Final Type	Dates	Original Type (Branstner 1995)
198	ELW	Mackinac ware (cf. Undecorated)	AD 900–1000	NA
199	ELW	cf. Bowerman Plain v. Cordmarked	AD 900	NA
200	LW	untyped (Generic Woodland, ELW/MLW)	NA	NA
201	MW	untyped (mini) (Hopewellian)	NA	LLW Mini Vessel?
202	ELW	Mackinac ware (mini)	AD 900–1000	? Mini Vessel?
204	LLW	Juntunen Linear Punctate	AD 1200–1300	NA
205	LLW	Juntunen Linear Punctate	cal AD 1220–77 (AMS)	NA
206	LLW	Juntunen Linear Punctate	AD 1200–1300	NA
207	LLW	untyped	AD 1200–1700	NA
208	LLW	untyped	AD 1200–1700	NA
209	LLW	Juntunen Linear Punctate	AD 1200–1300	NA
210	LLW	Juntunen ware	AD 1200–1300	NA
211	LLW	Juntunen Linear Punctate	AD 1200–1300	NA
212	LLW	Juntunen Linear Punctate	AD 1200–1300	NA
213	LLW	Juntunen ware (cf. Jab-and-Drag)	AD 1200–1300	NA
214	LLW	Juntunen ware (cf. Linear Punctate)	AD 1200–1300	NA
215	MLW	Bois Blanc ware	cal AD 1148–1224 (AMS)	NA
216	LLW	untyped	AD 1200–1600	NA
217	LLW	untyped	AD 1200–1600	NA
218	LLW	Juntunen ware (cf. Linear Punctate)	AD 1200–1300	NA

Cloudman Pottery Data (cont.)

Vessel	Ct.	Rim Radius (cm)	% Rim	Lip Thickness	Neck Thickness	Shoulder Thickness	Body Thickness	Temper 1	Temper 2	Temper 3	Exterior Sooting	Exterior Carbonization	Interior Carbonization	IC Type	Attrition
1	5	13	6	3.9	5.57	na	9.74	0.58	1.38	1.37	0	0	1	2	0
2	2	na	na	3.69	7.17	na	na	1.1	1.15	0.98	0	0	0	na	0
3	5	13	8	2.96	5.07	na	na	1.23	2.46	1.27	0	0	0	na	0
4	8	20	6	4.28	6.69	6.69	na	2.45	1.08	1.99	0	0	1	2	0
5	1	na	na	4.71	7.62	9.11	9.02	1.18	1.12	1.28	0	0	1	2	0
6	103	24	22	4.81	8.09	9.52	10.12	3.03	1.34	1.83	0	0	1	5	0
7	1	na	na	5.85	7.14	na	na	1.32	1.38	1.14	0	0	0	na	0
8	1	na	na	6.01	6.43	6.58	na	1.7	1.39	0.98	0	0	1	2	0
9	3	na	na	3.36	5.84	na	na	1.05	1.69	0.9	0	0	0	na	0
10	3	na	na	3.12	5.93	6.1	na	1.37	2.21	1.61	0	0	1	4	0
11	8	14	10	2.74	5.34	na	na	2.39	1.94	1.16	0	0	0	na	0
12	3	18	8	5.42	7.78	na	na	1.46	1.43	1.16	0	0	1	4	0
13	1	na	na	2.53	6.35	na	na	1.44	1.08	1.21	0	0	0	na	0
14	3	na	na	3.07	4.59	5.81	na	1.8	2.49	0.99	0	0	0	na	0
15	1	15	5	3.13	5.12	5.78	na	1.09	1.45	1.15	0	0	0	na	0
16	2	na	na	5.64	6.99	na	na	1.74	1.69	1.12	0	0	0	na	0
17	9	na	na	2.63	4.91	na	4.62	0.88	1.36	0.93	0	0	0	na	0
18	1	na	na	4.49	5.88	na	na	1.56	0.7	1.26	0	0	0	na	0
19	1	na	na	3.89	4.44	na	na	na	na	na	0	0	0	na	0
20	12	16	23	3.72	6.43	6.5	5.56	1.48	1.96	1.14	0	0	1	5	0
21	5	17	21	10.4	6.24	5.65	5.79	1.47	0.78	2.27	1	0	1	4	0
22	1	na	na	2.92	6.55	na	na	2.21	1.9	1.2	0	0	1	4	0
23	1	na	na	5.02	4.93	na	na	1.51	1.21	1.64	0	0	1	1	0
24	7	19	17	9.1	9.01	10.16	8.41	1.58	1.03	1.61	0	0	1	4	0
25	10	na	na	8.94	10.28	10.89	8.62	1.32	1.78	1.14	0	1	1	2	0

Appendix A   169

Cloudman Pottery Data (cont.)

Vessel	Ct.	Rim Radius (cm)	% Rim	Lip Thickness	Neck Thickness	Shoulder Thickness	Body Thickness	Temper 1	Temper 2	Temper 3	Exterior Sooting	Exterior Carbonization	Interior Carbonization	IC Type	Attrition
26	1	22	7	8.25	6.63	10.02	na	1.14	1.12	0.84	0	1	1	3	0
27	4	18	7	9.63	11.14	12.84	na	0.9	3.11	1.39	0	0	1	4	0
28	1	19	7	4.4	8.37	na	na	2.08	3.76	1.41	0	0	1	4	0
29	1	na	na	4.42	3.11	na	na	2.02	0.59	0.92	0	0	1	4	0
30	1	na	na	8.43	8.04	na	na	2.36	1.35	0.98	0	0	1	4	0
31	1	na	na	7.01	6.85	na	na	1.66	1.08	1.81	0	0	0	na	0
32	1	na	na	10.94	6.98	na	na	1.16	1.52	0.76	0	0	0	na	0
33	4	24	8	10.69	8.62	8.09	na	1.33	1.53	1.91	0	0	0	na	0
34	6	27	25	7.45	5.25	7.89	8.06	1.2	0.96	2.25	0	0	1	2	0
35	56	22	50	9.17	5.5	6.36	6.59	2.52	1.11	1.61	0	0	1	5	0
36	1	17	9	3.8	6.96	na	na	0.71	0.73	0.52	0	0	1	1	0
37	1	na	na	8.41	9.61	na	na	1.16	na	na	0	0	0	na	0
38	1	na	na	na	na	na	na	1.06	1.75	1.42	0	0	na	na	0
39	1	na	na	5.58	6.2	6.75	na	3.07	1.22	1.4	0	0	0	na	0
40/153	1	na	na	na	na	9.15	8.41	1.32	2.11	1.34	1	0	1	2	0
41	12	32	20	14.4	6.62	na	na	0.89	2.64	1.65	0	1	1	4	0
42	1	20	6	7.15	4.31	na	na	1.26	1.1	1.42	1	0	1	4	0
43	4	22	7	7.65	7.09	na	na	1.03	1.22	1.15	0	1	1	2	0
44	3	30	7	8.08	12.03	na	na	1.58	2.32	1.11	0	1	1	2	0
45	19	26	7	8.74	14.62	7.75	na	1.07	1.56	1.6	0	0	1	1	0
46	1	na	na	10.45	5.66	na	na	1.06	1.12	0.82	0	1	1	4	0
47	3	na	na	6.89	14.5	9.41	na	1.19	2.4	1.15	0	0	0	na	0
48	1	15	9	6.52	7.64	na	na	1.27	0.95	1.02	0	0	0	na	0
49	1	14	8	8.17	3.83	4.3	na	1.29	0.62	1.08	0	0	0	na	0
50	3	25	21	11.29	6.06	5.44	na	1.4	1.77	0.82	1	0	1	2	0

170   Appendix A

Cloudman Pottery Data (cont.)

Vessel	Ct.	Rim Radius (cm)	% Rim	Lip Thickness	Neck Thickness	Shoulder Thickness	Body Thickness	Temper 1	Temper 2	Temper 3	Exterior Sooting	Exterior Carbonization	Interior Carbonization	IC Type	Attrition
52	1	5	25	3.91	3.89	4.93	4.14	na	na	na	0	0	0	na	0
53	2	9	25	5.84	6.39	3.21	na	2.17	1.4	1.49	0	0	1	1	0
54	9	8	50	5.92	5.22	7.13	5.32	0.64	1.22	0.63	1	0	0	na	0
55	105	30	21	10.27	7.67	na	2.8	1.01	1.24	1.95	0	0	0	na	0
56	1	na	na	na	na	na	na	0.97	1.35	1.13	0	0	na	na	na
57	2	na	na	na	6.85	6.49	9.9	1.11	1.36	1.74	0	0	1	5	0
58	1	na	na	7.14	8.97	na	na	1.43	1.07	1.02	0	0	0	na	0
59	2	na	na	3.39	4.55	na	na	0.91	0.62	na	0	0	1	5	0
60	2	na	na	5.15	4.22	na	na	0.75	0.91	1.53	0	0	0	na	0
61	1	na	na	5.84	5.67	na	na	2.06	1.62	na	0	0	0	na	0
62	3	na	na	na	na	na	na	1.64	1.51	1.35	0	0	0	na	0
63	1	8	10	9.38	6.76	na	na	na	na	na	0	0	0	na	0
64	2	28	8	6.33	6	5.03	0	1.86	0.99	1.35	0	0	1	1	0
65	14	15	8	9.36	11.46	11.29	na	2.02	0.94	1.35	0	0	0	na	0
67	1	na	na	8.05	6.09	na	na	0.96	1.83	0.82	0	0	0	na	0
68	1	na	na	7.04	7.62	na	na	2.16	1.39	na	0	0	0	na	0
69	1	na	na	7.76	7.77	na	na	1.2	3.37	1.5	0	0	0	na	0
70	7	na	na	8.34	7.77	6.16	na	1.58	1.26	0.76	1	0	1	3	0
71	1	na	na	7.41	5.56	na	na	1.23	1.3	1.16	0	0	0	na	0
72	1	16	5	9.35	5.46	na	na	1.38	0.99	1.15	0	0	0	na	0
73	1	na	na	4.88	8.92	na	na	1.15	1.87	2.07	0	0	1	4	0
74	5	25	7	8.43	8.86	na	na	1.21	1.83	1.18	0	0	1	3	0
75	7	8	20	5.29	5.48	3.54	na	0.86	1.35	1.02	0	1	1	3	0
76	31	24	25	8.8	8.06	6.02	7.72	1.99	0.83	2.62	1	1	1	3	0
77	8	na	na	9.8	8.93	na	11.37	1.91	1.22	1.01	1	0	1	1	0

Cloudman Pottery Data (*cont.*)

Vessel	Ct.	Rim Radius (cm)	% Rim	Lip Thickness	Neck Thickness	Shoulder Thickness	Body Thickness	Temper 1	Temper 2	Temper 3	Exterior Sooting	Exterior Carbonization	Interior Carbonization	IC Type	Attrition
78	34	24	6	8.4	7.04	6.98	8.46	3.06	1.46	2.15	0	0	0	na	0
79	1	12	5	3.45	5.02	na	na	0.88	0.76	na	0	0	0	na	0
80	22	25	24	14.03	6.01	5.93	na	3.7	1.8	1.3	1	0	1	5	0
81	1	28	8	11.15	7.87	na	na	0.96	0.85	0.79	0	1	1	4	0
82	1	28	5	5.33	7.03	0	0	0.85	1.45	1.26	0	0	1	4	0
83	12	9	20	5.03	4.38	3.49	na	na	na	na	0	0	1	1	0
85	1	na	na	5.75	8.98	7.89	na	0.74	1.06	1.02	0	0	1	1	0
86	2	20	16	8	9.67	na	na	1.46	1	1.48	1	0	1	4	0
87	1	na	na	7.63	9.04	na	na	3.18	0.89	2.15	1	0	0	na	0
88	1	30	6	11.17	6.77	na	4.36	2.62	1.42	1.84	1	1	1	5	0
89	1	na	na	7.07	7.63	na	na	1.13	0.82	1.01	0	0	1	4	0
90	1	na	na	6.53	5.84	na	na	1.37	0.89	0.84	0	0	0	4	0
91	1	na	na	3.48	5.1	na	na	1.17	1.54	1.74	0	0	0	na	0
100	88	19	9	8.41	9.14	10.89	na	3.02	0.66	1.53	1	0	0	na	0
101	2	na	na	na	9.86	na	na	1.09	2.72	1.42	0	0	1	2	0
102	5	na	na	8.81	7.2	na	na	1.9	1.46	1.93	0	1	1	4	0
103	6	14	10	9.95	8.06	na	na	1.85	1.22	0.78	0	0	1	4	0
104	1	13	10	5.88	5.18	7.1	na	1.04	0.9	1.58	0	0	1	1	0
105	4	19	20	6.47	3.83	3.57	na	1.58	1.33	1.12	1	1	1	3	0
106	1	na	na	8.16	6.86	8.63	na	1.25	2.02	1.21	0	0	0	na	0
108	6	na	na	na	6.3	6.05	na	2.42	1.75	0.96	0	0	0	na	0
109	6	25	10	4.55	4.5	4.85	5.33	2.18	1.75	1.82	0	0	1	2	0
110	1	>18	na	5.49	6.36	na	na	1.5	1.4	1.19	0	0	0	na	0
112	2	na	na	5.06	4.45	na	na	0.77	1.15	1.82	0	1	1	1	0
113	1	na	na	4.42	5.84	na	na	2.06	1.42	1.5	0	0	0	na	0

Appendix A   171

Cloudman Pottery Data (cont.)

Vessel	Ct.	Rim Radius (cm)	% Rim	Lip Thickness	Neck Thickness	Shoulder Thickness	Body Thickness	Temper 1	Temper 2	Temper 3	Exterior Sooting	Exterior Carbonization	Interior Carbonization	IC Type	Attrition
114	1	na	na	4.82	6.21	na	na	1.96	0.95	1.16	0	1	1	5	0
115	1	na	na	7.22	9.79	na	na	2.48	1.63	1.41	0	0	0	na	0
116	4	14	9	6.3	4.29	na	na	2.32	1.03	2.01	1	0	1	5	0
117	2	12	7	9.03	5.01	5.02	na	1.37	1.35	1.24	0	0	0	na	0
118	3	na	na	4.51	4.23	na	na	1.09	1.68	1.02	0	1	1	4	0
120	3	20	19	8.02	7.79	5.53	na	2.32	1.05	1.45	0	0	1	1	0
121	19	18	20	7.14	6.84	5.49	na	5.58	2.92	1.97	0	0	0	na	0
122	5	25	7	9.58	7.14	na	na	1.18	0.82	0.88	0	1	1	1	0
123	1	25	5	9.53	5.68	na	na	1.9	1.14	1.18	0	0	1	5	0
124	1	na	na	10.64	6.44	na	na	5.86	1.41	0.98	1	1	1	4	0
125	4	13	6	5.28	5.38	na	na	1.28	1.02	1.9	0	0	0	na	0
126	3	25	6	10.42	7.62	7.48	na	1.52	1.72	1.68	0	0	0	na	0
127	2	na	na	8.58	6.24	na	na	2.63	2.14	1.18	0	0	0	na	0
128	11	24	7	9.25	4.29	na	na	1.87	1.1	1.4	0	0	1	4	0
129	3	na	na	8.82	4.08	na	na	0.95	1.39	1.31	0	0	0	na	0
130	1	26	5	10.19	6.08	na	na	2.45	3	1.04	0	0	0	na	0
131	19	25	5	7.6	7.79	na	na	1.33	0.87	1.64	0	0	1	5	0
132	2	16	10	8.71	6.31	na	na	1.33	1.05	1.31	0	0	1	4	0
133	23	na	na	9.11	8.31	na	na	1.81	2.25	1.94	0	0	1	4	0
134	1	na	na	9.89	6.67	na	na	1.1	1.17	na	0	0	1	5	0
135	2	na	na	5.35	7.39	na	na	1.22	1.13	0.74	0	0	0	na	0
136	1	na	na	7.3	6.68	na	na	1.08	1.1	1.71	0	0	1	4	0
137	2	na	na	6.62	7.49	na	na	1.47	1.5	1.28	0	0	0	na	0
138	1	20	9	10.63	9.18	na	na	1.69	3.66	1.35	0	0	0	na	0
139	6	na	na	9.24	7.45	na	na	1.16	1.01	1.2	0	0	1	4	0
140	1	na	na	5.81	6.07	na	na	1.34	3.43	1.48	0	0	0	na	0

Appendix A   173

Cloudman Pottery Data (cont.)

Vessel	Ct.	Rim Radius (cm)	% Rim	Lip Thickness	Neck Thickness	Shoulder Thickness	Body Thickness	Temper 1	Temper 2	Temper 3	Exterior Sooting	Exterior Carbonization	Interior Carbonization	IC Type	Attrition
141	1	19	6	9.65	7.52	6.56	na	2.55	3.15	1.36	0	0	0	na	0
142	5	20	9	9.16	7.36	6.75	na	1.36	3.4	1.41	0	0	0	na	0
143	1	na	na	na	na	na	na	1.37	1.81	1.24	0	0	na	na	na
144	1	na	na	5.96	7.28	na	na	1.51	1.08	1.26	0	0	0	na	0
145	3	17	6	8.13	7.76	na	na	0.86	1.77	1.37	0	1	1	4	0
146	4	18	16	8.52	7.21	5.92	na	1.76	0.94	1.8	0	1	1	3	0
147	3	17	17	5.75	4.02	na	na	1.37	1.45	1.23	0	1	1	1	0
148	1	17	16	8.06	6.46	na	na	1.38	1.23	1.22	0	0	0	na	0
149	1	na	na	7.92	5.83	na	na	1.32	1.41	1	0	1	1	4	0
150	21	21	15	6.56	6.7	5.69	3.89	1.28	0.87	1.34	0	1	1	3	0
151	1	na	na	8.15	7.57	na	na	2.3	1.19	1.05	1	0	0	na	0
152	2	na	na	7.35	7.95	na	na	1.32	1.25	1.58	0	0	1	1	0
154	2	na	na	na	na	na	na	0.89	0.75	0.78	0	0	1	2	0
155	3	18	10	13.06	8.63	0.19	na	1.59	1.07	0.71	0	0	0	na	0
156	3	na	na	6.51	8.48	na	na	2.34	1.54	1.27	0	0	0	na	0
157	1	na	na	na	na	na	na	1.15	0.97	0.82	0	0	na	na	0
158	1	na	na	5.95	8.17	0	0	0.79	1.28	1.1	0	0	0	4	0
159	1	na	na	6.62	8.57	na	na	1.3	2.02	0.66	0	0	1	4	0
160	3	na	na	7.1	8.36	na	na	1.88	0.79	1.42	0	0	1	4	0
161	2	na	na	5.26	6.92	na	na	1.23	1.11	0.8	0	1	1	3	0
162	5	27	20	6.8	7.63	7.63	6.66	1.45	1.72	1.52	0	1	1	4	0
163	1	na	na	7.39	10.01	na	na	1.56	1.3	1.1	0	0	1	4	0
164	14	21	10	7.62	8.9	na	na	2.17	1.8	1	0	0	0	na	0
165	1	na	na	4.52	5.86	7.73	na	1.61	1.91	1.12	0	0	1	5	0
166	48	28	20	6.22	6.6	7.51	10.03	1.65	1.53	1.11	0	1	1	1	0
167	1	na	na	5.74	6.61	na	na	na	na	na	0	1	1	1	0

174 Appendix A

Cloudman Pottery Data (cont.)

Vessel	Ct.	Rim Radius (cm)	% Rim	Lip Thickness	Neck Thickness	Shoulder Thickness	Body Thickness	Temper 1	Temper 2	Temper 3	Exterior Sooting	Exterior Carbonization	Interior Carbonization	IC Type	Attrition
168	1	na	na	5.45	5.12	na	na	4.11	1.56	1.04	0	0	0	na	0
169	1	14	5	3.68	5.15	na	na	1.19	1.27	1.17	0	0	0	na	0
170	8	15	5	3.49	4.12	5.55	na	1.37	0.99	1.73	0	0	0	na	0
171	1	na	na	4.34	5.58	na	na	1.23	0.93	1.42	0	0	0	na	0
172	2	26	7	10.31	7.97	6.72	na	1.43	1.36	1.26	1	0	1	4	0
173	12	17	23	10.49	8.01	8.45	na	1.43	2.15	1.16	1	1	1	1	0
174	6	na	na	3.92	4.06	7.47	na	1.18	1.46	0.68	0	1	1	1	0
175	19	na	na	9.52	3.44	3.08	6.38	1.45	1.25	1.73	0	0	1	1	0
176	1	na	na	8.43	4.26	na	na	1.94	1.16	1.74	0	0	1	4	0
177	2	na	na	7.82	6.56	na	na	1.16	0.74	1.28	0	0	1	4	0
178	1	na	na	5.83	5.29	na	na	1.06	0.89	1.03	0	1	1	4	0
179	1	25	7	8.06	9.2	na	na	1.13	0.9	1.64	0	1	1	5	0
180	1	12	5	5.57	3.93	na	na	1.45	0.79	0.69	0	0	0	na	0
181	2	na	na	10.34	10.13	na	na	0.77	1.6	2.22	0	0	0	na	0
182	1	7	14	4.19	6.69	5.7	na	0.74	na	na	0	0	0	na	0
183	2	na	na	6.6	12.56	na	na	1.04	0.64	1.13	0	0	0	na	0
184	1	na	na	8.89	5.71	na	na	1.27	1.01	1.24	0	0	0	na	0
185	1	na	na	9.23	7.97	na	na	1.35	1.58	0.69	0	0	0	na	0
186	1	na	na	na	na	na	na	1.29	0.76	0.87	0	0	0	na	0
187	1	na	na	6.59	na	na	na	1.57	1.47	1.1	0	0	0	na	0
188	1	na	na	na	5.25	na	na	0.8	0.65	1.03	1	0	0	na	0
189	1	na	na	3.38	4.07	na	na	2.77	1.31	1.26	0	0	0	na	0
190	1	na	na	5.31	na	na	na	1.2	na	na	0	0	0	na	0
191	9	26	23	12.44	7.91	7.48	na	1.89	1.75	1.85	0	1	1	2	0
192	114	16	21	10.49	7.7	6.35	5.27	1.32	1.81	0.77	1	0	1	3	0
193	82	20	22	9.4	6.81	6.03	6.14	0.84	1.21	1.93	1	0	1	3	0

Cloudman Pottery Data (*cont.*)

Vessel	Ct.	Rim Radius (cm)	% Rim	Lip Thickness	Neck Thickness	Shoulder Thickness	Body Thickness	Temper 1	Temper 2	Temper 3	Exterior Sooting	Exterior Carbonization	Interior Carbonization	IC Type	Attrition
194	1	19	7	5.01	4.74	na	na	1.02	1.05	0.81	0	0	1	4	0
195	1	na	na	na	na	na	na	1.98	0.68	1.45	0	0	na	na	0
196/203	2	na	na	10.75	8.75	na	na	2.21	0.87	1.1	0	0	1	4	0
197	3	na	na	8.89	6.98	na	na	0.98	2	1.48	0	0	1	5	0
198	9	26	6	7.63	6.83	7.23	na	2.18	1.12	1.73	0	0	0	na	0
199	13	na	na	6.91	4.94	na	na	1.51	1.3	1.03	0	0	0	na	0
200	36	10	18	6.03	6.64	9.43	7.79	3.47	3.13	2.64	0	0	1	2	0
201	3	5	20	5.76	5.57	6.74	5.15	0.95	na	na	0	0	0	na	0
202	4	6	27	4.15	4.52	2.78	3.71	na	na	na	0	0	1	2	0
204	19	26	19	8.91	5.98	4.15	4.2	1.38	1.9	1.07	0	0	1	3	0
205	2	16	20	7.64	8.55	5.19	na	1.05	1.58	1.17	0	1	0	na	0
206	4	30	6	7.77	8.35	na	na	1.67	0.78	1.37	0	0	0	na	0
207	1	na	na	7.01	6.88	na	na	1.2	0.87	1.27	0	0	1	1	0
208	1	na	na	3.98	6.89	5.43	na	1.52	0.82	1.29	0	0	0	na	0
209	1	13	8	6.21	9.12	11.23	na	1.29	1.39	1.44	0	0	0	na	0
210	1	na	na	4.4	6.49	9.15	na	1.45	0.7	0.86	0	0	0	na	0
211	1	na	na	6.9	8.35	5.65	na	3.18	0.81	1.16	0	0	1	5	0
212	1	na	na	8.47	8.44	na	na	1.18	1.31	1.28	0	1	1	1	0
213	1	na	na	5.47	6.56	7.67	na	1.22	0.67	0.88	0	0	0	na	0
214	7	8	10	7.86	8.73	7.46	na	1.21	0.83	0.9	0	0	1	4	0
215	3	na	na	6.45	8.65	11.26	na	1.19	1.51	1.13	0	1	1	1	0
216	2	30	5	7.3	8.61	8.37	6.59	1.47	1.31	1.33	0	0	0	na	0
217	1	na	na	9.72	6.04	na	na	0.82	1.24	0.85	0	0	0	na	0
218	1	na	na	8.03	6.58	na	na	2	1	1.64	0	1	1	4	0

APPENDIX B

Cloudman Pottery Vessels
Sampled for Microbotanical, Stable Isotope,
and Lipid Residue Analyses

Cloudman Pottery Vessels Sampled for Microbotanical, Stable Isotope, and Lipid Residue Analyses

Vessel	Period	Type	Microbotanical	Stable Isotope	Lipids	AMS
1	MW	Laurel Pseudo-scallop Shell	X	X	X	X
4	MW	Laurel Dentate Stamped	X	X		X
5	MW	Laurel Pseudo-scallop Shell	X	X		
6	MW	Laurel Dentate Rocker Stamped	X	X	X	
10	MW	Laurel Pseudo-scallop Shell	X	X		
12	MW	Laurel Dentate Stamped	X	X		
20	MW	Laurel Dentate Stamped			X	
22	MW	Laurel Pseudo-scallop Shell	X	X		
23	MW	Laurel Banked Linear Stamped	X	X		
28	MW	Laurel Pseudo-scallop Shell	X	X		
109	MW	Laurel Banked Linear Stamped	X	X	X	
112	MW	Laurel Banked Linear Stamped	X	X		
114	MW	Laurel Banked Linear Stamped	X			
131	MW	North Bay Linear Stamp			X	
35	MW/LW	Late Laurel (cross-hatched)	X	X	X	

Cloudman Pottery Vessels Sampled for Microbotanical, Stable Isotope, and Lipid Residue Analyses (*cont.*)

Vessel	Period	Type	Microbotanical	Stable Isotope	Lipids	AMS
118	MW/LW	Untyped	X			
8	ELW	Mackinac ware	X	X		
34	ELW	Mackinac ware	X	X	X	
41	ELW	Mackinac ware	X	X		
46	ELW	Mackinac ware	X			
50	ELW	Mackinac Banded	X	X		
55	ELW	Mackinac ware			X	
76	ELW	Mackinac Undecorated	X	X	X	
80	ELW	Mackinac Punctate	X	X	X	
81	ELW	Blackduck Banded	X	X		
88	ELW	Blackduck Banded	X	X		
100	ELW	Mackinac Punctate		X	X	
103	ELW	Mackinac Banded	X	X		X
105	ELW	Mackinac Punctate	X	X		X

Cloudman Pottery Vessels Sampled for Microbotanical, Stable Isotope, and Lipid Residue Analyses (*cont.*)

Vessel	Period	Type	Microbotanical	Stable Isotope	Lipids	AMS
120	ELW	Mackinac Banded	X	X		
122	ELW	Mackinac ware (cf. Punctate)	X	X		
124	ELW	Mackinac Banded	X	X		
132	ELW	Mackinac ware (cf. Punctate)	X	X		
173	ELW	Mackinac Banded	X	X	X	
174	ELW	Mackinac ware (cf. Punctate)	X	X		
175	ELW	Mackinac Punctate	X	X	X	
191	ELW	Mackinac Punctate		X	X	
193	ELW	Blackduck Banded	X	X	X	X
42	MLW	Bois Blanc ware	X	X		
215	MLW	Bois Blanc ware	X	X	X	X
24	LLW	"proto-Juntunen" ware (plain)			X	
25	LLW	Juntunen ware	X	X	X	
26	LLW	Juntunen ware	X	X		

Cloudman Pottery Vessels Sampled for Microbotanical, Stable Isotope, and Lipid Residue Analyses (cont.)

Vessel	Period	Type	Microbotanical	Stable Isotope	Lipids	AMS
101	LLW	Juntunen ware	X	X	X	
102	LLW	Juntunen Drag-and-Jab	X	X		X
152	LLW	Juntunen ware	X	X		
204	LLW	Juntunen Linear Punctate	X	X	X	
205	LLW	Juntunen Linear Punctate	X	X		X
213	LLW	Juntunen ware	X			
216	LLW	Untyped			X	
36	LP	Iroquoian-style	X	X		
40/153	LP	Iroquoian-style	X	X		
43	LP	Traverse Decorated v. Punctate	X	X	X	
70	LP	Iroquoian-style	X	X	X	X
75	LP	Traverse Plain v. Scalloped (mini)	X	X	X	
77	LP	Iroquoian-style			X	
146	LP	Iroquoian-style	X	X	X	X

Appendix B   181

Cloudman Pottery Vessels Sampled for Microbotanical, Stable Isotope, and Lipid Residue Analyses (*cont.*)

Vessel	Period	Type	Microbotanical	Stable Isotope	Lipids	AMS
150	LP	Traverse Plain v. Scalloped	X	X	X	X
162	LP	Iroquoian-style	X	X	X	X
164	LP	Iroquoian-style			X	
166	LP	Iroquoian-style			X	
179	LP	Iroquoian-style	X	X		X
Total			52	50	30	13

APPENDIX C

Selected Vessels from the Cloudman Pottery Assemblage

MIDDLE WOODLAND VESSELS

C1. Vessel 5, Laurel Pseudo-scallop Shell.

C2. Vessel 20, Laurel Dentate Stamped (oblique).

C3. Vessel 109, Laurel Banked Linear Stamped.

C4. Vessel 6, Laurel Dentate Rocker Stamped.

C5. Vessel 131, North Bay Linear Stamped.

MIDDLE WOODLAND/LATE WOODLAND TRANSITION VESSELS

C6. Vessel 35, Late Laurel (cf. Laurel Incised or Mackinac Banded).

C7. Vessel 33, untyped (incipient Blackduck?).

EARLY LATE WOODLAND VESSELS

C8. Vessel 80, Mackinac Punctate.

C9. Vessel 191, Mackinac Punctate.

C10. Vessel 50, Mackinac Banded.

C11. Vessel 120, Mackinac Banded.

C12. Vessel 76, Mackinac Undecorated.

C13. Vessel 55, Mackinac ware.

C14. Vessel 81, Blackduck Banded.

C15. Vessel 88, Blackduck Banded.

C16. Vessel 199, cf. Bowerman Plain v. Cordmarked.

EARLY LATE/MIDDLE LATE WOODLAND TRANSITION AND MIDDLE LATE WOODLAND VESSELS

C17. Vessel 200, untyped (ELW/MLW Transition).

C18. Vessel 42, Bois Blanc ware.

LATE LATE WOODLAND VESSELS

C19. Vessel 24, "Proto-Juntunen" ware (plain).

C20. Vessel 102, Juntunen Drag-and-Jab.

C21. Vessel 204, Juntunen Linear Punctate.

C22. Vessel 25, Juntunen ware.

Appendix C 187

LATE PRECONTACT VESSELS

C23. Vessel 43, Traverse Decorated v. Punctate.

C24. Vessel 150, Traverse Plain v. Scalloped.

C25. Vessel 162, Iroquoian-style (cf. Lawson Incised).

C26. Vessel 64, Iroquoian-style (cf. Ripley Plain).

C27. Vessel 74, Iroquoian-style (cf. Huron Incised).

C28. Vessel 156, Iroquoian-style (cf. Huron Incised).

C29. Vessel 166, Iroquoian-style (cf. Huron Incised).

MINIATURE VESSELS

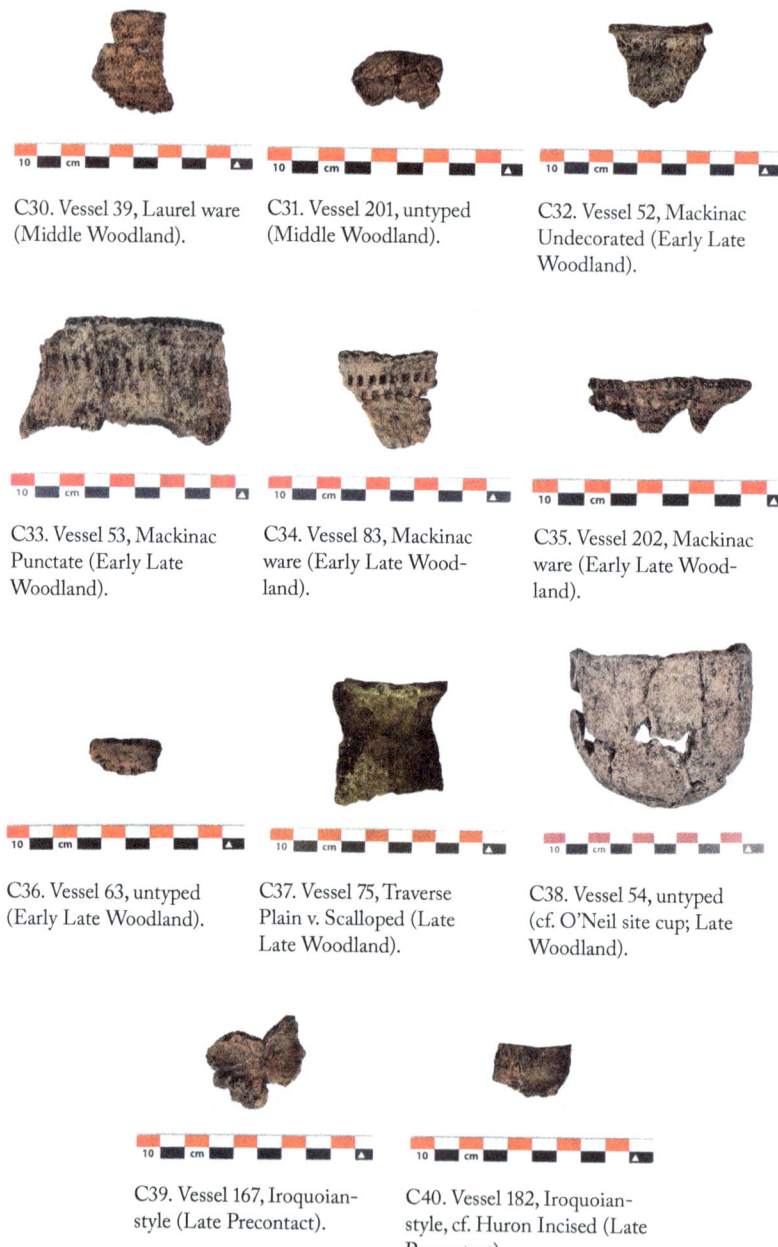

C30. Vessel 39, Laurel ware (Middle Woodland).

C31. Vessel 201, untyped (Middle Woodland).

C32. Vessel 52, Mackinac Undecorated (Early Late Woodland).

C33. Vessel 53, Mackinac Punctate (Early Late Woodland).

C34. Vessel 83, Mackinac ware (Early Late Woodland).

C35. Vessel 202, Mackinac ware (Early Late Woodland).

C36. Vessel 63, untyped (Early Late Woodland).

C37. Vessel 75, Traverse Plain v. Scalloped (Late Late Woodland).

C38. Vessel 54, untyped (cf. O'Neil site cup; Late Woodland).

C39. Vessel 167, Iroquoian-style (Late Precontact).

C40. Vessel 182, Iroquoian-style, cf. Huron Incised (Late Precontact).

REFERENCES

Abrams, E. M. 2009. "Hopewell Archaeology: A View from the Northern Woodlands." *Journal of Archaeological Research* 12 (2): 169–204.

Albert, Dennis A., Shirley R. Denton, and Burton V. Barnes. 1986. *Regional Landscape Ecosystems of Michigan*. Ann Arbor: School of Natural Resources, University of Michigan.

Albert, Rebecca K., Susan M. Kooiman, and William A. Lovis. 2018. "Temporal Analysis of Plant Diet at the Cloudman Site." Poster presented at the Michigan State University Undergraduate Research and Arts Forum, East Lansing.

Albert, Rebecca, Susan M. Kooiman, Caitlin Clark, and William A. Lovis. 2018. "Earliest Microbotanical Evidence for Maize in the Northern Lake Michigan Basin." *American Antiquity* 83 (2): 345–55.

Ambrose, Stanley H. 1987. "Chemical and Isotopic Techniques of Diet Reconstruction in Eastern North America." In *Emergent Horticultural Economies of the Eastern Woodlands*, edited by William F. Keegan, 88–107. Center for Archaeological Investigations, Occasional Paper No. 7. Carbondale: Southern Illinois University.

Anderson, David G., and Robert C. Mainfort Jr. 2002. "An Introduction to Woodland Archaeology in the Southeast." In *The Woodland Southeast*, edited by D. G. Anderson and R. C. Mainfort Jr., 1–19. Tuscaloosa: University of Alabama Press.

Appadurai, Arjun. 1981. "Gastro-Politics in Hindu South Asia." *American Ethnologist* 8 (3): 494–511.

Aronson, Meredith, James M. Skibo, and Miriam T. Stark. 1994. "Production and Use Technologies in Kalinga Pottery." In *Kalinga Ethnoarchaeology: Expanding Archaeological Method and Theory*, edited by William A. Longacre and James M. Skibo, 83–112. Washington, DC: Smithsonian Institution.

Arzigian, Constance. 2000. "Middle Woodland and Oneota Contexts for Wild Rice Exploitation in Southwestern Wisconsin." *Midcontinental Journal of Archaeology* 25: 245–68.

Atalay, Sonya, and Christine A. Hastorf. 2006. "Food, Meals, and Daily Activities: Food Habitus at Neolithic Catalhoyuk." *American Antiquity* 71 (2): 283–319.

Bamann, Susan, Robert Kuhn, James Molnar, and Dean Snow. 1992. "Iroquoian Archaeology." *Annual Review of Anthropology* 21: 435–60.

Baraga, Frederick. 1976. *Chippewa Indians, as Recorded by Rev. Frederick Baraga in 1847*. New York: Studia Slovenica.

Barrett, James H., Roelf P. Beukens, and Rebecca A. Nicholson. 2001. "Diet and Ethnicity during the Viking Colonization of Northern Scotland: Evidence from Fish Bones and Stable Carbon Isotopes." *Antiquity* 75: 145–54.

Bawaya, Michael. 2007. "Curation in Crisis." *Science* 317 (5841): 1025–26.

Benz, Charmaine M., and R. Todd Williamson, eds. 2005. *Diba Jimooyung, Telling Our Story: A History of the Saginaw Ojibwe Anishinabek*. Mt. Pleasant, MI: Saginaw Chippewa Indian Tribe of Michigan and the Ziibiwing Cultural Society.

Beoku-Betts, Josephine. 1995. "We Got Our Way of Cooking Things: Women, Food, and Preservation of Cultural Identity among the Gullah." *Gender and Society* 9 (5): 535–55.

Bergman, Ingela, Lars Ostlund, and Olle Zackrisson. 2004. "The Use of Plants as Regular Food in Ancient Subarctic Economies: A Case Study Based on Sami Use of Scots Pine Innerbark." *Arctic Anthropology* 41 (1): 1–13.

Bianchi, Thomas. 1974. "Description and Analysis of the Prehistoric Ceramic Materials Recovered on the Winter Site." Master's thesis, Western Michigan University, Kalamazoo.

Binford, Lewis R. 1968. "Post-Pleistocene Adaptations." In *New Perspectives in Archaeology*, edited by Sally Binford and Lewis R. Binford, 313–41. Chicago: Aldine.

———. 1980. "Willow Smoke and Dogs' Tails: Hunter-Gatherer Settlement Systems and Archaeological Site Formations." *American Antiquity* 45: 4–20.

Birch, Jennifer, and Ronald F. Williamson. 2012. *The Mantle Site: An Archaeological History of an Ancestral Wendat Community*. New York: AltaMira.

Blewett, William L., David P. Lusch, and Randall Schaetzl. 2009. "The Physical Landscape: A Glacial Legacy." In *Michigan Geography and Geology*, edited by R. Schaetzl, J. Darden, and Danita Brandt, 249–73. New York: Custom Publishing.

Blitz, John H. 1993. "Big Pots for Big Shots: Feasting and Storage in a Mississippian Community." *American Antiquity* 58 (1): 80–96.

Boyd, M., and C. Surette. 2010. "Northernmost Precontact Maize in North America." *American Antiquity* 75 (1): 117–33.

Boyd, M., C. Surette, A. Lints, and S. Hamilton. 2014. "Wild Rice (*Zizania* spp.), the Three Sisters, and the Woodland Tradition in Western and Central Canada." *Midwest Archaeological Conference Inc. Occasional Papers* 1: 7–32.

Boyd, M., C. Surette, J. Surette, I. Therriault, and S. Hamilton. 2013. "Holocene Paleoecology of a Wild Rice (*Zizania* sp.) Lake in Northwestern Ontario, Canada." *Journal of Paleolimnology* 50: 365–77.

Brandt, Kari L. 1996. "The Effects of Early Agriculture on Native North American Populations: Evidence from the Teeth and Skeleton." PhD dissertation, University of Michigan, Ann Arbor.

Branstner, Christine N. 1992. "National Register of Historic Places Archaeological Testing of 20CH6: A Multicomponent Site on Drummond Island, Michigan, 1991 Investigations." Report prepared for the Bureau of History, Michigan Department of State, Lansing.

———. 1995. "Archaeological Investigations at the Cloudman Site (20CH6): A Multicomponent Native American Occupation on Drummond Island, Michigan, 1992 and 1994 Excavations." Report prepared for Consortium of Archaeological Research, Department of Anthropology, Michigan State University, East Lansing.

Brashler, Janet G., Elizabeth B. Garland, Margaret B. Holman, William A. Lovis, and Susan R. Martin. 2000. "Adaptive Strategies and Socioeconomic Systems in Northern Great Lakes Riverine Environments: The Late Woodland of Michigan." In *Late Woodland Societies: Tradition and Transformation across the Midcontinent*, edited by T. E. Emerson, D. L. McElrath, and A. C. Fortier, 543–79. Lincoln: University of Nebraska Press.

Braun, David P. 1983. "Pots as Tools." In *Archaeological Hammers and Theories*, edited by J. A. Moore and A. S. Keene, 107–34. New York: Academic Press.

Braun, David P., and Stephen Plog. 1982. "Evolution of 'Tribal' Social Networks: Theory and Prehistoric North American Evidence." *American Antiquity* 47 (3): 504–25.

Braun, Gregory V. 2015. "Ritual, Materiality, and Memory in an Iroquoian Village." PhD dissertation, University of Toronto.

Bronitsky, Gordon, and Robert Hamer. 1986. "Experiments in Ceramic Technology: The Effects of Various Tempering Materials on Impact and Thermal-Shock Resistance." *American Antiquity* 51 (1): 89–101.

Brose, David S. 1970. *The Archaeology of Summer Island: Changing Settlement Systems in Northern Lake Michigan*. Anthropological Papers No. 41. Ann Arbor: Museum of Anthropology, University of Michigan.

Brose, David S., and Michael J. Hambacher. 1999. "The Middle Woodland in Northern Michigan." In *Retrieving Michigan's Buried Past: The Archaeology of the Great Lakes State*, edited by John R. Halsey, 173–92. Bloomfield Hills, MI: Cranbrook Institute of Science.

Burchill, Alexandra, and Matthew J. Boyd. 2015. "Analysis and Dietary Implications of Plant Microfossils on Middle Woodland Food Residues, Northern Minnesota." *Minnesota Archaeologist* 74: 107–21.

Carroll, Jon W. 2013. "Simulating Springwells: A Complex Systems Approach toward Understanding Late Prehistoric Social Interaction in the Great Lakes Region of North America." PhD dissertation, Michigan State University, East Lansing.

Chappuis, Eglantine, Vanesa Seriñá, Eugénia Martí, Enric Ballesteros, and Esperança Gacia. 2017. "Decrypting Stable-Isotope (δ^{13}C and δ^{15}N) Variability in Aquatic Plants." *Freshwater Biology* 62: 1807–18.

Chase, Brad. 2012. "Crafting Harappan Cuisine on the Saurashtran Frontier of the Indus Civilization." In *The Menial Art of Cooking*, edited by Sarah R. Graff and Enrique Rodríguez-Alegría, 145–72. Boulder: University Press of Colorado.

Childe, V. Gordon. [1936] 1951. *Man Makes Himself*. Reprint. New York: New American Library of World Literature.

Chilton, Elizabeth S. 1998. "The Cultural Origins of Technical Choice: Unraveling Algonquian and Iroquoian Ceramic Traditions in the Northeast." In *The Archaeology of Social Boundaries*, edited by Miriam Stark, 132–69. Washington, DC: Smithsonian Institution Press.

Chivis, Jeff. 2016. "The Introduction of Havana-Hopewell in West Michigan and Northwest Indiana: An Integrative Approach to the Identification of Communities, Interaction Networks, and Mobility Patterns." PhD dissertation, Michigan State University, East Lansing.

Chu, G. P. K. 1968. "Microstructure of Complex Ceramics." In *Ceramic Microstructures: Their Analysis, Significance, and Production*, edited by R. M. Fulrath and J. A. Pask, 828–62. New York: John Wiley.

Cleland, Charles E. 1982. "The Inland Shore Fishery of the Northern Great Lakes: Its Development and Importance in Prehistory." *American Antiquity* 47 (4): 761–84.

———. 1989. "Comments on 'A Reconsideration of Aboriginal Fishing Strategies in the Northern Great Lakes Region' by Susan R. Martin." *American Antiquity* 54 (3): 605–9.

———. 1999. "Cultural Transformation: The Archaeology of Historic Indian Sites in Michigan, 1670–1940." In *Retrieving Michigan's Buried Past: The Archaeology of the Great Lakes State*, edited by John R. Halsey, 279–90. Bloomfield Hills, MI: Cranbrook Institute of Science.

Cleland, Charles E., Margaret B. Holman, and J. Alan Holman. 1988. "The Mason-Quimby Line Revisited." *The Wisconsin Archeologist* 79 (1): 8–27.

Cloern, James E., Elizabeth A. Canuel, and David Harris. 2002. "Stable Carbon and Nitrogen Isotope Composition of Aquatic and Terrestrial Plants of the San Francisco Bay Estuarine System." *Limnology and Oceanography* 47 (3): 713–29.

Comer, P., and D. Albert. 1997. "Vegetation circa 1800 of Chippewa County, Michigan, East Part: An Interpretation of the General Land Office Surveys." Michigan Natural Features Inventory, Lansing. http://nmfi.anr.msu.edu/data/veg1800/chippewa_east.pdf; accessed March 7, 2018.

Comer, P., D. Albert, H. Wells, B. Hart, J. Raab, D. Price, D. Kashian, and R. Corner. 1995. *Michigan's Presettlement Vegetation, as Interpreted from the General Land Office Surveys 1816–1856.* Lansing: Michigan Natural Features Inventory.

Conway, Thor A. 1977. *Whitefish Island: A Remarkable Archaeological Site at Sault Ste. Marie, Ontario.* Ottawa: Ministry of Culture and Recreation, Historical Planning and Research Branch.

Cooper, Janet. 1996. "Cloudman Site (20CH6), Drummond Island, Michigan, Features 26 and 27, 1992 Excavations." Report prepared for the Consortium for Archaeological Research, Department of Anthropology, Michigan State University, East Lansing.

Craig, O. E., M. Forster, S. H. Andersen, E. Koch, P. Crombé, N. J. Milner, B. Stern, G. N. Bailey, and C. P. Heron. 2007. "Molecular and Isotopic Demonstration of the Processing of Aquatic Products in Northern European Prehistoric Pottery." *Archaeometry* 49 (1): 135–52.

Craig, O. E., H. Saul, A. Lucquin, Y. Nishida, K. Taché, L. Clarke, A. Thompson, D. T. Altoft, J. Uchiyama, M. Ajimoto, K. Gibbs, S. Isaksson, C. P. Heron, and P. Jordan. 2013. "Earliest Evidence for the Use of Pottery." *Nature* 496: 351–54.

Crawford, Gary W. 2011. "People and Plant Interaction in the Northeast." In *Subsistence Economies of Indigenous North America*, edited by Bruce D. Smith, 431–48. Washington, DC: Smithsonian Institution Scholarly Press.

Danziger, Edmund J. 1978. *The Chippewas of Lake Superior.* Norman: University of Oklahoma Press.

Demers, P. A. 1991. "Report on the St. Mary's River Archaeological Survey: Archaeological Reconnaissance and Limited Testing on the Lower St. Mary's River, Chippewa County, Michigan." Project. No. S90-281. Report submitted to the Bureau of History, Michigan Department of State, Lansing.

Densmore, Frances. [1929] 1979. *Chippewa Customs.* St. Paul: Minnesota Historical Society Press. Originally published as Bulletin No. 86, Bureau of American Ethnology. Washington, DC: Smithsonian Institution.

———. [1928] 2005. *Strength of the Earth: The Classic Guide to Ojibwe Uses of Native Plants.* St. Paul: Minnesota Historical Society Press. Originally published in "Uses of Plants by the Chippewa Indians." *Bureau of American Ethnology Annual Report* 44: 275–397.

Dorland, Steven G. H. 2018. "The Touch of a Child: An Analysis of Fingernail Impressions on Late Woodland Pottery to Identify Childhood Material Interactions." *Journal of Archaeological Science: Reports* 21: 298–304.

Dorothy, Lawrence G. 1978. "The Ceramics of the Sand Point Site (20BG14) Baraga County, Michigan: A Preliminary Description." Master's thesis, Western Michigan University, Kalamazoo.

———. 1980. "The Ceramics of the Sand Point Site (20BG14) Baraga County, Michigan: A Preliminary Description." *Michigan Archaeologist* 26 (3–4): 39–90.

Drake, Eric C., and Sean B. Dunham. 2004. "The Woodland Period Occupation of Grand Island." *Midcontinental Journal of Archaeology* 29 (2): 133–65.

Druc, Isabelle C., Kinya Inokuchi, and Laure Dussubieux. 2017. "LA-ICP-MS and Petrography to Assess Ceramic Interaction Networks and Production Patterns in Kuntur Wasi, Peru." *Journal of Archaeological Science: Reports* 12: 151–60.

Dunham, Sean B. 2008. "Wild Rice in the Eastern Upper Peninsula: A Review of the Evidence." Paper presented at the 2008 Annual Meetings of the Michigan Academy of Science, Arts & Letters, Botany and Plant Ecology Division, Kalamazoo.

———. 2009. "Nuts about Acorns: A Pilot Study on Acorn Use in Woodland Period Subsistence in the Eastern Upper Peninsula of Michigan." *The Wisconsin Archeologist* 90 (1–2): 113–30.

———. 2014. "Late Woodland Settlement and Subsistence Patterns in the Eastern Upper Peninsula of Michigan." PhD dissertation, Michigan State University, East Lansing.

———. 2017. "Location, Location, Location: A Foray into Persistent Places in da UP." Paper presented at the 61st Annual Meeting of the Midwest Archaeological Conference, Indianapolis, IN.

Dunham, Sean B., and Michael Hambacher. 2002. "Cultural Resource Evaluations: Hiawatha National Forest." Commonwealth Cultural Resources Group, Inc., Jackson, MI.

———. 2007. "Cultural Resource Evaluation: Bark Dock Site (FS 09-10-04-012/20CH95), Hiawatha National Forest, Chippewa County, Michigan." Commonwealth Cultural Resources Group, Inc., Jackson, MI.

Duwe, Samuel, and Hector Neff. 2007. "Glaze and Slip Pigment Analyses of Pueblo IV Period Ceramics from East-Central Arizona Using Time of Flight-Laser Ablation-Inductively Coupled Plasma-Mass Spectrometry (TOF-LA-ICP-MS)." *Journal of Archaeological Science* 34: 403–14.

Egan-Bruhy, Kathryn C. 2007. "20CH6. Cloudman Site Floral Table." On file at the Consortium for Archaeological Research, Department of Anthropology, Michigan State University, East Lansing.

———. 2014. "Ethnicity as Evidenced in Subsistence Patterns of Late Prehistoric Upper Great Lakes Populations." *Midwest Archaeological Conference Inc. Occasional Papers* 1: 7–32.

Ehrhardt, Kathleen L. 2009. "Copper Working Technologies, Context of Use, and Social Complexity in the Eastern Woodlands of Native North America." *Journal of World Prehistory* 22: 213–35.

Evershed, Richard P., Stephanie N. Dudd, Stephanie Charters, Hazel Mottram, Andrew W. Stott, Anthony Raven, Pim F. van Bergen, and Helen A. Bland. 1999. "Lipids as Carriers of Anthropogenic Signals from Prehistory." *Philosophical Transactions of the Royal Society B* 354 (1379): 19–31.

Falabella, F., L. Sanhueza, I. Correa, M. D. Glascock, T. J. Ferguson, and E. Fonseca. 2013. "Studying Technological Practices at a Local Level: Neutron Activation and Petrographic Analyses of Early Ceramic Period Pottery in Central Chile." *Archaeometry* 55 (1): 33–53.

Feathers, James K. 2006. "Explaining Shell-Tempered Pottery in Prehistoric Eastern North America." *Journal of Archaeological Method and Theory* 13 (2): 89–133.

Fischer, Anders, and Jan Heinemeier. 2003. "Freshwater Reservoir Effect in ^{14}C Dates of Food Residue on Pottery." *Radiocarbon* 45: 449–66.

Fischler, Claude. 1988. "Food, Self and Identity." *Social Science Information* 27 (2): 275–92.

Fitting, James E., David S. Brose, Henry T. Wright, and James Dinerstein. 1969. "The Goodwin-Gresham Site, 20IS8, Iosco County, Michigan." *The Wisconsin Archeologist* 50: 125–83.

Flannery, Kent V. 1973. "The Origins of Agriculture." *Annual Review of Anthropology* 2: 217–310.

Foster, William C. 2012. *Climate and Culture Change in North America AD 900–1600*. Austin: University of Texas Press.

Fournier, Michael R. 2007. "The Gyftakis Site: A Reevaluation of a Middle Woodland Site after 30 Years." Master's thesis, Western Michigan University, Kalamazoo.

Fox, William A. 1990a. "The Middle Woodland to Late Woodland Transition." In *The Archaeology of Southern Ontario to A.D. 1650*, edited by Chris J. Ellis and Neal Ferris, 171–88. Occasional Publication of the London Chapter, OAS, No. 5. London: Ontario Archaeological Society.

———. 1990b. "The Odawa." In *The Archaeology of Southern Ontario to A.D. 1650*, edited by Chris J. Ellis and Neal Ferris, 457–74. Occasional Publication of the London Chapter, OAS, No. 5. London: Ontario Archaeological Society.

Fox, William A., and Charles Garrad. 2004. "Hurons in an Algonquian Land." *Ontario Archaeology* 77–78: 121–34.

Franzen, John. 1975. "An Archaeological Survey of Chippewa County, Michigan." Michigan History Division, Michigan Department of State, Archaeological Survey Reports No. 5, Lansing.

Frederick, Kathryn M. 2019. "Storage, Decision-Making, and Risk Management in Non-Sedentary Societies." PhD dissertation, Michigan State University, East Lansing.

Garland, Elizabeth B., and Scott G. Beld. 1999. "The Early Woodland: Ceramics, Domesticated Plants, and Burial Mounds Foretell the Shape of the Future." In *Retrieving Michigan's Buried Past: The Archaeology of the Great Lakes State*, edited by John R. Halsey, 125–46. Bloomfield Hills, MI: Cranbrook Institute of Science.

Glascock, Michael D., and Hector Neff. 2003. "Neutron Activation Analysis and Provenance Research in Archaeology." *Measurement Science and Technology* 14: 1516–26.

Gremillion, Kristen J. 1996. "Early Agricultural Diet in Eastern North America: Evidence from Two Kentucky Rockshelters." *American Antiquity* 61 (3): 520–36.

———. 2004. "Seed Processing and the Origins of Food Production in Eastern North America." *American Antiquity* 69 (2): 215–33.

Guindon, François. 2009. "Iroquoian Pottery at Lake Abitibi: A Case Study of the Relationship between Hurons and Algonkians on the Canadian Shield." *Canadian Journal of Archaeology* 33: 65–91.

Hally, David J. 1983. "Use Alteration of Pottery Vessel Surfaces: An Important Source of Evidence for the Identification of Vessel Function." *North American Archaeologist* 4 (1): 3–26.

Halsey, John R. 1999. "Upper Mississippian in the Upper Peninsula." In *Retrieving Michigan's Buried Past: The Archaeology of the Great Lakes State*, edited by John R. Halsey, 272–78. Bloomfield Hills, MI: Cranbrook Institute of Science.

Hambacher, Michael J. 1992. "The Skegemog Point Site: Continuing Studies in the Cultural Dynamics of the Carolinian-Canadian Transition Zone." PhD dissertation, Michigan State University, East Lansing.

Hambacher, Michael J., and Margaret B. Holman. 1995. "Camp, Cache and Carry: The Porter Creek South Site (20MN100) and Cache Pits at 20MN31 in the Manistee National Forest." *Michigan Archaeologist* 41 (2–3): 47–94.

Hamilton, Scott, James Graham, and B. A. Nicholson. 2007. "Archaeological Site Distributions and Contents: Modeling Late Precontact Blackduck Land Use in the Northeastern Plains." *Canadian Journal of Archaeology* 31 (3): 93–136.

Hart, J., D. Asch, C. Scarry, and G. Crawford. 2002. "The Age of Common Bean in the North Eastern Woodlands." *American Antiquity* 76: 377–85.

Hart, John P. 2008. "Evolving the Three Sisters: The Changing Histories of Maize, Bean, and Squash in New and the Greater Northeast." In *Current Northeast Paleoethnobotany II*, edited by John P. Hart, 87–99. New York State Museum Bulletin 512. Albany: New York State Education Department.

———. 2012. "Pottery Wall Thinning as a Consequence of Increased Maize Processing: A Case Study from Central New York." *Journal of Archaeological Science* 39: 3470–74.

Hart, John P., and Hetty Jo Brumbach. 2009. "On Pottery Change and Northern Iroquoian Origins: An Assessment from the Finger Lakes Region of Central New York." *Journal of Anthropological Archaeology* 28: 367–81.

Hart, John P., and William A. Lovis. 2007. "A Multi-Regional Analysis of AMS and Radiometric Dates from Carbonized Food Residues." *Midcontinental Journal of Archaeology* 32: 201–61.

———. 2013. "Reevaluating What We Know about the Histories of Maize in Northeastern North America: A Review of Current Evidence." *Journal of Archaeological Research* 21 (2): 175–216.

Hart, John P., William A. Lovis, Gerald R. Urquhart, and Eleanora A. Reber. 2013. "Modeling Freshwater Reservoir Offsets on Radiocarbon-Dated Charred Cooking Residues." *American Antiquity* 78 (3): 536–52.

Hart, John P., William A. Lovis, Janet K. Schulenberg, and Gerald R. Urquhart. 2007. "Paleodietary Implications from Stable Carbon Isotope Analysis of Experimental Cooking Residues." *Journal of Archaeological Science* 34: 804–13.

Hart, John P., and C. Margaret Scarry. 1999. "The Age of Common Beans (*Phaseolus vulgaris*) in the Northeastern United States." *American Antiquity* 64 (4): 653–58.

Hart, John P., Karine Taché, and William A. Lovis. 2018. "Freshwater Reservoir Offsets and Food Crusts: Isotope, AMS, and Lipid Analyses of Experimental Cooking Residues." *PLoS ONE* 13 (4): e0196407. https://doi.org/10.1371/journal.pone.0196407.

Hart, John P., Robert G. Thompson, and Hetty Jo Brumbach. 2003. "Phytolith Evidence for Early Maize (*Zea mays*) in 2003 the Northern Finger Lakes Region of New York." *American Antiquity* 68 (4): 619–40.

Hart, John P., Termeh Shafie, Jennifer Birch, Susan Dermarkar, and Ronald F. Williamson. 2017. "Nation Building and Social Signaling in Southern Ontario: A.D. 1350–1650." *PLoS ONE* 11 (5): e0156178. https://doi.org/10.1371/journal.pone.0196407.

Hastorf, Christine A., and Michael J. DeNiro. 1985. "Reconstruction of Prehistoric Plant Production and Cooking Practices by a New Isotopic Method." *Nature* 315: 489–91.

Hastorf, Christine A., and Sissel Johannessen. 1994. "Becoming Corn-Eaters in Prehistoric America." In *Corn and Culture in the Prehistoric New World*, edited by Sissel Johannessen and Christine A. Hastorf, 427–43. University of Minnesota Publications in Anthropology No. 5. Boulder, CO: Westview Press.

Henning, Dale R. 1998. "The Oneota Tradition." In *Archaeology on the Great Plains*, edited by W. Raymond Wood, 345–414. Lawrence: University Press of Kansas.

Heron, Carl, and Oliver Craig. 2015. "Aquatic Resources in Food Crusts: Identification and Implication." *Radiocarbon* 57: 707–19.

Hilger, Inez. 1959. *Chippewa Child Life and Its Cultural Background*. Bureau of American Ethnology Bulletin 146. Washington, DC: Smithsonian Institution.

Hinsdale, W. 1931. *Archaeological Atlas of Michigan*. Michigan Handbook Series, X No. 4. Ann Arbor: University of Michigan Press.

Holman, J. Alan, and Danita Brandt. 2009. "Pleistocene Fauna." In *Michigan Geography and Geology*, edited by R. Schaetzl, J. Darden, and Danita Brandt, 106–14. New York: Custom Publishing.

Holman, Margaret B. 1978. "The Settlement System of the Mackinac Phase." PhD dissertation, Michigan State University, East Lansing.

———. 1984. "The Identification of Late Woodland Maple Sugaring Sites in the Upper Great Lakes." *Midcontinental Journal of Archaeology* 9 (1): 63–89.

Holman, Margaret B., and Janet. G. Brashler. 1999. "Economics, Material Culture, and Trade in the Late Woodland Lower Peninsula of Michigan." In *Retrieving Michigan's Buried Past: The Archaeology of the Great Lakes State*, edited by John R. Halsey, 212–20. Bloomfield Hills, MI: Cranbrook Institute of Science.

Holman, Margaret B., and Kathryn C. Egan. 1985. "Processing Maple Sap with Prehistoric Techniques." *Journal of Ethnobiology* 5 (1): 61–75.

Holman, Margaret B., and William A. Lovis. 2008. "The Social and Environmental Constraints on Mobility in the Late Prehistoric Upper Great Lakes Region." In *The Archaeology of Mobility: Old World and New World Nomadism*, edited by H. Bernard and W. Wandrich, 280–306. Los Angeles: Cotsen Institute of Archaeology, University of California, Los Angeles.

Howey, Meghan C. L. 2007. "Using Multi-Criteria Cost Surface Analysis to Explore Past Regional Landscapes: A Case Study of Ritual Activity and Social Interaction in Michigan, AD 1200–1600." *Journal of Archaeological Science* 34: 1830–46.

———. 2015. "Geospatial Landscape Permeability Modeling for Archaeology: A Case Study of Food Storage in Northern Michigan." *Journal of Archaeological Science* 64: 88–99.

Howey, Meghan C. L., and John O'Shea. 2002. "Thinking Outside the Circle: New Research at Michigan's Missaukee Earthworks." Paper presented at the 48th Midwest Archaeological Conference, Columbus, OH.

———. 2006. "Bear's Journey and the Study of Ritual in Archaeology." *American Antiquity* 71 (2): 261–82.

Howey, Meghan C. L., and Kathryn E. Parker. 2008. "Camp, Cache, Stay Awhile: Preliminary Considerations of the Social and Economic Processes of Cache Pits along Douglas Lake, Michigan." *Michigan Archaeologist* 54 (1–4): 19–44.

Howey, Meghan C. L., and Kathryn Frederick. 2016. "Immovable Food Storage Facilities, Knowledge, and Landscape in Non-Sedentary Societies: Perspectives from Northern Michigan." *Journal of Anthropological Archaeology* 42: 37–55.

Howey, Meghan C. L., Michael W. Palace, and Crystal H. McMichael. 2016. "Geospatial Modeling Approach to Monument Construction Using Michigan from A.D. 1000–1600 as a Case Study." *PNAS* 113 (27): 7443–48.

Huber, James K. 2001. "Palynological Investigations Related to Archaeological Sites and the Expansion of Wild Rice (*Zizania aquatica* L.) in Northeast Minnesota." Master's thesis, University of Minnesota.

Hupy, Christina M., and Catherine Yansa. 2009. "The Last 17,000 Years of Vegetation History." In Michigan Geography and Geology, edited by R. Schaetzl, J. Darden, and Danita Brandt, 91–105. New York: Custom Publishing.

Janzen, Donald E. 1968. *The Naomikong Point Site and the Dimensions of Laurel in the Lake Superior Basin*. Anthropological Papers No. 36. Ann Arbor: Museum of Anthropology, University of Michigan.

Johnson, Matthew. 2010. *Archaeological Theory: An Introduction*. Oxford: Wiley-Blackwell.

Jones, Siân. 1997. *The Archaeology of Ethnicity*. New York: Routledge.

Kalčik, Susan. 1984. "Ethnic Foodways in America: Symbol and the Performance of Identity." In *Ethnic and Regional Foodways in the United States: The Performance of Group Identity*, edited by Linda Kelly Brown and Kay Mussell, 37–65. Knoxville: University of Tennessee Press.

Kapp, Ronald O. 1999. "Michigan Late Pleistocene, Holocene, and Presettlement Vegetation and Climate." In *Retrieving Michigan's Buried Past: The Archaeology of the Great Lakes State*, edited by John R. Halsey, 31–58. Bloomfield Hills, MI: Cranbrook Institute of Science.

Katzenberg, M. Anne, and Susan Pfeiffer. 1995. "Nitrogen Isotope Evidence for Weaning Age in a Nineteenth Century Candian Skeletal Sample." In *Bodies of Evidence: Reconstructing History through Skeletal Analysis*, edited by Anne L. Grauer, 221–36. New York: Wiley-Liss.

Kenyon, Walter A. 1970. *Methodist Point*. Royal Ontario Museum Art and Archaeology, Occasional Paper 22. Toronto: Royal Ontario Museum.

Kincare, Kevin, and Grahame Larson. 2009. "Evolution of the Great Lakes." In *Michigan Geography and Geology*, edited by R. Schaetzl, J. Darden, and Danita Brandt, 174–90. New York: Custom Publishing.

Kobayashi, Masashi. 1994. "Use-Alteration Analysis of Kalinga Pottery: Interior Carbon Deposits of Cooking Pots." In *Kalinga Ethnoarchaeology: Expanding Archaeological Method and Theory*, edited by William A. Longacre and James M. Skibo, 127–68. Washington, DC: Smithsonian Institution Press.

Kooiman, Susan M. 2012. "Old Pots, New Approaches: A Functional Analysis of Woodland Pottery from Lake Superior's South Shore." Master's thesis, Illinois State University, Normal.

———. 2015a. "Pottery Function, Cooking, and Subsistence in the Upper Great Lakes: A View from the Middle Woodland Winter Site in Northern Michigan." Paper presented at the 80th Annual Meeting of the Society for American Archaeology, San Francisco, CA.

———. 2015b. "Sizing up the Past: Evaluating the Relationship between Rim Diameter and Volume in Late Woodland Upper Great Lakes Ceramic Jars." Paper presented at the 59th Annual Midwest Archaeological Conference, Milwaukee, WI, November.

———. 2016. "Woodland Pottery Function, Cooking, and Diet in the Upper Great Lakes of North America." *Midcontinental Journal of Archaeology* 41 (3): 1–25.

———. 2018. "A Multiproxy Analysis of Culinary, Technological, and Environmental Interactions in the Northern Great Lakes Region." PhD dissertation, Michigan State University, East Lansing.

Kooiman, Susan M., and Heather Walder. 2019. "Reconsidering the Chronology: Carbonized Food Residue AMS Dates and Compositional Analysis of a Curated Collection from the Upper Great Lakes." *American Antiquity* 84 (3): 495–515.

Kooiman, Susan M., Sean B. Dunham, and Christine Stephenson. 2019. "The Cloudman Site: A Multicomponent Woodland and Historic Period Site in the Northern Great Lakes." *The Wisconsin Archeologist* 100 (1–2): 57–68.

Kuhn, Robert D., and Robert E. Funk. 2000. "Boning Up on the Mohawk: An Overview of Mohawk Faunal Assemblages and Subsistence Patterns." *Archaeology of Eastern North America* 28: 29–62.

Larson, Curtis E. 1999. "A Century of Great Lakes Levels Research: Finished or Just Beginning?" In *Retrieving Michigan's Buried Past: The Archaeology of the Great Lakes State*, edited by John R. Halsey, 1–30. Bloomfield Hills, MI: Cranbrook Institute of Science.

Larson, Grahame, and Randall Schaetzl. 2001. "Origin and Evolution of the Great Lakes." *Journal of Great Lakes Research* 27 (4): 518–46.

Larson, Grahame J., and Kevin Kincare. 2009. "Late Quaternary History of the Eastern Mid-Continent Region, USA." In *Michigan Geography and Geology*, edited by R. Schaetzl, J. Darden, and Danita Brandt, 69–90. New York: Custom Publishing.

Ligman, Michael S. 2013. "'Put That in Your Pipe and Smoke It': An Exploratory Study of Native American Ceramic Tobacco Pipes at the James Fort Site in Virginia Using Portable X-Ray Fluorescence." Master's thesis, University of Massachusetts, Boston.

Linton, Ralph. 1944. "North American Cooking Pots." *American Antiquity* 9 (4): 369–80.

Lovis, William A. 1971. "The Holtz Site (20AN26), Antrim County, Michigan: A Preliminary Report." *Michigan Archaeologist* 17 (2): 49–64.

———. 1973. "Late Woodland Cultural Dynamics in the Northern Lower Peninsula of Michigan." PhD dissertation, Michigan State University, East Lansing.

———. 1978. "A Case Study of Construction Impacts on Archaeological Sites in Michigan's Inland Waterway." *Journal of Field Archaeology* 5 (3): 357–60.

———. 1990. "Curatorial Considerations for Systematic Research Collections: AMS Dating a Curated Ceramic Assemblage." *American Antiquity* 55 (2): 382–87.

———. 1999. "The Middle Archaic: Learning to Live in the Woodlands." In *Retrieving Michigan's Buried Past: The Archaeology of the Great Lakes State*, edited by John R. Halsey, 83–94. Bloomfield Hills, MI: Cranbrook Institute of Science.

———. 2009. "Between the Glaciers and Europeans: People from 12,000 to 400 Years Ago." In *Michigan Geography and Geology*, edited by R. Schaetzl, J. Darden, and Danita Brandt, 389–401. New York: Custom Publishing.

———. 2014. "An Up North Fishing Trip: Reinvestigating the Absolute Dated Archaeological Chronology of Northern Lake Michigan." Paper presented at the Museum of Anthropology, University of Michigan, Ann Arbor, April 3.

Lovis, W. A., R. E. Donahue, and M. B. Holman. 2005. "Long Distance Logistic Mobility as an Organizing Principle among Northern Hunter-Gatherers:

A Great Lakes Middle Holocene Settlement System." *American Antiquity* 70 (4): 669–93.

Lovis, William A., Alan F. Arbogast, and G. William Monaghan. 2012. *The Geoarchaeology of Lake Michigan Coastal Dunes*. Environmental Research Series No. 2. East Lansing: Michigan Department of Transportation and Michigan State University Press.

Lovis, William A., and John P. Hart. 2015. "Fishing for Dog Food: Ethnographic and Ethnohistoric Insights on the Freshwater Reservoir in Northeastern North America." *Radiocarbon* 57: 557–70.

Lovis, William A., Gerald R. Urquhart, Maria E. Raviele, and John P. Hart. 2011. "Hardwood Ash Nixtamalization May Lead to False Negatives for the Presence of Maize by Depleting Bulk $\delta^{13}C$ in Carbonized Residues." *Journal of Archaeological Science* 38: 2726–30.

Lovis, William A., Grace Rajnovich, and Aryn Bartley. 1998. "Exploratory Cluster Analysis, Temporal Change, and the Woodland Ceramics of the Portage Site at L'Arbre Croche." *The Wisconsin Archeologist* 79: 9–112.

Lovis, William A., Kathryn C. Egan-Bruhy, Beverly A. Smith, and G. William Monaghan. 2001. "Wetlands and Emergent Horticultural Economies in the Upper Great Lakes: A New Perspective from the Schultz Site." *American Antiquity* 66 (4): 615–32.

Lugenbeal, Edward. 1978. "The Blackduck Ceramics of the Smith Site (21KC3) and Their Implications for the History of Blackduck Ceramics and Culture in Northern Minnesota." *Midcontinental Journal of Archaeology* 3 (1): 45–68.

MacLean, Rachel, and Timothy Insoll. 1999. "The Social Context of Food Technology in Iron Age Gao, Mali." *World Archaeology* 31 (1): 78–92.

MacNeish, Richard S. 1952. *Iroquois Pottery Types: A Technique for the Study of Iroquois Prehistory*. National Museum of Canada Bulletin No. 124. Ottawa: Department of Resources and Development, National Museum of Canada.

Malainey, Mary. 2011. "Lipid Residue Analysis." In *A Consumer's Guide to Archaeological Science*, edited by Mary Malainey, 201–18. New York: Springer.

Malainey, Mary E., and Timothy Figol. 2015. "Methodology and Results of Lipid Residues Extracted from Naomikong Point and Sand Point Pottery." Report prepared for Susan Kooiman, Department of Anthropology, Michigan State University, East Lansing.

———. 2018. "Analysis of Lipid Residue Extracted from Archaeological Material from the Cloudman Site, 20CH6." Report prepared for Susan Kooiman, Department of Anthropology, Michigan State University, East Lansing.

Martin, Susan R. 1989. "A Reconsideration of Aboriginal Fishing Strategies in the Northern Great Lakes Region." *American Antiquity* 54 (3): 594–604.

———. 1999a. "A Site for All Seasons: Some Aspects of Life in the Upper Peninsula during Late Woodland Times." In *Retrieving Michigan's Buried Past: The Archaeology of the Great Lakes State*, edited by John R. Halsey, 221–27. Bloomfield Hills, MI: Cranbrook Institute of Science.

———. 1999b. *Wonderful Power: The Story of Ancient Copper Working in the Lake Superior Basin*. Detroit, MI: Wayne State University Press.

Mason, Carol I. 1986. "Prehistoric Maple Sugaring: A Sticky Subject." *North American Archaeologist* 7 (4): 305–11.

Mason, Carol I., and Margaret B. Holman. 2000. "Maple Sugaring in Prehistory: Tapping the Sources." In *Interpretations of Native North American Life: Material Contributions to Ethnohistory*, edited by M. S. Nassaney and E. S. Johnson. Gainesville: University Press of Florida.

Mason, Ronald J. 1966. *Two Stratified Sites on the Door Peninsula of Wisconsin*. Anthropological Papers No. 26. Ann Arbor: Museum of Anthropology, University of Michigan.

———. 1967. "The North Bay Component at the Porte des Morts Site, Door County, Wisconsin." *Wisconsin Archeologist* 48: 267–345.

———. 1970. "Hopewell, Middle Woodland, and the Laurel Culture: A Problem in Archeological Classification." *American Anthropologist* 72 (4): 802–15.

———. 1981. *Great Lakes Archaeology*. New York: Academic Press.

McElrath, Dale L., Andrew C. Fortier, and Thomas E. Emerson. 2009. "An Introduction to the Archaic Societies of the Midcontinent." In *Archaic Societies: Diversity and Complexity across the Midcontinent*, edited by A. C. Fortier, Dale L. McElrath, and T. E. Emerson, 3–21. Albany: State University of New York Press.

McElrath, Dale L., Thomas E. Emerson, and Andrew C. Fortier. 2000. "Social Evolution or Social Response? A Fresh Look at the 'Good Gray Cultures' after Four Decades of Midwest Research." In *Late Woodland Societies: Tradition and Transformation across the Midcontinent*, edited by T. Emerson, D. McElrath, and A. Fortier, 543–79. Lincoln: University of Nebraska Press.

McGovern, Patrick E., and Gretchen R. Hall. 2016. "Charting a Future Course for Organic Residue Analysis in Archaeology." *Journal of Archaeological Method and Theory* 23: 592–622.

McHale Milner, Claire. 1991. "Localization in Small-Scale Societies: Late Prehistoric Social Organization in the Western Great Lakes." In *Between Bands and States*, edited by Susan A. Gregg, 35–57. Occasional Paper No. 9. Carbondale: Center for Archaeological Investigations, Southern Illinois University.

———. 1998. "Ceramic Style, Social Differentiation, and Resource Uncertainty in the Late Precontact Upper Great Lakes." PhD dissertation, University of Michigan.

McPherron, Alan L. 1967. *The Juntunen Site and the Late Woodland Prehistory of the Upper Great Lakes Area*. Anthropological Papers No. 30. Ann Arbor: Museum of Anthropology, University of Michigan.

Miller, Melanie J., Helen L. Whelton, Jillian A. Swift, Sophia Maline, Simon Hammann, Lucy J. E. Cramp, Alexandra McCleary, Geoffrey Tayler, Kirsten Vacca, Fanya Becks, Richard P. Evershed, and Christine A. Hastorf. 2020. "Interpreting Ancient Food Practices: Stable Isotope and Molecular Analyses of Visible and Absorbed Residues from a Year-Long Cooking Experiment." *Nature: Scientific Reports* 10: 13704. https://doi.org/10.1038/s41598-020-70109-8.

Milligan, Heather E., Troy D. Pretzlaw, and Murray M. Humphries. 2010. "Stable Isotope Differentiation of Freshwater and Terrestrial Vascular Plants in Two Subarctic Regions." *Écoscience* 17 (3): 265–75.

Milner, George, D. Anderson, and M. Smith. 2001. "The Distribution of Eastern Woodlands Peoples at the Prehistoric and Historic Interface." In *Societies in Eclipse: Archaeology of the Eastern Woodlands Indians, A.D. 1400–1700*, edited by D. Brose, C. W. Cowan, and R. Mainfort, 9–18. Washington, DC: Smithsonian Institution Press.

Mithun, Marianne. 1999. *The Languages of Native North America*. Cambridge: Cambridge University Press.

Monaghan, G. William, and William A. Lovis. 2005. *Modeling Archaeological Site Burial in Southern Michigan: A Geoarchaeological Synthesis*. East Lansing: Michigan State University Press.

Monaghan, G. William, Timothy M. Schilling, and Kathryn E. Parker. 2014. "The Age and Distribution of Domesticated Beans (*Phaseolus vulgaris*) in Eastern North America: Implications for Agricultural Practices and Group Interactions." *Midwest Archaeological Conference Inc. Occasional Papers* 1: 33–52.

Monaghan, G. William, William A. Lovis, and Kathryn C. Egan-Bruhy. 2006. "Earliest *Cucurbita* from the Great Lakes, Northern USA." *Quaternary Research* 65: 216–22.

Montanari, Massimo. 2006. "Identity, Exchange, Traditions, and 'Origins.'" In *Food Is Culture*, edited by Carole Counihan and Penny Van Esterik, 133–37. New York: Columbia University Press.

Morgenstein, Maury, and Carol A. Redmount. 2005. "Using Portable Energy Dispersive X-Ray Fluorescence (EDXRF) Analysis for On-Site Study of Ceramic Sherds at El Hibeh, Egypt." *Journal of Archaeological Science* 32: 1613–23.

Morton, June D., and Henry P. Schwarcz. 2004. "Paleodietary Implications from Stable Isotopic Analysis of Residues on Prehistoric Ontario Ceramics." *Journal of Archaeological Science* 31: 503–17.

Muhammad, Allison June. 2010. "A Bioarchaeological Study of Late Woodland Population from Michigan: Frazer-Tyra Site (20SA9)." PhD dissertation, Wayne State University, Detroit, MI.

Nelson, Ben A. 1981. "Ethnoarchaeology and Paleodemography: A Test of Turner and Lofgren's Hypothesis." *Journal of Anthropological Research* 37 (2): 107–29.

Neubauer, Fernanda. 2016. "Late Archaic Hunter-Gatherer Lithic Technology and Function (Chipped Stone, Ground Stone, and Fire-Cracked Rock): A Study of Domestic Life, Foodways, and Seasonal Mobility on Grand Island in Michigan's Upper Peninsula." PhD dissertation, University of Wisconsin–Madison.

———. 2019. "Hunter-Gatherer Fall Social Aggregation: A Late Archaic Seasonal Mobility Model for Grand Island and Michigan's Upper Peninsula in the Great Lakes Region." *The Wisconsin Archeologist* 99 (1): 41–54.

O'Shea, John M. 1989. "The Role of Wild Resources in Small-Scale Agricultural Systems: Tales from the Lakes and the Plains." In *Bad Year Economics: Cultural Responses to Risk and Uncertainty*, edited by Paul Halstead and John O'Shea, 57–67. Cambridge: Cambridge University Press.

———. 2003. "Inland Foragers and the Adoption of Maize Agriculture in the Upper Great Lakes of North America." *Before Farming: The Archaeology and Anthropology of Hunter-Gatherers* 1 (3): 68–83.

O'Shea, John M., and Clare McHale Milner. 2002. "Material Indicators of Territory, Identity, and Interaction in a Prehistoric Tribal System." In *The Archaeology of Tribal Societies*, edited by W. A. Parkinson, 200–226. Ann Arbor, MI: International Monographs in Prehistory.

Parker, Bradley J., and Jason R. Kennedy. 2010. "A Quantitative Attribute Analysis of the Ubaid-Period Ceramic Corpus from Kenan Tepe." *Bulletin of the American Schools of Oriental Research* 358: 1–26.

Pearsall, Deborah M., and Christine A. Hastorf. 2011. "Reconstructing Past Life-Ways with Plants II: Human-Environment and Human-Human Interactions." In *Ethnobiology*, edited by E. N. Anderson, D. Pearsall, E. Hunn, and N. Turner, 173–87. Hoboken, NJ: Wiley-Blackwell.

Peelo, Sarah. 2011. "Pottery-Making in Spanish California: Creating Multi-Scalar Social Identity through Daily Practice." *American Antiquity* 76 (4): 642–66.

Perkl, Bradley E. 1998. "*Cucurbita pepo* from King Coulee, Southeastern Minnesota." *American Antiquity* 63 (2): 279–88.

Philippsen, Bente, Henrik Kjeldsen, Sönke Hartz, Harm Paulsen, Ingo Clausen, and Jan Heinemeier. 2010. "The Hardwater Effect in AMS ^{14}C Dating of Food Crusts on Pottery." *Nuclear Instruments and Methods in Physics Research B* 268: 995–98.

Potter, James M. 2000. "Pots, Parties, and Politics: Communal Feasting in the American Southwest." *American Antiquity* 65 (3): 471–92.

Pregitzer, Kurt S., David D. Reed, Theodore J. Bornhorst, David R. Foster, Glenn D. Mroz, Jason S. McLachlan, Peter E. Laks, Douglas D. Stokke, Patrick E. Martin, and Shannon E. Brown. 2000. "A Buried Spruce Forest Provides Evidence at the Stand and Landscape Scale for the Effects of Environment on Vegetation at the Pleistocene/Holocene Boundary." *Journal of Ecology* 88: 45–53.

Rajnovich, Grace. 2003. "The Laurel World: Time-Space Patterns of Ceramic Styles and Their Implications for Culture Change in the Upper Great Lakes in the First Millennium A.D." PhD dissertation, University of Michigan.

Ramsden, Peter G. 1990. "The Hurons: Archaeology and Culture History." In *The Archaeology of Southern Ontario to A.D. 1650*, edited by Chris J. Ellis and Neal Ferris, 361–84. Occasional Publication of the London Chapter, OAS, No. 5. London: Ontario Archaeological Society.

Raviele, Maria E. 2010. "Assessing Carbonized Archaeological Cooking Residues: Evaluation of Maize Phytolith Taphonomy and Density through Experimental Residue Analysis." PhD dissertation, Michigan State University, East Lansing.

Reber, Eleanor A., and John P. Hart. 2008. "Pine Resins and Pottery Sealing: Analysis of Absorbed and Visible Pottery Residues from Central New York State." *Archaeometry* 50: 999–1117.

Reid, C. S. "Paddy," and Grace Rajnovich. 1991. "Laurel: A Re-Evaluation of Spatial, Social and Temporal Paradigms." *Canadian Journal of Archaeology* 15: 193–234.

Rice, Prudence. 1987. *Pottery Analysis: A Sourcebook*. Chicago: University of Chicago Press.

———. 1996a. "Recent Ceramic Analysis 1: Function, Style, and Origins." *Journal of Archaeological Research* 4 (2): 133–63.

———. 1996b. "Recent Ceramic Analysis 2: Composition, Production, and Theory." *Journal of Archaeological Research* 4 (3): 165–202.

Richner, Jeffrey J. 1973. "Depositional History and Tool Industries at the Winter Site: A Lake Forest Middle Woodland Cultural Manifestation." Master's thesis, Western Michigan University, Kalamazoo.

Ritchie, William A. 1969. *The Archaeology of New York State*. Rev. ed. Garden City, NY: Natural History Press.

Robertson, James A., William A. Lovis, and John R. Halsey. 1999. "The Late Archaic: Hunter-Gatherers in an Uncertain Environment." In *Retrieving Michigan's Buried Past: The Archaeology of the Great Lakes State*, edited by John R. Halsey, 95–124. Bloomfield Hills, MI: Cranbrook Institute of Science.

Rodríguez-Alegría, Enrique, and Sarah R. Graff. 2012. "Introduction: The Menial Art of Cooking." In *The Menial Art of Cooking*, edited by Sarah R. Graff and Enrique Rodríguez-Alegría, 1–18. Boulder: University Press of Colorado.

Rogers, Edward S. 1962. *The Round Lake Ojibwa*. Art and Archaeology Division, Occasional Paper 5. Toronto: Ontario Department of Lands and Forests for the Royal Ontario Museum.

Ross, W. A. 1975. "Leslie M. Frost Natural Resources Centre Archaeological Resource Inventory." Manuscript on file, Ontario Ministry of Culture and Communications, Toronto.

Rye, O. S. 1976. "Keeping Your Temper under Control: Materials and the Manufacture of Papuan Pottery." *Archaeology and Physical Anthropology in Oceania* 11 (2): 106–37.

Sackett, James R. 1977. "The Meaning of Style in Archaeology: A General Model." *American Antiquity* 42 (3): 369–80.

Schiffer, Michael B. 1990. "The Influence of Surface Treatment on Heating Effectiveness of Ceramic Vessels." *Journal of Archaeological Science* 17: 373–81.

Schiffer, Michael B., and James M. Skibo. 1987. "Theory and Experiment in the Study of Technological Change." *Current Anthropology* 28 (5): 595–622.

———. 1997. "The Explanation of Artifact Variability." *American Antiquity* 62 (1): 27–50.

Schlanger, S. H. 1992. "Recognizing Persistent Places in Anasazi Settlement Systems." In *Space, Time, and Archaeological Landscapes*, edited by J. Rossignol and L. Wandsnider, 91–112. New York: Plenum Press.

Schoeninger, Margaret J. 1995. "Stable Isotope Studies in Human Evolution." *Evolutionary Anthropology* 4 (3): 83–98.

Schroeder, Sissel. 2004. "Current Research on Late Precontact Societies of the Midcontinental United States." *Journal of Archaeological Research* 124: 311–72.

Schwarcz, Henry P., and Margaret J. Schoeninger. 1991. "Stable Isotope Analyses in Human Nutritional Ecology." *American Journal of Physical Anthropology* 34: 283–321.

Scott, Elizabeth M. 1996. "Who Ate What? Archaeological Food Remains and Cultural Diversity." In *Case Studies in Environmental Archaeology*, edited by

Elizabeth J. Reitz, Lee A. Newsom, and Sylvia J. Scudder, 339–56. New York: Plenum Press.
Shapiro, Gary. 1984. "Ceramic Vessels, Site Permanence, and Group Size: A Mississippian Example." *American Antiquity* 49 (4): 696–712.
Shepard, Anna O. 1968. *Ceramics for the Archaeologist*. Washington, DC: Carnegie Institution.
Shott, Michael J. 1999. "The Early Archaic: Life after the Glaciers." In *Retrieving Michigan's Buried Past: The Archaeology of the Great Lakes State*, edited by John R. Halsey, 71–82. Bloomfield Hills, MI: Cranbrook Institute of Science.
Shott, Michael J., and Henry T. Wright. 1999. "The Paleo-Indians: Michigan's First People." In *Retrieving Michigan's Buried Past: The Archaeology of the Great Lakes State*, edited by John R. Halsey, 59–70. Bloomfield Hills, MI: Cranbrook Institute of Science.
Siegel, Sidney. 1956. *Nonparametric Statistics for the Behavioral Sciences*. New York: McGraw-Hill.
Simon, Mary L. 2011. "Evidence for Variability among Squash Seeds from the Hoxie Site (11CK4), Illinois." *Journal of Archaeological Science* 38: 2079–93.
Skibo, James. 1992. *Pottery Function: A Use-Alteration Perspective*. New York: Plenum Press.
———. 1994. "The Kalinga Cooking Pot: An Ethnoarchaeological and Experimental Study of Technological Change." In *Kalinga Ethnoarchaeology: Expanding Archaeological Method and Theory*, edited by William A. Longacre and James M. Skibo, 113–26. Washington, DC: Smithsonian Institution Press.
———. 2013. *Understanding Pottery Function*. Salt Lake City: University of Utah Press.
Skibo, James M., and Eric Blinman. 1999. "Exploring the Origins of Pottery on the Colorado Plateau." In *Pottery and People: A Dynamic Interaction*, edited by James M. Skibo and Gary M. Feinman, 171–83. Salt Lake City: University of Utah Press.
Skibo, James M., Mary E. Malainey, and Eric C. Drake. 2009. "Stone Boiling, Fire-Cracked Rock and Nut Oil: Exploring the Origins of Pottery Making on Grand Island." *The Wisconsin Archeologist* 90 (1–2): 47–64.
Skibo, James M., Mary E. Malainey, and Susan M. Kooiman. 2016. "Early Pottery in the North American Upper Great Lakes: Exploring Traces of Use." *Antiquity* 90: 1226–37.
Skibo, James M., Michael B. Schiffer, and Kenneth C. Reid. 1989. "Organic-Tempered Pottery: An Experimental Study." *American Antiquity* 54 (1): 122–46.

Skibo, James M., Tamara C. Butts, and Michael B. Schiffer. 1997. "Ceramic Surface Treatment and Abrasion Resistance: An Experimental Study." *Journal of Archaeological Science* 24: 311–17.

Smith, Beverly A. 1996. "Systems of Subsistence and Networks of Exchange in the Terminal Woodland and Early Historic Periods in the Upper Great Lakes." PhD dissertation, Michigan State University, East Lansing.

———. 2004. "The Gill Net's 'Native Country': The Inland Shore Fishery in the Northern Lake Michigan Basin." In *An Upper Great Lakes Archaeological Odyssey: Essays in Honor of Charles E. Cleland*, edited by William A. Lovis, 64–84. Detroit, MI: Wayne State University Press.

Smith, Bruce D. 2006. "Eastern North America as an Independent Center of Plant Domestication." *Proceedings of the National Academy of Science* 103 (33): 12223–28.

Smith, Bruce D., and Richard A. Yarnell. 2009. "Initial Formation of an Indigenous Crop Complex in Eastern North America at 3800 B.P." *PNAS* 106 (16): 6561–66. Open Access. www.pnas.org/cgi/doi/10.1073/pnas.0901846106.

Smith, David G. 1990. "Iroquoian Societies in Southern Ontario: Introduction and Historical Overview." In *The Archaeology of Southern Ontario to A.D. 1650*, edited by Chris J. Ellis and Neal Ferris, 279–90. Occasional Publication of the London Chapter, OAS, No. 5. London: Ontario Archaeological Society.

Smith, Monica L. 2006. "The Archaeology of Food Preference." *American Anthropologist* 108 (3): 480–93.

Snow, Dean R. 1980. "Early Horticultural Period." In *The Archaeology of New England*, edited by Dean R. Snow, 261–306. New York: Academic Press.

Speth, J., and K. Spielmann. 1983. "Energy Source Protein Metabolism and Hunter Gatherer Subsistence Strategies." *Journal of Anthropological Archaeology* 2: 1–31.

Speth, John D. 2015. "When Did Humans Learn to Boil?" *PaleoAnthropology* 2015: 54–67.

Spielmann, Katherine A. 2002. "Feasting, Craft Specialization, and the Ritual Mode of Production in Small-Scale Societies." *American Anthropologist* 104 (1): 195–207.

Stoltman, James B. 1973. *The Laurel Culture in Minnesota*. Minnesota Prehistoric Archaeology Series No. 8. St. Paul: Minnesota Historical Society.

———. 1989. "A Quantitative Approach to the Petrographic Analysis of Ceramic Thin Sections." *American Antiquity* 54 (1): 147–60.

Stoner, Wesley D. 2016. "The Analytical Nexus of Ceramic Paste Composition Studies: A Comparison of NAA, LA-ICP-MS, and Petrography in the Prehispanic Basin of Mexico." *Journal of Archaeological Science* 76: 31–47.

St-Pierre, Christian G., and Robert G. Thompson. 2015. "Phytolith Evidence for the Early Presence of Maize in Southern Quebec." *American Antiquity* 80: 408–15.

Striker, Sarah, Linda Howie, and Ronald F. Williamson. 2017. "Forming Pots and Community: Pottery Production and Potter Interaction in an Ancestral Wendat Village." In *Innovative Approaches and Explorations in Ceramic Studies*, edited by S. L. L. Varela, 53–69. Oxford: Archaeopress.

Stuiver, Minz, Paula J. Reimer, and Ron W. Reimer. 2017. CALIB 7.1. Electronic program. http://calib.org; accessed November 27, 2017.

———. 2018. CALIB 7.1. Electronic program. http://calib.org; accessed March 14, 2018.

Styles, Bonnie W. 2011. "Animal Use by Holocene Aboriginal Societies of the Northeast." In *The Subsistence Economies of Indigenous North American Societies*, edited by Bruce D. Smith, 449–82. Washington, DC: Smithsonian Institution Scholarly Press.

Surette, Clarence. 2008. "The Potential of Microfossil Use in Paleodiet and Paleoenvironmental Analysis in Northwestern Ontario." Master's thesis, Lakehead University, Thunder Bay, ONT.

Taché, Karine, and Oliver E. Craig. 2015. "Cooperative Harvesting of Aquatic Resources and the Beginning of Pottery Production in North-Eastern North America." *Antiquity* 89 (343): 177–90.

Tani, Masakazu. 1994. "Why Should More Pots Break in Larger Households? Mechanisms Underlying Population Estimates from Ceramics." In *Kalinga Ethnoarchaeology: Expanding Archaeological Method and Theory*, edited by William A. Longacre and James M. Skibo, 51–70. Washington, DC: Smithsonian Institution Press.

Terrell, E. E., P. M. Peterson, J. L. Reveal, and M. R. Duvall. 1997. "Taxonomy of North American Species *Zizania* (Poaceae)." *Sida* 17: 533–49.

Thompson, V. 2010. "The Rhythm of Space-Time and the Making of Monuments and Places during the Archaic." In *Trend, Tradition, and Turmoil: What Happened to the Southeastern Archaic*, edited by D. Thomas and M. Sanger, 217–28. New York: American Museum of Natural History.

Tooker, Elisabeth. 1991. *An Ethnography of the Huron Indians, 1615–1649*. Syracuse, NY: Syracuse University Press.

Trigger, Bruce G. 1976. *The Children of Aataentsic: A History of the Huron People to 1660*. Montreal: McGill-Queen's University Press.

Turner, Christy G., and Laurel Lofgren. 1966. "Household Size of Precontact Western Pueblo Indians." *Southwestern Journal of Anthropology* 22 (2): 117–32.

Twiss, Katheryn. 2012. "The Archaeology of Food and Social Diversity." *Journal of Archaeological Research* 20: 357–95.

Tykot, Robert H. 2016. "Using Nondestructive Portable X-Ray Fluorescence Spectrometers on Stone, Ceramics, Metal, and Other Materials in Museums: Advantages and Limitations." *Applied Spectroscopy* 70 (1): 42–56.

Valppu, Seppo H. 2000. "Paleoethnobotanical Investigations at the Big Rice Site: Laurel Culture Use of Wild Rice (*Zizania aquatica* L.) and Associated Radiocarbon Dates." In *Wild Rice Research and Management: Proceedings of the Wild Rice Research and Management Conference*, edited by L. S. Williamson, L. A. Dlutkowski, and McCammon Soltis, 27–39. Carlton, PA: Great Lakes Indian Fish and Wildlife Commission.

Vennum, Thomas. 1988. *Wild Rice and Ojibway People*. St. Paul: Minnesota Historical Society Press.

Voss, E. G., and A. Reznicek. 2012. *Michigan Flora: A Guide to the Identification and Occurrence of the Native and Naturalized Seed-Plants of the State*. 2 vols. Bloomfield Hills, MI: Cranbrook Institute of Science and University of Michigan Herbarium.

Walder, Heather. 2018. "Small Beads, Big Picture: Assessing Chronology, Exchange, and Population Movement through Compositional Analyses of Blue Glass Beads from the Upper Great Lakes." *Historical Archaeology* 52: 301–31. https://doi.org/10.1007/s41636-018-0100-4.

Wallis, Neill J., Thomas J. Pluckhahn, and Michael D. Glascock. 2016. "Sourcing Interaction Networks of the American Southeast: Neutron Activation Analysis of Swift Creek Complicated Stamped Pottery." *American Antiquity* 81 (4): 717–36.

Wallis, Wilson D., and Ruth Sawtell Wallis. 1955. *The Micmac Indians of Eastern Canada*. St. Paul: University of Minnesota Press.

Wandsnider, LuAnn. 1997. "The Roasted and the Boiled: Food Composition and Heat Treatment with Special Emphasis on Pit-Hearth Cooking." *Journal of Anthropological Archaeology* 16: 1–48.

Warrick, Gary. 2000. "The Precontact Iroquoian Occupation of Southern Ontario." *Journal of World Prehistory* 14 (4): 415–66.

Waugh, F. W. 1973. *Iroquois Foods and Food Preparation*. Anthropological Series No. 12, Memoir 86. Ottawa: Canada Department of Mines, Geological Survey.

White, Richard. 1991. *The Middle Ground: Indians, Empires and Republics in the Great Lakes Region, 1650–1815*. Cambridge: Cambridge University Press.

Wiessner, Polly. 1983. "Style and Social Information in Kalahari San Projectile Points." *American Antiquity* 48 (2): 253–76.

Williamson, Ronald F. 1990. "The Early Iroquoian Period of Southern Ontario." In *The Archaeology of Southern Ontario to A.D. 1650*, edited by Chris J. Ellis and Neal Ferris, 291–320. Occasional Publication of the London Chapter, OAS, No. 5. London: Ontario Archaeological Society.

Witgen, Michael. 2012. *An Infinity of Nations: How the Native New World Shaped Early North America*. Philadelphia: University of Pennsylvania Press.

Wobst, H. M. 1977. "Stylistic Behavior and Information Exchange." In *Papers for the Director: Research Essays in Honor of James B. Griffin*, edited by C. E. Cleland, 317–42. Anthropological Paper No. 61. Ann Arbor: University of Michigan Museum of Anthropology.

Wright, J. V. 1966. *The Pic River Site*. National Museum of Canada Bulletin 206. Ottawa: National Museum of Canada.

———. 1967. *The Laurel Tradition and the Middle Woodland Period*. National Museum of Canada Bulletin 217, Anthropological Series No. 79. Ottawa: National Museum of Canada.

———. 1973. *The Ontario Iroquois Tradition*. Facsimile ed. National Museum of Canada Bulletin 210. Ottawa: National Museum of Canada.

Yarnell, Richard A. 1964. *Aboriginal Relationships between Culture and Plant Life in the Upper Great Lakes Region*. Anthropological Papers No. 23. Ann Arbor: University of Michigan Museum of Anthropology.

INDEX

acorns
    at the Cloudman site, 118, 120–21, 126, 147, 149, 151, 157
    cooking and processing of, 16, 130–31, 139, 140, 145
    evidence in lipids, 118, 119, 147, 149
    Indigenous uses of, 130–31, 139, 140, 147
    role in subsistence, 3, 14, 29, 31, 36, 118, 127, 145, 149, 157
    as starchy resource, 3, 29, 40, 127, 145

actual function (pottery), 48, 53, 54, 94–95, 105

aggregation sites, 14, 15, 17, 19, 28, 30, 31, 106, 146, 150, 154

Albert, Rebecca, 113

Algoma ware, 72

Algonquian groups, 20, 23–24, 48, 130

American Indian. *See* Indigenous peoples, of the Northern Great Lakes

AMS dates/dating, 6, 57, 59, 76–77, 78–80, 81, 92, 121–22, 143–44, 148, 154

Anishinaabe/Anishinaabeg, 23, 25

aquatic resources
    cooking and processing of, 118–20, 147
    in Indigenous diet at the Cloudman site, 110–11, 118, 120, 123, 126, 127, 135, 149, 151
    faunal (*see* fish)
    floral, 110, 135, 148
    stable isotope signatures of, 110–11, 118, 119, 135, 147

Archaic period, 13–14

Arrowhead Drive site, 16, 37

assertive style, 45

attrition (of pottery), 48, 49, 54, 94

Baraga, Frederick, 132, 135, 138

beans, 22, 50, 117, 136, 140, 142, 154

berries
    at the Cloudman site, 119
    cooking and preparation, 133, 134, 139
    Indigenous uses of, 119, 133, 134, 137–38, 139, 140
    lipid signatures of, 113, 119

Binford, Lewis, 49

Blackduck ware
    at the Cloudman site, 64, 65, 66, 144, 150, 184, 185
    dates, 75, 76–77, 79, 92, 144
    description, 18, 66
    food residues and, 104, 110
    technical properties of, 91, 92

boiling
- as cooking technique, 3, 32, 39, 107, 122, 126, 139, 141, 145, 147, 151
- definition of, 32, 98
- foods
  - —acorns, 131
  - —fish, 135–36, 148
  - —maize, 38, 84, 115, 126, 131–32
  - —meat, 137
  - —squash, 117, 126, 132
  - —starchy resources, 3, 32, 39, 84, 147
  - —wild rice, 116, 126, 135, 141
- interior carbonization patterns of, 32, 49, 55, 98–107, 115–17, 126, 132, 141, 142, 146–47, 152

Bois Blanc Island, 20, 30

Bois Blanc ware
- at the Cloudman site, 64, 66, 67–68, 79, 144, 186
- dates, 18, 67, 76–77, 79, 144
- description, 18, 67

Bowerman ware, 18, 65, 66–67, 150, 185

Branstner, Christine, 34, 35, 53, 59–60, 61, 65, 66, 75, 76, 80, 81, 144

Braun, David, 5, 37–38, 47

cache pits, 19–20

carbohydrates, 50

carbon (element)
- in AMS dating, 57
- stable isotopes of, 56, 109–11, 120

carbonization
- definition, 48, 94
- exterior, 54, 94, 95, 96
- interior, 39, 48, 54, 94, 95, 96, 105, 146
- —patterns of, 16, 32, 49, 54–55, 75, 94, 97–104, 105, 122, 126, 132, 140, 141, 142, 146, 152
- —preservation of, 96

ceramic analysis. *See* pottery: analysis

Chippewa. *See* Ojibwe

Chippewa County, Michigan, 35

Cleland, Charles, 28–29, 35–36

climate, 6, 10–12, 124, 125, 149, 153, 156

Cloudman site
- components/occupations, 33–34, 35, 36, 61, 78–80, 151–54
- dates of occupation, 4, 61, 75–78, 144
- description and geographic setting, 2, 3, 10, 33–34, 88, 146, 148–49
- environmental setting, 36–37, 110, 122–24, 147
- excavations, 4, 34–36
- seasonality, 120–21

cluster analysis, 115–17

collars (pottery)
- description, 89
- and Iroquoian-style pottery, 71
- and Juntunen ware, 68

compositional analysis, 46

conifer product, 113

Contact ("Protohistoric") period, 20, 21, 22–25, 34, 35, 76, 78, 81, 130, 133, 134, 142, 144

cooking
- changes in, 3, 4, 6, 7, 32, 52, 54, 93, 123
- at the Cloudman site, 146–47, 151–54
- in ethnographic accounts, 40–41, 88, 109–20
- food residues and, 55–57, 109–20
- identity and, 51, 103–4, 124–26, 139–42, 150
- interior carbonization evidence of, 3, 7, 48, 55, 94–108
- methods and practices, 2, 3, 7, 16–17, 32–33, 37–40, 49, 51, 109, 115–17, 126
- technology and
  - —organic vessels, 16–17, 97, 105
  - —pottery, 3, 4, 6, 16–17, 32–33, 37–40, 46–47, 54, 83–94, 117–18, 140

Index 215

corn. *See* maize
corn soup, 136, 140
cuisine
   at the Cloudman site, 117–20, 126–27, 137, 138
   cooking and, 103–4, 117, 139–42, 146
   definition of, 40, 49–50
   environment and, 32, 127, 156
   identity and, 40, 50, 117, 125, 142, 150–51, 154–55
   proxies for, 7, 109, 117–20
   technology/pottery and, 32, 37, 40, 43, 52, 91, 117–20

Densmore, Frances, 118, 130, 133
diachronic change
   in culinary behaviors, 6, 39, 109, 111–18, 139–42, 146–49, 151–54
   in pottery technology, 4, 6, 38, 59, 75, 81, 84–90, 94, 95, 143–46, 151–54
diet
   at the Cloudman site, 109, 113, 114, 120, 122–24, 126, 127, 147–49, 151, 154
   definition of, 49
   identity and, 40, 124–25
   of Indigenous peoples, 20, 22, 30, 38, 40, 119, 129, 133, 136, 137, 138, 139, 141
   methods of investigation, 5, 6, 33, 39, 53, 55, 56, 113, 120, 127, 156, 157
   nutrition and, 49–50
dietary analysis, 1, 41, 117, 120, 143, 151, 156
dog burials, 24, 31, 37, 39, 146, 154
domesticated/cultivated foods
   at the Cloudman site, 121–22, 148
   in the Northern Great Lakes, 3, 13, 17, 109, 148

Door Peninsula, Wisconsin, 29, 30, 62
Drummond Island, Michigan
   archaeology of, 20, 33, 36, 136, 154–55
   environment and presettlement vegetation, 36, 118, 136, 153
   geography of, 2, 33, 34, 36, 153, 154–55
Dunham, Sean, 17, 29, 38, 127, 145

Early Iroquois, 21
Early Late Woodland
   cuisine and subsistence, 103, 104, 105, 107, 114, 123, 126, 146, 148, 149, 152
   dates, 77, 79, 80, 92
   lifeways and mobility, 19, 29, 31
   pottery, 18, 31, 35, 60–61, 65–67, 74–75, 84–87, 89–90, 92, 93, 94, 95, 103, 104, 105, 106, 107, 144, 145, 150, 151, 152, 185, 188
earthen enclosures, 19–20, 30, 31
Eastern Agricultural Complex (EAC), 13
Eastern Upper Peninsula of Michigan, 11, 18, 20, 29, 30, 33, 36, 38, 118, 127, 151–52, 155
Eastern Woodlands of North America, 11, 13, 14, 17, 22, 50, 55, 84, 145
emblemic style, 45
environment
   of the Cloudman site, 36–37, 122–24, 125, 127, 153, 156
   human cultural adaptation and, 7, 25–26, 29, 31–32, 49, 125, 156, 157
   of the Northern Great Lakes, 10–12, 25–26, 29, 31–32, 147–49
ethnographic accounts, of Indigenous food and cooking, 6, 40, 41, 97, 118, 127, 129–42, 148, 150, 157
ethnographic analogy, 7, 129, 143, 151
ethnographic bias, 129–30

ethnohistoric accounts, 6, 40, 41, 125, 127, 129–42, 148
European-made trade goods, 36
experimental archaeology, 156
exterior carbonization. *See under* carbonization
exterior sooting, 39, 48, 54, 94, 95, 105
extralocal social relationships, 19, 31

fats, role in nutrition, 50
fatty acids. *See* lipids
faunal remains, 36–37, 119, 120, 138
feasting, 31, 51
fish
  cooking and preparation of, 57, 120, 134, 135–36, 138, 139, 140
  fall-spawning, 3, 15, 28, 29, 30, 37, 120, 127, 149
  residue signatures of, 110, 113, 119, 135, 147, 148
  role in diet and subsistence, 13, 24, 25, 28, 29, 32, 37, 109, 149, 157
  spring-spawning, 15, 28, 121
fishing (activity), 12, 14, 15, 16, 17, 22, 25, 28, 119, 121
food, definition of, 50–51
foodways, 2, 4, 6, 7, 9, 13, 41, 43, 49, 52, 84, 130
foraging-collecting spectrum, 49
freshwater reservoir effect (FRE), 57
functional analysis, of pottery, 5, 6, 7, 43, 53–55, 57, 83–108, 143, 156, 157

Grand Island, Michigan, 14, 16
Great Lakes region (definition), 9, 10

Hambacher, Michael, 67, 72
Hart, John, 38, 84, 111, 120
hazelnuts, 36, 118–19, 121, 131
heating effectiveness (pottery), 47, 48, 89, 90, 106, 135, 145
Hilger, Inez, 130–33, 136

Historic period, 31, 34, 35, 112, 119, 129, 130, 131, 136, 141, 150, 154
hominy, 131, 133, 138, 140
Hopewell, 14, 73, 74
horticulture, 21, 23, 119, 121, 124, 149
Howey, Meghan, 19–20
hunter-gatherers, 13, 22, 23, 24, 25, 31, 45, 49, 50, 119
Huron Incised pottery, 71, 74
Huron. *See* Wendat, and Wendat-Petun groups

identity, 19, 40, 44–52, 83, 91, 94, 103, 105, 109, 124–25, 133, 142, 149–51, 154–55
Indigenous peoples, of the Northern Great Lakes, 1, 2, 4, 5, 6, 7, 13–25, 40, 41, 50, 78, 114, 117, 129, 132, 138, 142, 143
Initial Woodland, 15. *See also* Middle Woodland
inland shore fishery, 28
intended function (pottery), 47, 48, 84–94
intensification, of resources,
  at the Cloudman site, 123, 149
  as subsistence strategy, 32, 38, 51–52
interior carbonization. *See under* carbonization
Iroquoian
  cuisine/subsistence, 41, 112, 114, 115, 116, 117, 124, 125, 129, 130–42, 150, 151, 154
  ethnographic accounts of, 130–42
  language, 20
  pottery, 19, 23, 36, 48, 70, 145
  society and identity, 6, 18, 20–22, 24, 41, 48, 155
Iroquoian period, 20–22
Iroquoian-style pottery, 70–72, 74, 75, 76–78, 80, 81, 84, 87, 89, 91–93, 104, 105, 106, 110, 115, 116, 124, 125, 144, 149, 153, 154, 155, 187, 188

Jaccard's coefficient, 115–16
Juntunen sequence, 18, 63–69
Juntunen site, 20, 22, 30, 67, 114, 152
Juntunen ware
  at the Cloudman site, 35, 68–69, 76–78, 79, 150, 152, 155
  dates, 18, 31, 76–78, 79, 80, 144
  description and style, 18, 31, 68, 70, 89, 153, 186
  residues/use alteration, 104, 115, 116, 141, 155
  technical properties of, 91–92
  varieties, 68–69, 80, 92

Kruskal-Wallis test, 103

Lake Huron, 2, 9, 33, 36
Lake Superior, 3, 9, 10, 11, 14, 22, 23, 24, 25, 30, 135
Late Late Woodland
  cuisine/subsistence, 29, 30, 103–4, 105, 114, 115–16, 123, 125, 127, 141, 146, 148–49, 150, 153
  dates, 23, 76–77, 78, 79–80
  lifeways and mobility, 18, 19, 29, 30, 125, 152, 153
  pottery, 6, 18, 30, 31, 35, 53, 60–61, 68–69, 74–75, 80, 84–87, 89–90, 92, 93–94, 95, 105, 106, 125, 135, 141, 144, 145, 150, 152, 186, 188
Late Precontact
  cuisine/subsistence, 19, 22, 103–5, 106, 107, 114, 115, 120, 123, 124, 125, 126, 133, 141, 146–47, 148–49, 150
  cultural history, 22–25
  dates, 23, 77–78, 79, 80, 144
  pottery, 22, 33, 37, 60–61, 70–73, 74–75, 80, 85–87, 89–90, 92–93, 94, 95, 107, 117, 133, 135, 144, 145, 148, 150, 153, 154, 155, 187, 188
  ritual behavior, 19, 22, 31
  social relationships and identity, 19, 20, 22–25, 33, 80, 154
Late Woodland
  component of the Cloudman site, 35
  cultural history, 17–20
  dates, 14, 17, 34
  pottery, 18, 30–32, 35, 38, 39, 40, 60, 63, 64, 69, 79, 84, 86, 87, 88, 93, 107, 184
  sites, 17
  social and settlement patterns, 17–20, 28–30, 31–32, 40, 45, 106, 150, 152
  subsistence, 2–3, 28–30, 32, 37, 95, 103, 105, 106, 113, 122, 127, 139, 145, 148, 149, 152–53
  See also Early Late Woodland; Late Late Woodland; Middle Late Woodland
Laurel culture, 16, 19, 151
Laurel ware
  at the Cloudman site, 35, 61–62, 63, 64, 73–74, 78–79, 150, 151, 184, 188
  dates, 76–77, 78–79, 121–22, 144, 151
  description/style, 15, 16, 18, 61–62, 63, 73
  geographic distribution, 15, 30
  residues/use alteration, 104, 116, 121–22, 148
  technical properties of, 38, 88, 91–92
  varieties, 104, 116, 121–22, 148
Lawson ware, 71, 187
legacy collections, 4, 5, 33
life history, 94
lipid residue analysis, 16, 43, 56–57, 58, 112–13, 118, 119, 143, 147
lipids, 16, 39, 55, 56, 57, 112, 121, 124, 135, 147, 149
Little Ice Age, 124, 154
locale provisioning, 152

localization (social), 18, 19, 30, 125, 150, 153
logistic mobility, 29
low fat content foods, 113, 119, 137

Mackinac ware
  at the Cloudman site, 35, 65–66, 74, 79, 144, 150, 184–85, 188
  dates, 18, 76–77, 79, 144
  description/style, 63, 65–66, 67, 74
  geographic distribution, 37, 92
  residues/use alteration traces, 104, 116
  technical properties of, 91–92
  varieties, 65–66
macrobotanical remains, 36, 118, 119, 121, 131, 136, 138, 157
maize
  AMS dates, 22
  at the Cloudman site, 36, 113–17, 118–27, 135, 139, 148, 149, 150, 151, 153–54, 156, 157
  cooking and preparation, 38, 84, 115–17, 118, 126, 131–32, 145, 151, 152
  cultivation/agriculture, 17, 20, 21, 22, 30, 36, 50, 52, 124, 125, 127, 149, 153–54
  ethnographic accounts of, 131–32, 140, 141, 142, 150
  in food residues, 56, 109–11, 113–17, 119–20, 123, 135, 139, 141, 148, 150, 151–52, 153–54
  in the Great Lakes, 3, 17, 21–22, 24, 29, 30, 50, 127, 149
Malainey, Mary, 16–17, 56–57, 112–13
maple sugar, 132, 134, 137–39, 140, 142
McHale Milner, Claire, 31, 35, 38, 45
meat, preparations of, 24, 119, 130, 132, 134, 136, 137, 139, 140
Medieval Climatic Optimum, 12, 29, 123–24, 127, 148, 153, 156
medium fat content foods, 113, 119

Michigan State University, 35
microbotanical analysis, 43, 55–56, 58, 108, 109, 113–17, 120, 138, 139, 143, 157
microbotanical remains, 39, 55, 115, 117, 123, 132, 133, 135, 147, 148, 153, 154
Middle Late Woodland
  dates, 77, 79
  pottery, 61, 64, 67–68, 76, 95, 144, 186
Middle Ontario Iroquoian period, 21
Middle Woodland
  component of the Cloudman site, 35
  cuisine/subsistence, 28–29, 32, 33, 38, 39, 102–3, 104, 105, 107, 112, 114, 115, 117, 121–22, 123, 126, 127, 140, 141, 146, 147, 148, 151
  cultural history, 14–17
  dates, 14, 34, 77–78, 80, 121–22, 144, 151
  lifeways and mobility, 14–17, 19, 20, 28–29, 30, 40, 45, 106, 145, 150, 152
  pottery, 6, 14, 15, 16, 18, 30, 31, 32, 35, 37–40, 45, 60–65, 73–74, 78, 84–88, 89–90, 91–92, 93–94, 95, 104, 106, 113, 121–22, 144, 145, 148, 150, 151, 152, 184, 188
  sites, 16
Mid-Holocene Climatic Optimum, 12
miniature pottery vessels, 60–61, 73–75, 188
mobility
  group/population, 15, 18, 88, 151
  logistic, 29, 49
  residential, 19, 29, 31, 49
mounds
  at the Cloudman site, 34–35, 39, 88, 146, 152–53
  in the Great Lakes, 14, 19, 20, 31, 88, 153
multiproxy analysis, 52–53, 58, 156, 157

Naomikong Point site, 16, 32, 33, 38, 39, 84, 88
Native Americans, 127, 129, 141. *See also* Indigenous peoples, of the Northern Great Lakes
nitrogen (stable isotopes), 56, 109–10, 111, 148
nixtamalization, 115, 126, 131, 132, 152
North Bay ware, 15, 30, 61, 62–63, 79, 184
Northern Great Lakes
　cooking behaviors, 98, 103, 105, 120, 124, 126, 129, 132, 134, 142, 146–47
　description and geographic setting, 1, 9, 10, 24, 25–26
　earthworks, 19–20, 31, 152–53
　environment/climate, 10–12, 49, 122–24, 147–49
　important archaeological sites of, 16, 17, 31, 37
　origins of pottery in, 15, 16–17
　subsistence and settlement patterns, 2–4, 13–14, 15–16, 17–20, 22–25, 27–30, 31–32, 33, 38, 40, 115, 118, 120, 121–22, 123–24, 127, 146–49, 151, 152, 155, 157
nutrition, 49–51, 117
nuts
　at the Cloudman site, 36, 118–19, 120, 121, 123, 126, 149, 151
　in ethnographic accounts, 118, 131

Odawa, 22, 23–25, 36, 70, 76, 80, 81, 125, 133, 144, 150, 155
Ojibwe
　culture history of, 23–25
　ethnographic accounts of diet and cooking, 41, 112, 118–19, 125, 129–42, 147, 150
omnivore's paradox, 50

O'Neil
　site, 17, 69–70, 74–75
　ware, 64, 69–70, 74–75, 188
Ontario, 6, 9, 10, 15, 16, 20–22, 23, 24, 76, 80, 122, 136, 155
organic vessels/containers, 16–17, 97, 105, 141
O'Shea, John, 109, 123
othering, 51
Ottawa. *See* Odawa

palatability, of food, 38, 84, 115, 126, 135, 145, 152
Paleoindian period, 11, 13
parching, 98, 133, 134
performance characteristics, 47–48, 130
persistent places, 14, 106, 152
petrographic analysis, 46
Petun. *See* Tionnontati; Wendat, and Wendat-Petun groups
phytoliths, 55, 113, 114, 115, 121, 122, 132, 134, 141, 148, 150, 152
pollen, 55
Potagannissing River, 20, 33, 35, 123
pottery
　analysis, 5, 6, 7, 43, 53–55, 57–58, 83, 156, 157
　decoration, 5, 44, 45, 47, 53, 63, 70, 93, 106
　function, 4, 6, 32, 43, 46–49, 52, 53, 81, 83–108, 126, 151, 156
　—ceremonial/ritual, 5, 38, 39, 83, 88, 152, 146
　—utilitarian, 5, 38, 39, 45, 46, 83, 88
　manufacture, 6, 47, 48, 51, 60, 62, 64, 69, 72, 73, 88, 93, 97, 130, 152, 155
　morphology/shape, 32, 45, 47, 53, 54, 61, 67, 87
　paste, 46, 47, 93, 106
　rim diameter (vessel size/volume/capacity), 37, 38, 54, 84, 86–88, 91, 92, 145

pottery (*cont.*)
   style, 6, 7, 17, 18, 19, 29, 30–32, 40, 43–45, 52, 83, 125, 153
     —communication and, 43–45
     —definition, 43–44
     —identity and, 19, 44–45, 47, 157
     —visibility and, 45
   taxonomy/typology/typological categories, 5, 6, 7, 21, 35, 43, 44, 46, 53, 59–75, 90, 104
   as technology, 4, 7, 32–33, 52, 83, 107, 143, 145–46, 157
   vessel fill levels, 16, 105, 97–98, 146
   vessel strength, 48, 84, 106, 145
   vessel wall thickness, 32, 37, 38, 47, 54, 84, 88–90, 91, 93–94, 106, 145
Princess Point, 20–21
protein, 49, 50, 113
protein starvation, 50
Protohistoric period. *See* Contact ("Protohistoric") period

rabbit starvation. *See* protein starvation
residential mobility, 19, 29, 31, 49
residues
   absorbed, 4, 6, 16, 33, 39, 43, 53, 56–57, 94, 109, 112–13, 117, 118, 119, 123, 126–27, 130, 137, 138, 143, 147, 156, 157
   adhered, 4, 6, 33, 39, 43, 48, 53, 55, 56, 59, 76, 94, 96, 97–108, 109–11, 113–15, 117, 122, 125, 126–27, 132, 135, 136, 138, 141–42, 143, 147–48, 150–51, 153, 154, 156–57
   AMS dating of, 6, 43, 57, 76, 122, 143–44, 155
Ripley Plain ware, 71, 187
risk buffering, 22, 29, 31, 44, 49, 50
rituals, 19, 24, 30, 39, 51–52, 146, 153
roasting, 49, 98, 119, 132
roots, as foodstuff, 113, 119, 136, 138, 139
Round Lake Ojibwe, 136, 138, 139

sagamité, 140
Sami, 50
Sand Point site, 17, 20, 22, 31, 32, 33, 38, 39, 84, 88
Sandy Lake ware, 64
Schiffer, Michael, 47, 94
Schultz site, 122
Schultz Thick pottery, 14
Scott Point site, 17, 37
Shepard, Anna, 46
Skegemog Point site, 67, 72
Skegemog ware, 18
Skibo, James, 16, 47–49, 53
Smith, Beverly, 24–25, 28
squash
   AMS dates of, 121–22, 148
   at the Cloudman site, 113–18, 120–23, 125, 126, 127, 135, 148–49, 151, 154, 157
   in Eastern North America, 13, 22
   ethnographic accounts of, 132–33, 136, 139, 140, 141, 142
   microbotanical remains of, 55, 113–17, 135, 148–49, 151, 154
St. Mary's River, 33, 35
stable isotope analysis, 43, 56, 58, 109–11, 136, 143, 147
stable isotopes, 6, 39, 43, 53, 55, 56, 108, 109–11, 115, 119, 123, 124, 126, 136, 138, 143, 147, 156, 157
starches (plant), 55, 113, 148, 150
starchy resources, 3, 29, 32, 38–39, 40, 84, 89, 98, 107, 109, 127, 145, 147
stewing
   as a cooking technique, 3, 32, 39, 102–4, 117, 142, 146–47, 151, 154
   definition, 32, 98, 141
   foods
     —acorns, 131
     —fish, 140
     —maize, 115, 126, 132, 140, 151
     —squash, 117, 126, 132, 141

—wild rice, 116, 126, 134, 141
interior carbonization patterns, 49, 55, 98–105, 126, 141, 146–47
Straits of Mackinac, 18, 20, 22, 30, 45
subsistence
and settlement patterns, 2, 4, 6, 12, 18, 20, 27–30, 32, 33, 49, 159, 156, 157
strategies, 18, 22, 28, 37, 39, 40, 51
Summer Island, 16, 28, 37
surface treatment (pottery), 53, 68, 75
symbolic communication/symboling, 44–45, 51
synchronic variation
in culinary behaviors, 40, 103–4, 107, 109, 149
in pottery technology, 40, 83, 91–93, 94, 107, 149

technical choice, 47, 152
technical properties, of pottery, 5, 37, 40, 47, 59, 83–94, 104, 107
temper pottery, 16, 22, 46, 47, 48, 73, 75, 106, 155
temper size, 4, 37, 38, 48, 54, 84–86, 91–92, 93–94, 106, 107, 135, 145, 152, 154
Terminal Woodland, 17. *See also* Late Woodland
terrestrial resources, 12, 56, 110, 113, 118, 120
thermal conductivity, 38. *See also* heating effectiveness
thermal shock resistance, 38, 47, 48, 84, 106, 135, 145, 152
Three Sisters, 22, 117, 125, 133, 142, 151, 154
Tionnontati, 20
Tooker, Elisabeth, 118, 130–33, 136, 140
Traverse ware
at the Cloudman site, 68, 70, 72–73, 74–75, 76–78, 80, 144, 150, 153–55, 187, 188

dates, 18, 76–78, 80, 144, 155
description/style, 18, 72–73, 75, 187, 188
residues/use-alteration traces and, 104, 115, 116, 125, 133, 149, 150, 154
technical properties of, 91, 92 154

Upper Great Lakes, 9, 17, 25, 29, 30, 79, 87, 123, 127, 138
Upper Mississippian (Oneota), 19, 22–23
Upper Peninsula of Michigan
environment and geography of, 11, 12, 118, 153, 155
mounds of, 20
pottery of, 15, 16, 18, 19, 22, 23, 30, 31, 76, 92
use alteration traces, 7, 39, 48–49, 54, 83, 94–108, 143, 151

vegetables, 134, 136, 137–38, 140

Waugh, F. W., 118, 125, 130, 131–33, 136–38, 140
Weissner, Polly, 44–45
Welch's unpaired t-test, 84–85, 86–87, 90, 92
Wendat, and Wendat-Petun groups
archaeology and cultural background, 20–24
diet, 118, 125, 130, 132
maize and, 114
pottery, 71, 155
wild rice
AMS dates, 121–22
at the Cloudman site, 36, 37, 113–18, 120, 121–22, 123–24, 125, 126, 127, 133, 142, 145, 148, 149, 151–53, 156, 157
cooking and preparation, 116–17, 126, 133–35, 140–42, 145, 152

wild rice (*cont.*)
   ethnographic accounts of, 125, 133–35, 136, 137, 139–42, 150
   in food residues, 55, 113–17, 119, 120, 121–22, 123, 133, 139, 141, 148, 150, 151, 152
   in the Great Lakes region, 3, 15, 29, 31, 50, 122, 127, 145, 149
   growing conditions/environment, 123–24, 149, 153, 156

Winter site, 16, 32, 33, 79
Wobst, Martin, 44–45
Woodland period. *See* Early Late Woodland; Late Woodland; Late Late Woodland; Middle Late Woodland; Middle Woodland

Younger Dryas, 11

SUSAN M. KOOIMAN
is assistant professor of anthropology
at Southern Illinois University Edwardsville.

www.ingramcontent.com/pod-product-compliance
Lightning Source LLC
Chambersburg PA
CBHW071408300426
44114CB00016B/2226